ECONOMICS AND AUSTERITY IN EUROPE

The full impact of austerity policies across Europe is still being assessed, but it is clear that their gendered impacts have been consistently severe, structural and manifold. They have also been, until now, under-researched and under-estimated.

This book brings together the research of leading feminist economists in the area of gender and austerity economics to perform a rigorous gender-impact analysis both at national and pan-European levels. The chapters not only offer thorough evidence for the detrimental gender-impact of austerity policies across Europe, but they also provide readers with concrete suggestions of alternative policies that national governments and the European Union should adopt. With a combination of country case studies and cross-country empirical analysis, this book reveals the scope and channels through which women and men have been impacted by austerity policies in Europe, and goes on to offer readers the opportunity to assess the feasibility and implications of a feminist alternative to continued austerity.

Economics and Austerity in Europe will be invaluable to social science students and researchers, as well to as policy-makers searching not just for a Plan B to continued austerity policies but for a Plan F – a feminist economic strategy to stimulate sustainable economic recovery.

Hannah Bargawi is Lecturer in Economics at the School of Oriental and African Studies (SOAS), University of London, UK.

Giovanni Cozzi is Senior Lecturer in Economics at the University of Greenwich, London, and a member of the Greenwich Political Economy Research Centre (GPERC), UK.

Susan Himmelweit is Emeritus Professor of Economics at the Open University, UK.

Routledge IAFFE Advances in Feminist Economics

IAFFE aims to increase the visibility and range of economic research on gender; facilitate communication among scholars, policymakers, and activists concerned with women's wellbeing and empowerment; promote discussions among policymakers about interventions which serve women's needs; educate economists, policymakers, and the general public about feminist perspectives on economic issues; foster feminist evaluations of economics as a discipline; expose the gender blindness characteristic of much social science and the ways in which this impoverishes all research even research that does not explicitly concern women's issues; help expand opportunities for women, especially women from underrepresented groups, within economics; and, encourage the inclusion of feminist perspectives in the teaching of economics. The IAFFE book series pursues the aims of the organization by providing a forum in which scholars have space to develop their ideas at length and in detail. The series exemplifies the value of feminist research and the high standard of IAFFE sponsored scholarship.

For a full list of titles in this series, please visit www.routledge.com/series/IAFFE

11 **Women and Austerity**
The economic crisis and the future for gender equality
Edited by Maria Karamessini and Jill Rubery

12 **New Frontiers in Feminist Political Economy**
Edited by Shirin M. Rai and Georgina Waylen

13 **Gender and Climate Change Financing**
Coming out of the margin
Mariama Williams

14 **Feminist Economics and Public Policy**
Edited by Jim Campbell and Morag Gillespie

15 **Economics and Austerity in Europe**
Gendered impacts and sustainable alternatives
Edited by Hannah Bargawi, Giovanni Cozzi and Susan Himmelweit

ECONOMICS AND AUSTERITY IN EUROPE

Gendered impacts and sustainable alternatives

Edited by Hannah Bargawi, Giovanni Cozzi and Susan Himmelweit

First published 2017
by Routledge
2 Park Square, Milton Park, Abingdon, Oxon OX14 4RN

and by Routledge
711 Third Avenue, New York, NY 10017

Routledge is an imprint of the Taylor & Francis Group, an informa business

© 2017 selection and editorial matter, Hannah Bargawi, Giovanni Cozzi
and Susan Himmelweit; individual chapters, the contributors

The right of Hannah Bargawi, Giovanni Cozzi and Susan Himmelweit to
be identified as the authors of the editorial material, and of the authors for
their individual chapters, has been asserted in accordance with sections 77
and 78 of the Copyright, Designs and Patents Act 1988.

All rights reserved. No part of this book may be reprinted or reproduced or
utilised in any form or by any electronic, mechanical, or other means, now
known or hereafter invented, including photocopying and recording, or in
any information storage or retrieval system, without permission in writing
from the publishers.

Trademark notice: Product or corporate names may be trademarks or
registered trademarks, and are used only for identification and explanation
without intent to infringe.

British Library Cataloguing in Publication Data
A catalogue record for this book is available from the British Library

Library of Congress Cataloging in Publication Data
A catalog record has been requested for this book

ISBN: 978-1-138-64607-0 (hbk)
ISBN: 978-1-138-64608-7 (pbk)
ISBN: 978-1-315-62776-2 (ebk)

Typeset in Bembo
by Saxon Graphics Ltd, Derby

CONTENTS

List of figures	*vii*
List of tables	*ix*
Notes on contributors	*xi*
Foreword: Zita Gurmai	*xvii*
Acknowledgments	*xix*
Abbreviations	*xxi*

Introduction: austerity and after – the case for a gendered approach   1
Hannah Bargawi, Giovanni Cozzi and Susan Himmelweit

PART I
Theorising on gender, austerity and policy alternatives   13

1 A gender-equitable macroeconomic framework for Europe   15
Diane Elson

2 A feminist alternative to austerity: the purple economy as a gender-egalitarian strategy for employment generation   27
Ipek Ilkkaracan

3 The role of gender equality in an equality-led sustainable development strategy   40
Özlem Onaran

vi Contents

PART II
Case studies on the impact of austerity policies on women and men

57

4 Crisis, policy responses and gender: the Italian experience 59
Giovanna Vertova

5 Gender equality and economic crisis: Ireland and the EU 76
Ursula Barry

6 The effects of the economic crisis and austerity on gender
equality in Spain and the Spanish regions 91
Elvira González Gago

7 The gender impact of austerity in the UK under the
Conservative–Liberal Democrat Coalition Government,
2010–15 113
Howard Reed

PART III
Alternative policies, the role of social infrastructure and the care economy

135

8 Making the case for a gender-aware, investment-led recovery
for Europe 137
Hannah Bargawi and Giovanni Cozzi

9 A European gendered investment plan with formal childcare
as a cornerstone 155
Lars Andersen and Signe Dahl

10 Costing a feminist plan for a caring economy: the case of free
universal childcare in the UK 168
Jerome De Henau

Conclusion: explaining austerity and its gender impact 189
Susan Himmelweit

Index *204*

FIGURES

6.1	The Spanish economic crisis: evolution of main macroeconomic variables	93
6.2	Evolution of regional economic indicators	94
6.3	Evolution of employment and unemployment rates by sex	102
7.1	Cumulative impact of tax and social security reforms between 2010 and 2015 in cash terms	115
7.2	Cumulative impact of tax and social security reforms between 2010 and 2015 as a percentage of net income	116
7.3	Distributional impact of tax, benefit and tax credit changes, 2010–15, in cash terms by gendered household type	117
7.4	Distributional impact of tax, benefit and tax credit changes, 2010–15, as a percentage of net income by gendered household type	118
7.5	Distributional impact of changes to direct taxes and social security at the individual level in cash terms: men and women by household income decile	120
7.6	Distributional impact of changes to direct taxes and social security at the individual level as a percentage of net income: men and women by household income decile	120
7.7	Distributional impacts of cuts to spending on public services (excluding social security) over the 2010–15 Parliament: annual cash equivalent by income decile	124
7.8	Distributional impacts of cuts to spending on public services (excluding social security) over the 2010–15 Parliament: as a percentage of net income plus value of services received, by income decile	125

viii Figures

7.9	Distributional impacts of cuts to spending on public services (excluding social security) over the 2010–15 Parliament: annual cash equivalent, by gendered household type	126
7.10	Distributional impacts of cuts to spending on public services (excluding social security) over the 2010–15 Parliament: as a percentage of net income plus value of services received, by gendered household type	127
7.11	Combined impact of tax/benefit measures and cuts to other public services, by income decile	128
7.12	Combined impact of tax/benefit measures and cuts to other public services, by gendered household type	129
9.1	Main reasons for part-time employment in the EU, 2014	156
9.2	Share of 0–3 year old children in childcare and female activity rate (25–49 years)	158
9.3	Effect on EU employment (male/female)	164

TABLES

4.1	The theoretical framework	63
4.2	Feminisation rate of employment, 2008	68
4.3	The three stages of the Italian PS (absolute change, thousands)	69
4.4	The three stages of unemployment and inactivity (absolute change, thousands)	70
5.1	EU falling employment rates	78
6.1	Evolution 2008–2014 of regional budget devoted to welfare policies (%)	99
6.2	Evolution of female and male regional employment rates	105
6.3	Evolution of regional female and male unemployment rates	107
7.1	Implied reductions in each category of spending accounting for population change	123
7.A1	Tax and social security reforms included in the analysis	133
7.A2	Spending categories in the Landman Economics public spending model	134
8.1	Projected private investment as % of GDP	147
8.2	Female employment as % of male employment	147
8.3	Projected average GDP growth (%)	148
8.4	Projected total employment (in millions)	149
8.5	Government spending as % of GDP	150
8.6	Projections for government debt and fiscal sustainability	150
9.1	Growth and employment effects on selected regions and countries, cumulative effect 2016–20	165
9.2	Examples of spill-over effects to EU countries that are not part of the strategy, cumulative effect 2016–20	166
10.1	Number of children and staff ratios	171
10.2	Childcare workers' annual and hourly pay and weekly hours (2014)	172

x Tables

10.3	Total cost of free universal full-time childcare	173
10.4	Number of jobs created in childcare services (universal full-time coverage)	173
10.5	Job creation in childcare and other sectors	175
10.6	Net household income gains from employment with and without Universal Credit and childcare costs (couples on median wages and with two pre-school children)	178
10.7	Tax revenue from job creation and net funding needs	179
10.8	Cost of free childcare for alternative hours and coverage	182

CONTRIBUTORS

Lars Andersen is Director of the Economic Council for the Labour Movement (ECLM), Denmark. He has an MSc in Economics and is a member of the editorial board of the *Danish Journal of Economics*, member of the Advisory Board at Institute of Economics, University of Copenhagen, former external Associate Professor and external examiner at Copenhagen Business School, and a former member of the Board of the Danish Research Council. Lars was formerly an economist in the ECLM and Statistics Bureau of Denmark.

Hannah Bargawi is Lecturer in Economics, School of Oriental and African Studies (SOAS), University of London. Before joining the Economics department, she worked at the Centre for Development Policy and Research at SOAS. She participated in the EU-funded AUGUR project, which utilised a global macroeconomic model to investigate scenarios for Europe and the world in 2030. Dr Bargawi has been involved in numerous other research and consultancy projects for international agencies such as the Asian Development Bank, the International Labour Organization and the United Nations Development Programme. Her current research focuses on the changing position, role and pay of both men and women in the labour market in Europe, considering whether or not recent austerity policies have had particularly gendered impacts and what an alternative, gender-equitable macroeconomic framework might look like.

Ursula Barry is an Associate Professor in the School of Social Policy, Social Work and Social Justice at University College Dublin. Her research interests include the economic and social position of Irish women; women, inequality and public policy; gender and the labour market; Irish economic and social policy; comparative policy perspectives in different EU countries; and poverty, inequality and social inclusion in Ireland and the EU. Ursula Barry was the Irish Expert on the EU Research Network

xii Contributors

on Gender Equality and Employment (ENEGE) until 2015, and is currently working on EU Networks on Equality Data and Women and Poverty. She has written extensively on gender equality, feminism and reproductive rights in Ireland. She co-authored (with Dr Pauline Jackson) the chapter on 'Ireland in Crisis 2008–2012: Women, austerity and inequality', in *Women and Austerity – the future for gender equality policy* (2014), edited by Jill Rubery and Maria Karamessini.

Giovanni Cozzi is Senior Lecturer in Economics at the University of Greenwich, London, UK, and a member of the Greenwich Political Economy Research Centre (GPERC). He was Senior Economist at the Foundation for European Progressive Studies (FEPS), Brussels, Belgium, and Research Fellow at the Centre for Development Policy and Research (CDPR) at the School of Oriental and African Studies. At CDPR he collaborated on a three-year European Commission FP7-funded project assessing the Challenges for Europe in the World of 2030 (AUGUR). His current research is on fiscal policies, the role of social and physical investment in promoting sustainable growth and employment for women and men, and the role of development banks. Several of his research publications employ the Cambridge Alphametrics Model (CAM), a Structuralist growth model, to project alternative macroeconomic scenarios and their policy implications.

Signe Dahl is Senior Economist at ECLM (Economic Council of the Labour Movement) in Copenhagen. Signe holds a Master of Science in Economics from the University of Copenhagen. She has also taken parts of the economic master's degree at the American University in Washington DC and the University of Hyderabad in India. Signe works with the analysis of international economics and the development in growth, prosperity and welfare in Europe. Signe has developed a wide range of analyses and reports on the harming effects of austerity on the European economy as well as the effects of an increase in the investment level on the European economy, including green and relevant investments' impact on the economic structures and the social return of increased labour force and education in Europe. Signe is also responsible for ECLM's international macroeconomic model HEIMDAL. Signe participates in several international networks.

Jerome De Henau is Senior Lecturer at the Open University, UK. A socio-economist with a PhD from the Free University of Brussels, his research interests are in gender analysis of economic issues and social policy. He has recently led a project on simulating gendered employment effects of investing in care in various OECD countries (funded by ITUC), and was co-investigator in an ESRC grant on "Gender and intrahousehold entitlements. A cross-national longitudinal analysis" (GenIX). His previous research projects include "Within-Household Inequalities and Public Policy" (WHIPP) as part of the Gender Equality Network (GENet) funded by the ESRC (2006–2010); investigating parenthood and employment in Europe (project Pepsi, funded by the Belgian Federal Government 2006–2008); fertility in Europe and the influence of employment conditions and

Contributors **xiii**

public policies (project MOCHO, funded by the European Commission 2001–2004); long-term care organisation in Belgium (2002–2003); and gender inequality in academia (2001–2003). He is a member of the International Association for Feminist Economics and the UK Women's Budget Group.

Diane Elson is Emeritus Professor of Sociology at the University of Essex, UK, and a Research Associate of the Center for Women's Global Leadership, Rutgers University, USA. She is currently a member of the UN Committee for Development Policy, and adviser to UN Women. In 2016 she was awarded the Leontief Prize for Advancing the Frontiers of Economic Thought. She is a former Vice President of the International Association for Feminist Economics and is currently chair of the UK Women's Budget Group, a network of academics, policy analysts and activists that scrutinises UK government budgets for their impact on gender inequality and women's rights. She has published widely on gender equality and economic policy, including articles in *World Development*, *Journal of International Development*, *Feminist Economics*, *Journal of Human Development and Capabilities*, and *International Review of Applied Economics*.

Susan Himmelweit is Emeritus Professor of Economics at the Open University, UK. Her research is on gender issues in economics, particularly those located at the boundary between the economy and the household. Her current research is on theoretical and policy issues to do with austerity, gender inequality and the care infrastructure of society. She is a founder member and past chair of the UK Women's Budget Group, a think tank analysing and commenting on the gender aspects of economic policy. She was President of the International Association for Feminist Economics in 2009 and is on the editorial board of its journal *Feminist Economics*.

Ipek Ilkkaracan is Professor of Economics at Istanbul Technical University, Faculty of Management, and Associate Director of the ITU Women's Studies Center. She holds a BA in Political Science from Swarthmore College, Pennsylvania and an MA and PhD in Economics from the New School for Social Research, New York. Her research focuses on the care economy, work–life balance and time-use; gender inequalities in labour markets; and macroeconomics of wages and unemployment. She has published in refereed journals such as *Applied Economics*, *Development*, *Feminist Economics*, *Labour* and *Topics in Middle Eastern and North African Economies*. Her 2010 book entitled *Work–Life Balance Policies in 7 OECD Countries: Towards Gender Equality in Labor Markets* was the first-ever publication in Turkish on the issue of work–life balance. Ilkkaracan is an Associate Editor of *Feminist Economics* (an SSCI journal), expert on Turkey in the European Network of Experts on Gender Equality (ENEGE) and a board member of the Middle Eastern Economics Association (MEEA). She is also the founding member of the Gender and Macroeconomics European Network (GEM-Europe), the ITU Women's Studies Center, the Women's Employment and Labor Initiative (KEIG Platform) and Women for Women's Human Rights – New Ways in Turkey.

xiv Contributors

Elvira González Gago is a senior economist specialising in employment, social cohesion and gender policies. She was director of the Centre for Economic Studies Tomillo for ten years. She has been the Spanish national expert of the network of labour market experts of the European Employment Policy Observatory since 2005 and the Spanish member of the European Network of Experts on Gender Equality (ENEGE) since 2008. She has also worked as consultant for the OECD, European Parliament, and public and private Spanish institutions, such as the Ministry for Social Services, the Ministry for Equal Opportunities and the respective departments of various Spanish regions. Through her work, which has resulted in publications in English, Spanish and German, she has gained a deep knowledge and understanding of how the situation of women evolves with (the absence of) gender-sensitive policies and of the obstacles to work on.

Zita Gurmai is a former Member of the European Parliament, vice-chair of the Committee on Women's Rights and Gender Equality in the 2004–2009 term, member of the Committee on Regional Development between 2009 and 2014 and also substitute in the Committee on Transport and Tourism in the last term. She was elected President of the PES (Party of European Socialists) Women in 2004. She is also Vice-President of the Foundation for European Progressive Studies. After finishing at the University of Economic Sciences in Budapest, Zita Gurmai worked in the private sphere, in numerous companies. She finally turned to politics in 1995, becoming the chargé d'affaires of the Women's Organisation of the Hungarian Socialist Party, which she has chaired since 2001. She became vice-chair of the Socialist International in 1999 and 2003 until 2008. She was a member of the Hungarian Parliament between 2002 and 2004.

Özlem Onaran is Director of the Greenwich Political Economy Research Centre (GPERC) and Professor of Economics at the University of Greenwich, UK. Özlem has done extensive research on issues of inequality, wage-led growth, employment, globalization and crises. She has directed research projects for the International Labour Organization, the Vienna Chamber of Labour and the Austrian Science Foundation, and is currently working on two projects funded by the Institute for New Economic Thinking and the Foundation of European Progressive Studies. She is a member of the Scientific Committee of the Foundation of European Progressive Studies, the Scientific Advisory Board of the Hans Boeckler Foundation, the Coordinating Committee of the Research Network Macroeconomics and Macroeconomic Policies, and the Policy Advisory Group of the Women's Budget Group, and is a research associate at the Political Economy Research Institute of the University of Massachusetts, Amherst. She has more than 70 articles in books and peer-reviewed journals such as *Cambridge Journal of Economics, World Development, Environment and Planning A, Public Choice, Economic Inquiry, European Journal of Industrial Relations, International Review of Applied Economics, Structural Change and Economic Dynamics, Eastern European Economics* and *Review of Political Economy*.

Howard Reed is Director of the economic research consultancy Landman Economics, which he founded in 2008. Before founding Landman Economics Howard was Chief Economist at the Institute for Public Policy Research. Landman Economics specialises in combining research of high policy relevance with cutting-edge microsimulation and econometric modelling in a number of economic research fields including labour markets, taxation, health economics and policy evaluation. Landman Economics has conducted a range of analyses of the distributional impact of UK tax and benefit policies since 2008 for a wide selection of clients including the UK Trades Union Congress, the Women's Budget Group, the Office of the Children's Commissioner in England and the Equality and Human Rights Commission.

Giovanna Vertova is Assistant Professor at the University of Bergamo, Italy, where she teaches International Political Economy, Development Economics and Political Economy. Her current research interests are the economics of globalisation, national systems of innovation and feminist economics. Vertova edited *The Changing Economic Geography of Globalization* (2006), *Lo spazio del Capitale* (2009) and, more recently, *The Great Recession and the Contradictions of Contemporary Capitalism* (2014) with Riccardo Bellofiore.

FOREWORD

When the financial and economic crisis hit, many saw this as an opportunity to overcome the flaws of the neoliberal system and to start work towards a political alternative that would lead to inclusive and shared growth. Alternatives did prevail – however, unfortunately these were (and still are) exclusionary alternatives that were largely promoted and backed by the far right. As a result, we are now witnessing a curious and dangerous alliance between the neoliberal system and a return to very traditional, conservative views.

More importantly, these views have served as an underpinning for the austerity measures that have had significant societal consequences. The institutional framework for gender equality has been downgraded in many countries, erroneously seen as an unnecessary expense, given the strong budgetary constraints imposed by austerity measures. Consequently, gender mainstreaming has almost completely disappeared in both the policy design and implementation phases. The effects of austerity have also been felt beyond the government sector. In the NGO scene, competition for scarce financial resources has led in many situations to detrimental competition instead of collaboration. Academia has also been impacted as departments and institutes that focused specifically on gender were either closed down or merged with other disciplines.

Sadly, the political sphere at the EU level has been as disappointing as that of its member states. The "Strategy on equality between women and men" came to an end in 2015 and since then we have waited in vain for a new comprehensive five-year plan. It is high time the European Commission issued a strategy beyond a mere staff document that could encourage European women to believe that greater efforts were being made to achieve equality. The draft Maternity Leave Directive became the victim of the European Commission's Regulatory Fitness and Performance Programme, as many member states were not open to negotiation on

xviii Foreword

the lengthening of full-paid maternity leave (the current Directive prescribes a mere 14 weeks, well below both ILO and WHO recommendations).

The Roadmap entitled "New start to address the challenges of work–life balance faced by working families" is supposed to give a new impetus to a better framework on the issue; however, in its current form, it fails to address many of the challenges ahead, e.g. it states clearly that it will not bring up the controversial issues of either the length or payment of maternity leave. Further, the Roadmap does not address the issues of changing family compositions and increased mobility of young families – instead, it is still firmly rooted in the traditional family model. Its aim is to facilitate the entry of women into the labour market; however, it does not focus on the quality of work and does not take into account the changing character of work, measures that are needed to improve the situation of women in the most difficult social and employment conditions. In this context, it seems that the Roadmap pushes many women against their will into the labour market, rather than emancipating and empowering them. The language of the text also reflects this approach – it does not aim to put the EU once more at the forefront of the gender agenda and it does not strive for a societal transformation.

Against this background, this publication puts forward progressive and inclusive political and economic alternatives. Rather than fine-tuning the neoliberal system – which would inexorably lead to greater inequality – the strategy proposed here is to promote a fairer, more caring and just society. It is the duty of our progressive family to come with an alternative that boldly challenges the system itself. This volume (as well as the project, meetings and seminars that gave light to it) is indeed a major step in the right direction.

Zita Gurmai
FEPS Vice President

ACKNOWLEDGMENTS

This edited volume is the outcome of original work that stems from the international project "Beyond Austerity, Towards, Employment: a Gender Aware Framework". This collaborative project was set up by the Foundation for European Progressive Studies (FEPS) with the collaboration of the Economic Council for the Labour Movement (ECLM), the Think Tank for Action on Social Change (TASC), the Open University and the School of Oriental and African Studies (SOAS), University of London. We are very grateful to all these institutions for supporting this project. We are particularly grateful to Dr Ernst Stetter, Secretary General of FEPS, Zita Gurmai, Vice President of FEPS, Lars Andersen, Managing Director of ECLM, David Begg, Director of TASC, and Nat O'Connor, former director of TASC.

The original work in this book is the result of many discussions and meetings among participants of the "Beyond Austerity, Towards Employment: a Gender Aware Framework" project. The inception seminar held in Brussels at FEPS in February 2014 allowed the project and research to be informed by comments from academics, policy-makers and civil society organisers. We extend our thanks to participants of this event and in particular Professor Marcella Corsi of La Sapienza, Università di Roma, for her support and input. Further project events helped inform the research, including an event co-organised by the Fundació Rafael Campalans, in Barcelona, and a final dissemination event in Brussels in March 2015. We are grateful to the Fundació's director, Esther Niubó, and the event organisers in Brussels and Barcelona. In particular, thanks to Ischi Graus, Judit Tanczos, Elva Bova.

We would also like to thank Beth Tasker and Rebecca Omonira for editing all the contributions with great care and attention. Thanks also to Routledge, the IAFFE Series Editor Jill Rubery and two anonymous referees.

Last, but not least, we thank the authors of this volume who enthusiastically participated in the seminars, and have contributed their long research experience and expertise to this project.

ABBREVIATIONS

ALMP	Active Labour Market Policies
BCS	British Crime Survey
BHPS	British Household Panel Survey
CAM	Cambridge Alphametrics Macroeconomic Model
CEO	Chief Executive Officer
COFOG	Classification of Functions of Government
DWP	Department for Work and Pensions
EA-18	Euro Area
EC	European Commission
ECB	European Central Bank
ECLM	Economic Council of the Labour Movement
EES	European Employment Strategy
EIB	European Investment Bank
EIG	Early Intervention Grant
EMU	European Monetary Union
ENEGE	European Network for Gender, Employment and Social Inclusion
EPSU	European Public Service Union
ESA	European System of National Accounts
ESRI	Economic and Social Research Institute
EU	European Union
EU SILC	European Union Statistics on Income and Living Conditions
EU-28	European Union 28 member state countries
EWL	European Women's Lobby
FRS	Family Resources Survey
FEPS	Foundation for European Progressive Studies
FTE	Full-time equivalent
GET	Global Employment Trends – International Labour Organization

xxii Abbreviations

GDP	Gross Domestic Product
GLS	General Lifestyle Survey
GPERC	Greenwich Political Economy Research Centre
GPG	Gender pay gap
HMRC	Her Majesty's Revenue and Customs
IFS	Institute for Fiscal Studies
ILO	International Labour Organization
IMF	International Monetary Fund
ITC	Innovation, Technology and Communication
LCF	Living Costs and Food Survey
LFS	Labour Force Surveys
NEF	New Economics Foundation
NHS	National Health Service
NGO	Non-governmental organisation
OECD	Organisation for Economic Co-operation and Development
OFCE	Observatoire Français des Conjonctures Économiques
ONS	Office for National Statistics
PESA	Public Expenditure Statistical Analyses
PS	Production System
PSIRU	Public Services International Research Unit
R&D	Research and Development
SNP	Scottish National Party
SOAS	School of Oriental and African Studies
SOC	Standard Occupational Classification
SPA	State Pension Age
SRS	Social Reproduction System
TASC	Think Tank on Social Change
UC	Universal Credit
UK	United Kingdom
UN	United Nations
UNEP	United Nations Environment Programme
US	United States
USC	Universal Social Charge
VAT	Value Added Tax
WBG	Women's Budget Group
WHO	World Health Organization

INTRODUCTION

Austerity and after – the case for a gendered approach

Hannah Bargawi, Giovanni Cozzi and Susan Himmelweit

Aims, structure and theoretical framework of the book

This edited volume, *Economics and Austerity in Europe: Gendered impacts and sustainable alternatives*, explores two major arguments. The first is that while austerity policies have had differential impacts across Europe, their *gendered* impacts have been severe, structural and manifold, and so far have been under-researched and underestimated. Thus one of the core objectives of this book is to use rigorous analysis to shed more light on the gendered impact of austerity policies both at EU and country level.

The second argument is that an alternative to continued austerity is not only possible and indeed required from the perspective of sustainable growth, employment generation and promoting equity more generally, but it is also necessary in order to address gender inequalities. As such, another central objective and theme of the book is to demonstrate the desirability and viability of investment in care and social infrastructure as a gender-aware policy alternative that would also address Europe's macroeconomic difficulties.

In order to achieve these two objectives, the book has been split into three parts. The first part makes the case for why and how gender equity needs to be addressed in macroeconomic policy-making by demonstrating the links between gender equality, employment and sustainable growth. As such, the three chapters that make up this part provide a theoretical framework from which later chapters draw to build a gendered approach to austerity and propose an alternative vision for Europe.

The second part of the volume explores concrete case studies of austerity policies, focusing on their differential gender impacts and policy alternatives across European countries. The cases of Ireland, Italy, Spain and the United Kingdom are considered, providing a wide range of experiences and policy trajectories from which lessons for other countries in Europe and beyond can be drawn. These case studies not only explore the common gendered impact of austerity policies across Europe, but they also help to identify country-specific gender patterns and how these have been impacted by austerity policies. These countries have been chosen as amongst those in Western Europe that have experienced some of the harshest austerity measures, whether self-imposed (as in the United Kingdom) or in cases where these policies have been externally imposed or recommended within the context of the Eurozone crisis (such as in Italy and Spain).

The third part of the book builds on the lessons from parts one and two and considers the question of what should come after austerity. Its chapters use various quantitative and econometric tools and models to assess the gender impact of alternative economic policies. It proposes and discusses ways for policy-makers to move beyond the current austerity consensus, highlighting the necessity of adopting gender-sensitive alternatives for long-term economic viability.

Finally, the conclusion returns to the theme of why austerity policies have been imposed when they have been so ineffective in addressing Europe's economic problems. It argues that policy has in practice been driven by a different agenda – a disengagement from public involvement in social reproduction and its reprivatisation – that has inevitably impacted adversely on women. It is this agenda that needs to be challenged if progress in tackling gender inequalities is to be made.

Austerity defined

The rise of austerity in our economic, political and social vocabulary is not new. In macroeconomic terms, Blyth's (2013: 12) definition of austerity is worth noting:

> Austerity is a form of voluntary deflation in which the economy adjusts through the reduction of wages, prices, and public spending to restore competitiveness, which is (supposedly) best achieved by cutting the state's budget, debts, and deficits. Doing so, its advocates believe, will inspire "business confidence" since the government will neither be "crowding-out" the market for investment by sucking up all the available capital through the issuance of debt, nor adding to the nation's already "too big" debt.

The rationale for fiscal retrenchment during recession relies at its most basic on the argument that it will generate business confidence and policy credibility so that fiscal consolidation in the short run will lead to higher economic growth, driven by private investment in the medium to long term. This has become known as "expansionary fiscal austerity" (Alesina and Ardagna 2009).

The intellectual roots of austerity economics date back to 19th century classical liberal economists such as Adam Smith and David Ricardo (Blyth 2013). However, the recent revival of austerity economics is more closely related to economic theories of the 1970s and 1980s and their application to the sovereign debt crises in emerging and developing countries during that time. The argument that fiscal deficits crowd out private investment and must therefore be curtailed, even during recessions, was forcefully pushed by the International Monetary Fund during that period (Polak 1997) and remains a persistent belief among many policy-makers today (Ostry et al. 2015).

This argument appeared to receive support in Europe from the experiences of Ireland and Denmark in the late 1980s. In an analysis of the policy responses to the 1980s economic crises in these two countries, Giavazzi and Pagano (1990) asserted that reductions in government spending had a positive impact on investors' confidence and that these reductions, coupled with moderate tax cuts, were expansionary and helped spearhead economic recovery.

However, the economic environment of the 1980s was very different from now. Fiscal consolidation in Ireland and Denmark occurred at a time of favourable economic circumstances, which included access to new European fiscal revenues, a currency devaluation in Ireland prior to entering the European Exchange Rate Mechanism, and the opening up of the European single market (Konzelmann 2012). Thus, it is questionable whether the Irish and Danish cases can be used to make any case for "expansionary fiscal austerity" today.

Further, it is unlikely that higher levels of public spending would crowd out private investment. As Stiglitz (2015) has argued, in the current economic situation public investment is more likely to crowd-in private investment than crowd it out. Rather, public investment in both physical and social infrastructure is essential to generate a sustainable economic recovery. On the one hand, investment in physical infrastructure (in sectors such as renewable energy and the green economy, transport and telecommunication) creates demand in the short term for new goods and services, and in the medium term stimulates productivity and growth through an expanded stock of physical capital and higher efficiency. On the other hand, investment in social infrastructure (i.e. investment in nurseries, hospitals, prisons, community housing and more generally in public services providing care, health, education and training) fosters employment and poverty reduction in the short term and increases the stock of human capital and human capacity in the longer term, again stimulating productivity and growth (ILO 2014). From a gender perspective, investment in social infrastructure not only has the advantage of directly and indirectly generating more employment in total, it reduces gender inequality in employment opportunities, which investment in physical infrastructure tends to worsen (De Henau et al. 2016).

Reinhart and Rogoff (2010) claimed to have provided empirical backing for the original theoretical arguments for austerity, suggesting that a debt-to-GDP ratio above 90% would prove inimical to economic growth. However, this and other empirical analyses of the links between government debt and growth continue to be marred by data concerns and a nagging question over causality, i.e. is it low growth that causes rising debt-to-GDP ratios or does causality run the other way around (Herndon et al. 2013)? The above arguments for pro-cyclical austerity have struggled to find traction among academic economists and empirical evidence of its success remains elusive (Sawyer 2012).

Nevertheless, European policy-makers have adopted deficit reduction policies on an unprecedented scale in response to the 2008 financial crisis. Analogies drawn between government and household budgets have also been used to popularise the belief (not grounded in economic theory) that governments should live within their means (Wren-Lewis 2015). It would appear that political motivations rather than economic arguments have driven the agenda for austerity across Europe (Blyth 2013; Wren-Lewis 2015).

Tracing the European policy discourse

The origins of fiscal retrenchment in Europe can be traced back to the creation of the European single market in the late 1980s. During this period policy priorities shifted drastically from a commitment to full employment towards combating inflation and increasing labour market flexibility. At the turn of the 1980s, laissez-faire economic liberalism was put forward as the solution to economic problems that were deemed to be the result of earlier Keynesian policies and state intervention in the economy (Petit 2012). Countries were urged to contain government expenditures (especially on welfare) to prevent budget deficits fuelling inflation. Governments were also encouraged to grant independence to central banks to enable them to use interest rates to keep inflation under control.

Indeed, across Europe since the early 1980s fiscal policy has been seen as a tool to discourage fiscal profligacy and budget deficits that lead to unsustainable public debt (Arestis and Sawyer 2010). This is exemplified by the Stability and Growth Pact, which demands that countries keep their fiscal deficit to an arbitrary 3% of Gross Domestic Product (GDP) limit in any year. It is also reflected in the 60% debt-to-GDP ratio imposed under the same pact (Arestis and Sawyer 2010). In the United Kingdom this position is reflected in the Charter for Budget Responsibility (HM Treasury 2015), which states that UK governments must run absolute budget surpluses when the economy is growing. In addition, another institutional arrangement set up in the 1990s in the EU is the complete separation between the monetary authorities and the fiscal authorities (in the shape of national governments) and the absence of a European Treasury. Thus, there is no significant fiscal policy operated at the European level (Irvin and Izurieta 2011).

Such rules imposed by the European Union, which arbitrarily specify a fixed limit on government borrowing, fail to recognise that borrowing serves as a mechanism for distributing the cost of adjustment to shocks over time. In addition, constraints on government borrowing reduce the flexibility of national governments' fiscal policy and make fiscal coordination very difficult (Arestis et al. 2001). Thus, by way of its specific design, the EU has removed active fiscal policy from the domain of national policy-makers, and has constrained it to a mere tool for balancing budgets. The adoption of such an economic stance at the European level meant that the response to the economic crisis of 2008 was severely curtailed. Confronted with a potential public debt crisis, increased budget deficits resulting from the global financial crisis and large bank bailouts, one by one European countries implemented harsh cuts to government spending in an attempt to spearhead economic growth and create jobs. However, it soon became evident that such policies were having the opposite effect.

Over the past four years European institutions have begun to recognise that at the root of European economic stagnation lay inadequately low levels of investment. To this end, several European policy-makers argued that the way out of stagnation and high unemployment would be through the combination of budget consolidation and debt control with stronger employment and social cohesion (Rasmussen and Schulz 2010). In other words, appropriately paced fiscal consolidation (austerity) should go hand in hand with growth-enhancing policies (Buti and Padoan 2012). At economic policy level this translated into two main initiatives: the Compact for Growth and Jobs (June 2012); and European Commission President Jean-Claude Juncker's Investment Plan for Europe (November 2014).

However, these measures are likely to prove inadequate to significantly stimulate economic growth and reduce unemployment in Europe. There are two main reasons for this. First, these initiatives are very small. The Juncker Plan, for instance, only represents an annual investment boost of approximately 0.75% of EU GDP and this is clearly not sufficient to stimulate economic recovery in Europe. Further, the potential positive effects of these initiatives are significantly dampened by continued austerity policies. In a recent study, Griffith-Jones and Cozzi (2016) argued that Europe would need at least an additional €530 billion of investment over the period 2015–20 and that the combination of the Juncker Plan with continued austerity policies would lead to a very low growth rate of 1.5% across the EU for the period 2015–20, thus, well below the pre-crisis period of 2000–08 when European average GDP growth stood at 2.3%.

Austerity and gender analysis

Understanding the gender impact of policies requires assessing their impact on all known gender inequalities – e.g. in employment rates, in earnings, in hourly wages rates, skill levels and employment incentives. It also requires assessing their impact on less obviously "economic" variables, such as the amount of time spent on unpaid work, the gender distribution of caring labour, and gender roles and opportunities more generally.

Such gender-impact assessment is important for all policies whatever their aim, not only for those primarily designed to reduce gender inequality. This is for a number of reasons. First, recognising and quantifying differential gender impacts on a number of dimensions is the first stage in mitigating any worsening effects on corresponding gender inequalities and in choosing policies that ameliorate them. Legislation in some jurisdictions, such as the UK and the EU, requires this to be done wherever possible (European Commission 2010).

Secondly, understanding potential gender impacts can improve the efficiency of policy-making, whatever its goals. This is because men and women differ in their behavioural responses to any policy change due to the fact that they occupy different social positions and are affected in distinct ways by social norms (Seguino 2013; Himmelweit 2002; De Henau and Himmelweit 2013). Evidence from developing countries has repeatedly shown the negative effects on growth, employment and productivity of reforms that are not gender aware (Elson 1995; Fontana and Rodgers 2005; Seguino 2000).

This book uses gender-impact analysis of austerity policies to show how they have set back gender equality in various dimensions and, in consequence, have hampered the achievement of a sustainable recovery. This analysis is also proactive – alternative policies are proposed to achieve such a recovery while also reducing gender inequalities.

Austerity policies are having detrimental effects on long-term economic growth and employment across Europe (see e.g. Griffith-Jones and Cozzi 2016; Dauderstaedt and Hillebrandt 2013; Bagaria et al. 2012; Griffith-Jones et al. 2012; Sawyer 2012). They are also significantly shifting the burden of fiscal adjustments on to women. Karamessini and Rubery (2013) warned that austerity measures risk reversing progress towards gender equality by undermining important employment and social welfare measures. Corsi and D'Ippoliti (2013) stressed that, as main beneficiaries of public expenditure schemes, as providers of services that complement or substitute for public provisioning (e.g. of care) and because they are overrepresented in the public sector, women are likely to feel the impacts of austerity policies particularly severely.

The European Women's Lobby (2012) reports that increasing precariousness has begun to significantly affect lone mothers and female pensioners, due to their greater reliance on state-funded services under threat from cutbacks. In the United Kingdom, cuts to benefits and tax credits are negatively impacting lone parents in particular, who are predominantly women, while cuts to public services and especially cuts to spending on health, social care and public housing impact most on lone parents and single pensioners, who again tend to be predominantly women (Reed, Ch.7 in this volume). This is also evident in Ireland, where public sector cuts have had a disproportionate negative impact on lone parents, large families, unemployed households, travellers and people with disabilities. These groups are particularly at risk of poverty and deprivation (Barry, Ch.5 in this volume).

Cuts in government expenditure have also led to a reduction in female-dominated public sector jobs, pay and working conditions. A study conducted by the European Federation of Public Services Unions in 2010–11 in four European countries revealed public sector job cuts to have been a widespread feature of austerity policies, with women's employment disproportionately affected (EPSU 2011). For instance, in Italy cuts in local public services as a result of reduced transfers from national to regional and local public authorities have led to women withdrawing from the labour market due to an increased difficulty in balancing paid work with family responsibilities (Vertova, Ch.4 in this volume). In Spain, public sector wage cuts and increases in civil servants' working hours have affected women more than men due to their higher participation in public employment (Gago, Ch.6 in this volume).

Introduction **7**

The overall picture that emerges from the chapters in this volume is that there are clear gender effects of austerity policies across Europe. Women are feeling the impact of such policies both directly via their reduced employment in the public sector, and indirectly via the reduction of public sector spending on crucial care, health and education services that have, in the past, supported working women. Women are also the greater users of public services, both directly for themselves and because they are more likely to live in households with other users.

Developing a gendered alternative to austerity

The negative impact of austerity policies on growth and employment has led to the emergence of alternative policy proposals for a sustainable economic recovery in Europe. Several of these proposals have focused on the need to adopt an investment-led expansionary macroeconomic framework in order to create growth and jobs in Europe (e.g. Griffith-Jones and Cozzi 2016; Stiglitz 2015; Varoufakis et al. 2013; Bagaria et al. 2012; McKinley and Cozzi 2011 among others).

In a recent study, the International Labour Organization (ILO) (2014) stressed the need for a more integrated approach to economic recovery that combines social protection, employment and taxation policies. In particular, it argued that the better financing of health and social protection systems, and their coordination with employment and taxation policies, could lead to sustainable growth and reduce poverty (ILO 2014).

Concurrently, a number of scholars have begun to demonstrate what a feminist alternative to austerity might constitute in concrete policy terms (Annesley 2014; Perrons and Plomien 2013). In the United Kingdom, the UK and Scottish Women's Budget Groups (2015) have put forward a "Feminist economic strategy" – Plan F – to create a caring and sustainable economy, reduce gender inequality in the labour market and stimulate employment by investing in social as well as physical infrastructure and using fiscal policy to reduce income inequality. This plan recommends a reversal of current and planned expenditure cuts that have particularly adverse effects on women, reforming social security to ensure a fairer sharing of care and the costs of caring, and improving the conditions of both paid and unpaid care work. While this plan would partly pay for itself in increased revenues from employment, Plan F also advocates taking effective action on tax avoidance, cutting spending on nuclear weapons and a progressive reversal of previous tax cuts.

Book structure

Part 1 of this volume presents the core theoretical framework for the exploration of gender, austerity and policy alternatives in Europe. Chapter 1 by Diane Elson provides an overview of the need for a gender-equitable macroeconomic framework and the importance of investing in a caring economy for an inclusive and equitable recovery. Elson draws on feminist principles to explain the need for a gender-equitable alternative to the current macroeconomic trajectory, and citing a number of feminist contributions outlines the content of such alternative policies.

Chapter 2 by Ipek Ilkkaracan introduces a vision for a new economic order in which the better-known green economy is complemented by a "purple" economy (purple being the symbolic colour adopted by the feminist movement in countries around the world). The green economy accounts for the value of ecosystems in the design of production and consumption processes in order to enable their sustainability. In a similar vein, the purple economy implies the need for an investment plan in social care infrastructure, and emphasises the employment generation potential of such purple investments. Ilkkaracan evaluates how a purple investment plan could spearhead economic recovery in Europe, while improving gender equality and the sustainability of caring labour.

Chapter 3 by Özlem Onaran concludes Part 1 by outlining the cornerstones of a macroeconomic model that can be used to analyse the various channels through which gender equality can influence growth and employment outcomes. The chapter assesses the main features that a post-Keynesian/neo-Kaleckian demand-led growth model with endogenous changes in productivity and employment and a role for public spending would require in order to incorporate gender-relevant categories in the behavioural functions that determine private aggregate demand.

Part 2 of this volume presents several case studies on the impact of austerity policies on men and women in Europe, and aims to demonstrate that country-specific gender-impact analysis is a necessary tool to design effective economic policies for sustainable and equitable growth. Chapter 4 by Giovanna Vertova looks specifically at the Italian case by first presenting a theoretical framework that integrates different dimensions of a gender analysis and emphasises the role of the production and reproduction systems, both of which are required to create human well-being. The second part of the chapter uses this theoretical framework to analyse the gender impact of the crisis and austerity policies in Italy.

Chapter 5 by Ursula Barry explores the gendered impact of austerity in the Irish context, considering in particular the policy processes at European and national level. Barry demonstrates how policy-making processes have not been informed by gendered analyses, either in their design or their implementation. The result has been a dangerous loss of commitment to gender equality principles within the EU and in Ireland in particular.

Chapter 6 by Elvira Gonzáles Gago considers gender equality in Spain, tracing the evolution of policies since the global economic crisis. Gago's conclusions support the findings of the other case studies in this volume, showing how Spain's policy responses to the global economic crisis have been gender-blind and that women have fared worse than men in the post-crisis period. The chapter also demonstrates the importance of considering regional differences in order to appreciate fully the gender impact of austerity in Spain.

The final chapter in this part, Chapter 7 by Howard Reed, takes the distributional issues further and considers the differential impacts of austerity policies in the United Kingdom, ultimately revealing the regressive and gender inequitable outcomes of the UK government's policy agenda. Reed's analysis of the combined impact of tax and welfare changes shows women's losses as a share of their household's income to be around twice as large as men's, and that already vulnerable groups (such as lone parents and single pensioners, both of whom are predominantly female) suffer disproportionately from these changes.

Part 3 of this volume builds upon the theoretical and empirical debates presented in Parts 1 and 2 and discusses gender-aware alternative policies for equitable and sustainable recovery in Europe. As such, the chapters within this part demonstrate the content and feasibility of adopting alternative policies to austerity and the necessity that these address gender equality issues. Chapter 8 by Hannah Bargawi and Giovanni Cozzi contrasts and evaluates the medium-term effects of two alternative scenarios for Europe: continued austerity vis-à-vis a gendered-expansionary macroeconomic framework. Using the Cambridge Alphametrics Model (CAM), a structuralist growth model that has its intellectual roots in Keynesian economics, the chapter demonstrates the economic feasibility of a gendered-expansionary macroeconomic scenario as an alternative to austerity policies. Such a strategy is economically viable and leads to substantial gains in terms of job creation for women and men, as well as accelerated growth and lower government debt and fiscal deficits.

Chapter 9 by Lars Andersen and Signe Dahl presents a gender investment plan that would promote equality between men and women by balancing childcare responsibilities and creating jobs for women. This plan stands on two pillars. First, substantial investment in developing, extending and subsidising childcare systems should increase the female labour force and ensure that no parent is excluded from the labour market by childcare responsibilities. Secondly, the increased female labour force would be employed by an upsurge in the demand for female labour created by such public investment. This chapter demonstrates that a gendered investment plan with childcare at its heart would promote equality between men and women.

Chapter 10 by Jerome De Henau presents a costed alternative strategy for the United Kingdom to achieve a caring economy that works for the people and for gender equality, by investing in high-quality caring services and supporting more equitable sharing of unpaid care between men and women. This would require better government funding of social infrastructure (e.g. care, health, education and training services, social security and housing), which would improve both well-being and productivity, not only day to day but in ways that persist over time and that benefit future generations.

Drawing from the theoretical and empirical evidence presented throughout this volume, the book concludes with a contribution by Susan Himmelweit on austerity and its gender impact. This chapter explores the background and rationale for the adoption of policies that have held back recovery and set back gender equality throughout Europe. It does so in part by examining trends that were emerging well before the financial crisis hit, as well as providing critical reflections on the impact of austerity on men and women and on the care economy.

References

Alesina, A. and S. Ardagna. 2009. "Large Changes in Fiscal Policy: Taxes Versus Spending." Working Paper No.15438. Cambridge, MA: National Bureau of Economic Research (NBER).

Annesley, C. 2014. *UK Austerity Policy: A Feminist Perspective.* Berlin: Friedrich Ebert Stiftung.

Arestis, P. and M. Sawyer. 2010. "The Return of Fiscal Policy." *Journal of Post Keynesian Economics* 32: 112–130.

Arestis, P., K. Mccauley and M. Sawyer. 2001. "An Alternative Stability Pact for the European Union." *Cambridge Journal of Economics* 25: 112–130.

Bagaria, N., D. Holland and J. Van Reenen. 2012. "Fiscal Consolidation in a Depression." *National Institute Economic Review* 221.

Blyth, M. 2013. *Austerity: The History of a Dangerous Idea.* Oxford: Oxford University Press.

Buti, M. and P.C. Padoan. 2012. "From a Vicious to a Virtuous Circle in the Eurozone – the Time is Ripe." Vox CEPR's Policy Portal. www.voxeu.org/article/vicious-virtuous-circle-eurozone (accessed 29 February 2016).

Corsi, M. and C. D'Ippoliti. 2013. "Class and Gender in Europe, Before and During the Economic Crisis." Working Papers CEB 13-027, Universite Libre de Bruxelles.

Dauderstaedt, M. and E. Hillebrandt (eds). 2013. *Alternatives to Austerity: Progressive Growth Strategies for Europe.* Berlin: Fridrich-Ebert Stiftung.

De Henau, J. and S. Himmelweit. 2013. "Examining Public Policy from a Gendered Intra-household Perspective: Changes in Family-related Policies in the UK, Australia and Germany since the Mid-nineties." *Oñati Socio-Legal Series* 3(7).

De Henau, J., S. Himmelweit, Z. Łapniewska and D. Perrons. 2016. *Investing in the Care Economy: A Gender Analysis of Employment Stimulus in Seven OECD Countries.* Report by the UK Women's Budget Group. Brussels: International Trade Union Congress.

Elson, D. 1995. "Gender Awareness in Modeling Structural Adjustment." *World Development* 23(11): 1851–1868.

European Commission. 2010 "Strategy for Equality between Women and Men 2010–2015." Communication from the Commission. Luxembourg: Publications Office of the European Union.

EPSU. 2011. *Widening the Gender Gap: The Impact of Public Sector Pay and Job Cuts on the Employment and Working Conditions of Women in Four Countries.* Brussels: EPSU.

European Women's Lobby. 2012. *The Price of Austerity: The Impact on Women's Rights and Gender Equality in Europe.* Brussels: EWL.

Fontana, M. and Y. van der Meulen Rodgers. 2005. "Gender Dimensions in the Analysis of Macro-Poverty Linkages." *Development Policy Review* 23(3): 333–349

Giavazzi, F. and M. Pagano. 1990. "Can Severe Fiscal Contractions Be Expansionary? Tales of Two Small European Countries." *NBER Macroeconomics Annual* 5: 75–122.

Griffith-Jones, S. and G. Cozzi. 2016. "Investment-led Growth: A Solution to the European Crisis." In M. Jacobs and M. Mazzuccato (eds). *Rethinking Capitalism: Economic Policies for Sustainable and Equitable Economic Growth.* London: Wiley-Blackwell.

Griffith-Jones, S., M. Kollatz-Ahnen, L. Andersen and S. Hansen. 2012. "Shifting Europe from Austerity to Growth: A Proposed Investment Programme for 2012–2015." FEPS-IPD-ECLM Policy Brief.

HM Treasury. 2015. *Charter for Budget Responsibility. Summer Budget 2015 Update.* London: HM Treasury.

Herndon, T., M. Ash and R. Pollin. 2013. "Does High Public Debt Consistently Stifle Economic Growth? A Critique of Reinhart and Rogoff." Amherst, MA: PERI Working Paper 322.

Himmelweit, S. 2002. "Making Visible the Hidden Economy: The Case for Gender-impact Analysis of Economic Policy." *Feminist Economics* 8(1): 49–70.

International Labour Organization. 2014. *Social Protection Global Policy Trends 2010–2015: From Fiscal Consolidation to Expanding Social Protection: Key to Crisis Recovery, Inclusive Development and Social Justice.* Geneva: ILO.

Irvin, G. and A. Izurieta. 2011. "Fundamental Flaws in the European Project." *Economic & Political WEEKLY* 6: 14–16.

Karamessini, M. and J. Rubery (eds). 2013. *Women and Austerity: The Economic Crisis and the Future for Gender Equality.* Oxford: Routledge.

Karamessini, M. and J. Rubery. 2014. "The Challenge of Austerity for Equality: A Consideration of Eight European Countries in the Crisis." In A. Eydoux, A. Math and H. Périvier (eds). *European Labour Markets in Times of Crisis: A Gender Perspective. Debates and Policies.* Paris: OFCE 135: 15–40.

Konzelmann, S. 2015. "The Political Economics of Austerity." *Cambridge Journal of Economics* 38: 701–741.

McKinley, T. and G. Cozzi 2011 "Fiscal Contraction or Fiscal Expansion in the US: Which Will Promote Growth and Employment?" CDPR Development Viewpoint No. 66. London: Centre for Development Policy and Research.

Ostry, J., A.R. Ghosh and R. Espinoza. 2015. "When Should Public Debt Be Reduced?" IMF Staff Discussion Paper SDN/15/10. Washington DC.

Perrons, D. and A. Plomien. 2013. "Gender, Inequality and the Crisis." In M. Karamessini and J. Rubery (eds). *Women and Austerity: The Economic Crisis and the Future for Gender Equality.* Oxford: Routledge.

Petit, P. 2012. "Building Faith in a Common Currency: Can the Eurozone Get beyond the Common Market Logic?" *Cambridge Journal of Economics* 36: 271–281.

Polak, J. 1997. "The IMF Monetary Model at Forty." IMF Working Paper 97/49. Washington DC.

Rasmussen, P. and M. Schulz. 2010. "It's Time for a New Deal on European Economic Policy." PES. http://pes.eu/en/news/its-time-new-deal-european-economic-policy (accessed 1 March 2016).

Reinhart, C. and K. Rogoff. 2010. "Growth in a Time of Debt." *American Economic Review* 100(2): 573–578.

Sawyer, M. 2012. "Fiscal Austerity: The 'Cure' which Makes the Patient Worse." Policy Paper. London: CLASS.

Seguino, S. 2000. "Gender Inequality and Economic Growth: A Cross-country Analysis." *World Development* 28(7): 1211–1230.

Seguino, S. 2013. "From Micro-level Gender Relations to the Macro Economy and Back Again." In D. Figart and T. Warnecke (eds). *Handbook of Research on Gender and Economic Life.* Cheltenham: Edward Elgar.

Stiglitz, J. 2015. "Stimulating the Economy in an Era of Debt and Deficit." *The Economists' Voice* (March).

UK and Scottish Women's Budget Groups. 2015. "Plan F: A Feminist Economic Strategy for a Caring and Sustainable Economy." http://wbg.org.uk/wp-content/uploads/2015/02/PLAN-F-2015.pdf (accessed 28 December 2015).

Varoufakis, Y., S. Holland and J.K. Galbraith. 2013. "A Modest Proposal for Resolving the Eurozone Crisis." Version 4.0. https://varoufakis.files.wordpress.com/2013/07/a-modest-proposal-for-resolving-the-eurozone-crisis-version-4-0-final1.pdf (accessed 29 February 2016).

Wren-Lewis, S. 2015. "The Austerity Con." *London Review of Books* 37(4): 9–11.

PART I

Theorising on gender, austerity and policy alternatives

1

A GENDER-EQUITABLE MACROECONOMIC FRAMEWORK FOR EUROPE

Diane Elson

Introduction

In 2008 European countries were hit by a severe financial crisis, in which several leading banks had to be bailed out. Private sector financial firms lost confidence in one another and inter-bank lending dried up. The credit crunch led to a recession, with falling employment and output. In the period 2008–10, governments in many countries tried to counteract this by providing a fiscal stimulus, taking measures to increase public expenditure and cut taxes. As a result, the recession did not turn into a depression, and the downward spiral in output and employment was halted. However, the recession caused government budget deficits to rise in many EU countries, as tax receipts fell and statutory welfare payments, such as unemployment benefits, rose; and large payments were made to bail out the banks. Consequently, the debt-to-GDP ratios in many EU countries rose, in some cases substantially. By May 2010, the financial crisis of 2008 (which was a crisis in the private sector financial system) had morphed into a crisis in public finance in several EU countries, including Ireland, Greece and Portugal, which were unable to continue to borrow at affordable rates of interest in international financial markets. In return for loans from the European Central Bank, the European Commission and the IMF, governments of these countries were required to adopt austerity policies, mainly comprising deep cuts in public expenditure. Doubts were also cast over the solvency of Spain and Italy, and austerity policies were introduced by their governments to try to avert a crisis. Even in some countries where there was no problem in servicing public debt, such as the UK, deep cuts in public expenditure were introduced. Austerity policies led to a second recession in 2012 in several EU countries, including Italy, Spain, Portugal, Greece, Austria and the Netherlands. By the end of 2015, there were signs that output was beginning to recover, but in many countries unemployment remained high, and many people who wanted

16 Diane Elson

full-time secure salaried employment were forced to accept precarious part-time work and/or become self-employed for very low returns. As this book shows, women were disproportionately hit by the austerity measures. On average a larger proportion of women's income tends to come from social security payments, so cuts to social security tend to hit women harder than men. Cuts to public health and care services tend to hit women harder than men because women make more use of these services than men, not only to meet their own needs but also to assist them in taking care of others. Women still bear ultimate responsibility for the care of their families, neighbours and communities, and when public services are cut, women frequently have to increase their hours of unpaid care work. In many countries a greater share of women's employment than men's is in the public sector, so cuts to spending on public services tends to lead to larger job losses for women than for men.

We need a gender-equitable macroeconomic policy framework for Europe based on the principles set out in this chapter. Governments must expand their understanding of the economy to include non-market and unpaid work; recognize, reduce and redistribute unpaid work; dethrone GDP as the premier indicator; invest in social as well as physical infrastructure; put more emphasis on raising taxes on well-off people and companies; and transform the governance of finance so that finance is directed to socially useful ends.

Expand the understanding of the economy to include non-market and unpaid work

Women are disadvantaged by policies that are based on economic models that do not include unpaid work. It is important to recognize that economies do not just consist of the production of goods and services by paid work, they include the production of goods and services through unpaid work in households and communities. Unpaid production makes an important contribution to the well-being of those who benefit from it and produces a vital input for the economy: labour. Though conventional economic analysis takes labour to be an externally given resource endowment, like land labour should be seen as a produced means of production. To produce labour for the economy, on a daily and an intergenerational basis, unpaid work is required, such as shopping, preparing meals, cleaning and providing interpersonal care for members of families and communities. This unpaid work is disproportionately done by women and girls (Picchio 1992; Folbre 1994; Elson 1998).

Gender equality has all too often been reduced to questions of women's participation in markets, with little consideration of the terms of that participation. There has been in many countries a squeeze on time available to provide unpaid care for family and friends, as women have increased their participation in paid work, but men have not increased their participation in unpaid work to the same extent. Meanwhile public provision of infrastructure that reduces unpaid work has been inadequate.

Time use studies throw light on all uses of labour: market and non-market, paid and unpaid, and assist in understanding all dimensions of labour use. A system has been developed for conducting comparable time use studies in European countries, initially in 2000 and updated in 2008 (Eurostat 2009). Fifteen countries[1] have conducted studies using these guidelines and sex-disaggregated data can be found in a database organised by Sweden Statistics.[2]

On the basis of time use data, it is possible to construct satellite accounts which place a money value on unpaid work and its output, so as to compare this with GDP. The European System of Accounts 2010 does not include unpaid production of household services as part of GDP, though it does include a satellite account covering this production. Some European countries have produced satellite accounts. For instance, the UK's Office for National Statistics produced a household satellite account in 2002 (Holloway et al. 2002). Satellite accounts suggest that unpaid production of household services is quite large in relation to GDP. It amounts to about 35% of conventionally measured GDP in France (on average across the period 1995–2006), about 40% in Finland and 30% in the United States over the same period (Stiglitz et al. 2009: 36). However, neither time use data nor satellite accounts are produced on a regular basis, and up-to-date data and estimates are not widely available, so that it is rarely possible to track changes throughout the course of an economic crisis.

If we consider unpaid work as well as paid work, it becomes clear that many macroeconomic policies are not gender-neutral in their impact. For instance, attempts to reduce a government budget deficit by cutting public expenditure are likely to impact more on women than on men. This is because women tend to make greater use of public services than men, and are frequently required to increase their unpaid work when public services are cut. In addition, a higher proportion of women's employment than men's employment tends to be in the public sector. Moreover, social security payments often make up a greater share of women's incomes than men's, because women earn less in the labour market.

Recognize, reduce and redistribute unpaid work

A gender-equitable macroeconomic policy framework should recognize the importance of unpaid work by ensuring that there are regular updates of time use studies by national statistical offices and by considering unpaid work in all economic and social policy decisions. For instance, policymakers must be alert to the risk that policies created ostensibly to improve the efficiency of health services might instead transfer work from the public health service, where it is paid, to families and communities, where it is unpaid. An example of such transfers is the introduction of day surgery, where patients do not stay in hospital to recover from surgery, but are discharged into the care of a relative or friend, who must care for them for at least twenty-four hours, and often longer.

Rather than increasing unpaid work, policy should: promote its reduction, eliminate some kinds of unpaid work altogether (one example of this would be better housing and affordable energy leading to a reduction in some kinds of housework) and provide paid services that substitute for other kinds of unpaid work (such as care work). It is as a result of public investment (and the increased production of commodities that substitute for unpaid work, such as washing machines) that the amount of time spent on unpaid work in Europe has tended to decline.

However, the aim is not to abolish unpaid work completely. We all need time free from care, but also time free for the care of our family and friends. There is a benefit both to giving and receiving personal care. But when providing unpaid care is an obligation that takes up a lot of time, day in and day out with no respite, it becomes a burden. Governments should use economic policy to promote the equal sharing of a manageable quantity of unpaid care work between women and men.

The most obvious way to do this is to ensure that paid leave for domestic care responsibilities is equally available to men and women, and that men are given incentives to use this leave. Governments can introduce statutory paid leave for new fathers as well as new mothers, and ensure that pay for paternity and maternity leave is a high proportion of the salary forgone. Norway provides a good example (Rønsen and Kitterød 2015). In the mid-1990s, paid parental leave totalled 52 weeks with 9 weeks reserved for mothers, 4 weeks reserved for fathers and 39 weeks available for either parent. The leave was paid at 80% of wages. By 2010, paid parental leave totalled 56 weeks, and leave reserved for fathers had been extended to 10 weeks, while leave reserved for mothers stayed at nine weeks. After the paid leave, each parent may take up to one year of unpaid leave with job protection. The introduction and extension of parental leave reserved for fathers has increased the take-up of parental leave among fathers, and employers have become accustomed to men taking several weeks of leave during the first year of a child's life, which helps to promote gender equality in the labour market.

It is also important that all social security benefits related to children should be designed so that they are paid to the main carer rather than automatically paid to the mother of the children. This applies to cash transfers like child benefit and also to the provision of credits in the state pension system to cover contributions of those who take time out of the labour market to care for children.

Employment regulations should be designed to ensure that employers provide flexible working arrangements of a kind that benefit employees. Measures should be introduced to promote a shorter 'normal' working week in paid employment and to abolish the penalties faced by part-time workers, in terms of worse hourly pay and conditions. A 30-hour week in paid work as the norm for both women and men would do much to enable an equal redistribution of unpaid work. Economies need to be rebalanced, recognizing that we all, women and men alike, need both time to provide unpaid care for our families and friends, but also time free from the obligation to provide such care; and that we all, women and men alike, have a right to decent paid work that can be combined with caring responsibilities without penalty.

Dethrone GDP as the premier indicator

To support the creation of a gender-equitable economy production of various kinds needs to be expanded, but the growth of GDP in itself is not a good indicator of increases in well-being if GDP measures production, valuing goods and services at market prices, but market prices do not reflect the full costs and benefits to society of the goods and services produced.

The issue of how to improve measurement of economic performance and social progress was considered by a commission of eminent economists (including two feminist economists, Bina Agarwal and Nancy Folbre) set up by the President of France in 2008. Their report contains some useful conclusions for establishing a gender-equitable macroeconomic framework for Europe (Stiglitz et al. 2009). They recommend that more attention be paid to other indicators produced by the system of national accounts, such as real household consumption (a measure that would exclude government spending on services such as prisons, military and rectifying environmental damage such as oil-spills). Real household income should be monitored, adjusting not only for taxes and transfers but also for receipt of government services in kind (i.e. for which no charges are made). The commission also recommends going beyond the system of national accounts to produce a plural system of indicators. These could include measures of non-market production through household satellite accounts and the construction of multi-dimensional well-being indicators that, alongside income, would include enjoyment of health, education, satisfying work, voice, social connections, environment and security. Information should not only be given for the average household or individual, but should pay attention to inequalities between households and individuals, including gender inequality. Implementation of these recommendations would be helpful for developing a gender-equitable macroeconomic framework and monitoring progress.

Nevertheless, in the immediate future attention is likely to be focused on growth of output and employment. Here it is important to go beyond aggregates and recognize that some outputs and employment may damage rather than contribute to a gender-equitable economy, just as some outputs and employment damage rather than contribute to environmental sustainability. For instance, while 'entertainment' services (such as strip clubs, pole-dancing clubs and escort agencies) may provide employment for women, they reinforce sexist attitudes that permeate wider society and make it harder to construct a gender-equitable economy. On the other hand, there are some kinds of output and employment that actively contribute to a more gender-equitable economy: good quality, publicly provided care services staffed by well-trained, well-paid people, men as well as women.

The UK Women's Budget Group has developed a plan for gender-equitable economic recovery in the UK that has at its centre the growth of public care, health, education and training services, affordable environmentally sustainable housing, renewable energy and environmentally friendly public transport (WBG

2015b). This would improve well-being and productivity in gender-equitable ways benefiting people not only today but in years to come. The growth in output of these areas (and comparable activities, chosen according to needs in specific European countries) should be monitored as well as growth of GDP.

Similarly, it is important to go beyond aggregate measures on employment and job creation: for instance, there should be monitoring, with gender-disaggregated data, of the proportion of employment that is part-time, self-employed, provides an income above the national minimum wage, and has access to benefits such as paid holidays, parental leave and occupational pensions. The aggregate employment and job creation data may suggest that recovery is underway, but the growth may be in low-income, poor quality employment. Attention also has to be paid to occupational segregation, because a gender-equitable economy requires that occupational segregation be reduced, both through more women entering male-dominated activities (such as construction) and more men entering female-dominated activities, such as care services. So rather than focusing only on aggregate data of growth of GDP and employment, attention needs to be focused on what types of output are growing and what types of employment are growing, and appropriate indicators constructed.

Invest in social as well as physical infrastructure

Public spending on physical infrastructure like transport facilities, communication systems and power generation and other utilities is defined as public investment in the system of national accounts. The rationale is that this spending increases the stock of capital assets and provides additional benefits (in the form of additional output and well-being) not just in the year when the spending is carried out but also in future years during the life of the asset. These additional benefits accrue directly through the output produced by the assets, and also indirectly through enhancing the availability and productivity of labour in many sectors of the economy. Thus improved transport and communications infrastructure enables more people to enter the labour market and reduces the time they have to spend travelling to work.

A well-known and widely accepted principle of public finance allows governments to finance public investment by borrowing (Musgrave 1939; Musgrave 1959: 556–75). The rationale for this so-called 'golden rule' is that since public investment provides a stream of benefits for people in the future, it is appropriate for future generations to contribute to financing those investments via taxation to pay the costs of borrowing. Future generations inherit the obligation to service public debt, but in exchange they receive a corresponding stock of assets.

Public spending on the on-going delivery of services such as education, health and care also enhances future output and human well-being directly through creating and maintaining what some economists call 'human capital'. The indirect benefits are delivered through enabling more women to participate in the paid economy, both because the amount of unpaid work they have to do is reduced, and because these services provide paid jobs for women. These services should be understood as providing a social infrastructure, comparable to physical infrastructure. For instance, spending on childcare and early years education can substantially increase both women's labour force participation, and the learning abilities of children with gains to future output, productivity and well-being (Campbell et al. 2013).

However, spending on the on-going costs of these services, on salaries and on material inputs, is classified in the system of national accounts as public consumption, not investment. An example is the spending on the salaries of nursery assistants and teachers who provide early years care and education services, and the money spent on materials (paper, pencils, books, etc.). This is classified as public consumption and not treated as creating assets that will produce future streams of output and well-being (though building new nurseries and schools does count as public investment). Applying the 'golden rule' permits governments to borrow to build the physical infrastructure that will contribute to future output and well-being, but not the social infrastructure.

The way that public investment is defined in the European System of National Accounts (ESA) is not set in stone. ESA 2010 now counts military expenditure on weapons systems (comprising vehicles and other equipment such as warships, submarines, military aircrafts, tanks, missile carriers and launchers, etc.) as investment (Eurostat 2013: 74 and 443). An implication of this change is that a UK government could borrow to build a new Trident submarine and nuclear missile system without breaching the 'golden rule'. In the context of the Eurozone, enabling a government in the Eurozone area to count public spending on weapons systems as public investment makes it easier for them to comply with the highly restrictive fiscal rules established for the Eurozone, set out in the Stability and Growth Pact (Truger 2015).

The ways in which investment is defined in the ESA 2010 should be challenged, and a case made to include spending on social infrastructure as public investment. The Commission on the Measurement of Economic Performance and Social Progress recommended that the definition of assets should be widened, so that, for instance, expenditure on health should be seen as investment in human capital not final consumption (Stiglitz et al. 2009). In addition, the interpretation of the 'golden rule' should be modified, so that the spending it covers excludes expenditure on military weapons systems and includes spending on education, health, childcare and early years education, as suggested by Truger (2015).

When governments have responded to falling rates of growth and rising unemployment with public investment, they have usually focused on physical infrastructure, such as roads and railways, not social infrastructure, and on physical capital rather than human capital. Public investment in social infrastructure can provide decently paid jobs for many women and an increasing number of men, reduce the amount of unpaid work that women have to do and create direct and indirect increases in output and well-being for years to come.

22 Diane Elson

Put more emphasis on raising taxes on well-off people and companies

Fiscal policies in Europe have disproportionately focused on cutting expenditure on social infrastructure and social security, while doing little to raise tax revenue. A government's capacity to reduce gender inequality is shaped by the tax revenue it raises. A high level of tax revenue enables governments to fund the services, social security and infrastructure that make it easier for women to undertake paid work, and to provide jobs for women in the public sector that are often of better quality than those in the private sector.

Competition to attract multinational businesses and their highly paid executives has led to cuts in corporation and capital gains taxes, tax holidays and other exemptions. Cross-border cooperation on the taxation of corporations has failed to keep pace with globalization. As a result, tax avoidance schemes have proliferated and the political clout of wealthy people enables them to engage in tax evasion with little fear of prosecution. Governments have turned to indirect taxes like VAT to raise revenue, but such taxes fall most heavily on poor households, and hit single mothers particularly hard.

In successive reports[3] on the British government's budgets since 2008, the Women's Budget Group has shown how failure to raise more tax revenue in equitable ways has disproportionately impacted on women. The deficit reduction strategy introduced in July 2010 placed overwhelming emphasis on cutting expenditure rather than raising tax revenue, and the main revenue raising measure was an increase in VAT. Of the £26 billion 'savings' made by the UK government since June 2010 through cuts to social security spending and changes to direct taxes, £22 billion came from women, according to parliamentary analysis published in autumn 2014. This equates to 85% of the total with just 15% coming from men.[4] The Women's Budget Group carried out its own analysis, which considered changes to indirect and direct taxes, cuts to public services and cuts to social security, and found that single women were particularly hard hit (Women's Budget Group 2013). While introducing cuts to spending on public services and social security, the government also reduced taxes (Women's Budget Group 2014). The income threshold for the payment of income tax was raised, a measure that will cost £12 billion a year – the majority of which will go to men and those on higher incomes. The Women's Budget Group estimates that at least 21 million workers aged 16 and above will not benefit at all, of whom 63% are women. Duty on beer was cut and duty on petrol was frozen, benefiting men more than women, because women tend to buy less beer and fuel than men (Women's Budget Group 2014).

Governments across Europe pay lip service to raising more revenue through combating tax avoidance and evasion but many fail to enact effective measures. A report on Spain illustrates the problems (Center for Economic and Social Rights 2015). Large companies benefit from generous tax incentives and privileges. In 2012, while small and medium enterprises effectively paid close to 16% of their income in tax, large businesses effectively paid just 5.3% (both were lower than

A gender-equitable macroeconomic framework **23**

the 30% nominal rate that year). Large companies are estimated to have used tax breaks to avoid paying €19 billion in 2012: three times the budget for social security benefits for families and children in 2015. Thirty-three of the 35 companies which make up Spain's benchmark stock market index have direct subsidiaries in tax havens.

Tax avoidance and evasion is a gender-equality issue, as is made clear in the contributions to a special gender issue of the Tax Justice Bulletin (Nelson 2015). The construction of a gender-equitable macroeconomic framework requires attention to taxation as well as to expenditure.

Transform finance so that it is socially useful

The economic crisis in Europe began as a financial crisis. Banks were allowed to borrow excessively against too little capital, and to undertake risky innovations (including the introduction of mortgage-backed securities and credit default swaps) without any external overview of how much risk was building up in the financial system as a whole. Many new financial products were traded 'over-the-counter' to specific clients without any transparency, rather than on open markets. In the years preceding the financial crisis, governments changed laws to facilitate the development of these complex new financial products. Central banks failed to regulate adequately, partly because of a lack of understanding of these new financial products, and provided uncritical support for the enormous growth of individual banks that became 'too big to fail'. Looked at as a whole, the changes in regulation further increased systemic risk. When it became clear that the crisis threatened the ability of banks to discharge their obligations to depositors, and with a potential 'run on the banks' looming, governments stepped in to 'bail out' the large banks. Most of the banks retained the same leadership that had so mismanaged them. These actions prevented depositors from losing their money, but did not prevent the drying up of credit or the knock-on effects to the rest of the economy.

Women were included in the financial sector as borrowers, though often subject to discrimination and given worse terms than men, whether borrowing to buy homes or to operate small businesses. However, women were largely absent from the key decision-making bodies in the financial sector, both private and public (Schuberth and Young 2011). Some commentators have advanced the view that if more women had been at the helm, excessive risk taking would have been avoided and there would not have been a financial crisis.[5] However, although the employment of more women in key decision-making positions in the financial sector and the governance of finance may help in transforming behaviour, it is possible that women themselves may embrace macho norms in order to survive and achieve promotion.

Following the financial crisis, some new regulatory structures were put in place and a European banking union is being created (Young 2014: 35–38). However, there is still a need for thorough-going reform of financial governance. The vast

24 Diane Elson

majority of bank loans do not support new business investment but instead fund either increased consumption or the purchase of already existing assets, in particular urban property, driving up prices but not increasing supply (Turner 2015: 6). Public policy should seek to produce a different allocation of credit than would result from purely private decisions, deliberately counteracting the private bias toward urban property and instead favouring other potentially more socially valuable forms of credit allocation (Turner 2015: 11). As well as better regulation of profit-driven financial firms, more support needs to be given to financial firms that are organised around a different culture, described by Crespo and Van Staveren (2011) as an 'ethics of care'. Such organisations include cooperative banks and credit unions, which would be less likely to discriminate against women.

Alongside financial governance reforms to improve the supply of loans, attention must be paid to the drivers of the demand for loans. In some countries the apparent recovery of output in 2015 is underpinned by increases of household debt to very high levels. In the UK household debt stood at 144% of household income in 2015, and was forecast by the Office for Budget Responsibility to rise to 167% by 2020, almost the ratio that prevailed just before the financial crisis (Women's Budget Group 2015a). Cutbacks to social security and public services, and loss of income, push some people into taking on more debt than they can afford. Research into why people had debt problems by a UK debt charity, StepChange, found that the biggest cause was loss of employment and reduction of working hours, followed by illness, divorce, an elderly parent needing additional care and the birth of a new baby. Single parents are the worst-affected group. Women make up the majority of people contacting StepChange for advice on debt problems: in 2014 women comprised 57% of clients, up from 54% in 2012 (StepChange 2014).

The governance of the financial sector has important implications for fiscal policy. If there are no far-reaching reforms to the financial sector, then the potential for another financial crisis is high. This encourages finance ministers to argue that reducing public debt and building a budget surplus must be key objectives of fiscal policy. Failure to transform the financial sector tends to foster an 'austerity bias' in fiscal policy, with the continuation of adverse implications for gender equality.

Conclusions

Even though there are signs of recovery of output, unemployment is high and employment precarious, and the safety net of the welfare state has been seriously weakened. Women are disproportionately at risk. If there is to be a gender-equitable recovery, a different set of principles are needed to guide macroeconomic policy. This chapter has argued that governments must to expand their understanding of the economy to include non-market and unpaid work; recognize, reduce and redistribute unpaid work; dethrone GDP as the premier indicator; invest in social as well as physical infrastructure; put more emphasis on raising taxes on well-off people and companies; and transform the governance of finance so that finance is directed to socially useful ends. If finance ministers and other policy officials took note of these principles, there would be much more likelihood of a recovery that restores progress to gender equality in Europe.

Notes

1 The countries are Belgium, Bulgaria, Estonia, France, Finland, Germany, Italy, Latvia, Lithuania, Norway, Poland, Slovenia, Spain, Sweden and UK.
2 Harmonized European Time Use Survey, Sweden Statistics. www.h5.scb.se/tus/tus/default.htm
3 See www.wbg.org.uk
4 www.thetimes.co.uk/tto/news/politics/article4303623.ece
5 The so-called Lehman Sisters hypothesis (Kristof 2009).

References

Campbell, J., D. Elson and A. McKay. 2013. "The Economic Case for Investing in High Quality Childcare and Early Years Education." WISE Briefing Sheet, Women in Scotland's Economy Research Centre. Glasgow Caledonian University.

Center for Economic and Social Rights (2015). *Fact Sheet No. 14.* Spain. www.cesr.org/downloads/FACTSHEET_Spain_2015_web.pdf (accessed 21 April 2016).

Crespo, R. and I. Van Staveren. 2011. "Would we have had this crisis if women had been running the financial sector?" *Journal of Sustainable Finance and Investment* 1: 3–4, 241–50.

Elson, D. 1998. "The economic, the political and the domestic: businesses, states and households in the organisation of production." *New Political Economy* 3(2): 189–208.

Eurostat. 2009. "Harmonized European Time Use Surveys. 2008 Guidelines." Office for Official Publications of the European Communities. Luxembourg.

Eurostat. 2013. "European System of Accounts ESA 2010." Publications Office of the European Union. Luxembourg.

Folbre, N. 1994. *Who Pays for the Kids? Gender and the Structures of Constraint.* London: Routledge.

Holloway, S., S. Short and S. Tamplin. 2002. "Household Satellite Account." Office of National Statistics. London.

Kristof, N. 2009. "Mistresses of the Universe." *New York Times* (9 February).

Musgrave, R. A. 1939. "The nature of budgetary balance and the case for a capital-budget." *American Economic Review* 29: 260–71.

Musgrave, R. A. 1959. *The Theory of Public Finance. A Study in Public Economy.* New York: McGraw-Hill.

Nelson, L. (ed.) 2015. *Tax Justice Bulletin: Gender Edition.* www.taxjustice.net/wpcontent/uploads/2013/04/TJF_2015_Women.pdf (accessed 21 April 2016).

Picchio, A. 1992. *Social Reproduction: The Political Economy of the Labour Market.* Cambridge: Cambridge University Press.

Rønsen, M and R. Kitterød. 2015. "Gender-equalizing family policies and mother's entry into paid work: recent evidence from Norway." *Feminist Economics* 21(1): 59–89.

Schuberth, H. and B. Young. 2011. "The Role of Gender in the Governance of the Financial Sector." In B. Young, I. Bakker and D. Elson (eds). *Financial Governance from a Feminist Perspective.* London: Routledge.

StepChange. 2014. "Personal Debt 2014: Statistics Yearbook." www.stepchange.org/Portals/0/documents/media/reports/statisticsyearbooks/StepChangeDebtCharity StatisticsYearbook2014.pdf (accessed 21 April 2016).

Stiglitz, J., A. Sen and J-P. Fitoussi. 2009. "Report by the Commission on the Measurement of Economic Performance and Social Progress." www.insee.fr/fr/publications-et-services/dossiers_web/stiglitz/doc-commission/RAPPORT_anglais.pdf (accessed 21 April 2016).

Truger, A. 2015. "Implementing the Golden Rule for Public Investment in Europe: Safeguarding Public Investment and Supporting the Recovery." Materialien zu Wirtschaftund und Gesellschaft Nr. 138. Abteilung Wirtschaftswissenschaft und Statistik der Kammer für Arbeiter und Angestellte für Wien.

Turner, A. 2015. *Between Debt and the Devil: Money, Credit, and Fixing Global Finance.* Princeton: Princeton University Press.

Women's Budget Group. 2013. "To ensure economic recovery for women, we need Plan F." http://wbg.org.uk/pdfs/WBG-briefing_Sept-2013_final.pdf_(accessed 21 April 2016).

Women's Budget Group. 2014. "Giveaways to men, paid for by women." http://wbg.org.uk/wp-content/uploads/2014/03/Budget-Briefing-2014.pdf (accessed 21 April 2016).

Women's Budget Group. 2015a. "The impact on women of the Autumn Statement and Comprehensive Spending Review." http://wbg.org.uk/2015assessments/wbg_afs_csr_2015_report_2015_12_07_final3/ (accessed 21 April 2016).

Women's Budget Group. 2015b. "Plan F: A Feminist Economic Strategy for a Caring and Sustainable Economy." http://wbg.org.uk/wp-content/uploads/2015/02/PLAN-F-2015.pdf (accessed 21 April 2016).

Young, B. 2014. "Financial Crisis: Causes, Policy Responses and Future Challenges. Outcomes of EU Funded Research." Brussels: European Commission.

2

A FEMINIST ALTERNATIVE TO AUSTERITY

The purple economy as a gender-egalitarian strategy for employment generation

Ipek Ilkkaracan

Introduction

The slow pace of economic recovery and the persistent unemployment problem in Europe are testimony to the limited success of austerity policies as a remedy for economic recession. The need for alternative policies towards a sustainable recovery based on employment generation is urgent. The green economy vision of a sustainable economic order has been suggested as a solution to the environmental crisis; in the context of the recent global economic crisis, this vision has been extended to entail solutions to the economic crisis and the problem of rising unemployment through green jobs. The "purple economy" vision proposed in Ilkkaracan (2013) that is based on a gender-equitable economic order has been put forth as a remedy to the crisis of care. This chapter evaluates if and how the purple economy has the potential to serve as a strategy for the generation of "purple jobs" in Europe and hence may provide an alternative to austerity.

The purple economy – based on the symbolic purple colour adopted by the feminist movement in some countries around the world – suggests an alternative vision for a sustainable and gender-egalitarian economic order. It is organised around the sustainability of caring labour through a redistributive internalisation of the costs of care into the workings of the system (just as the green economy is organised around the sustainability of provisioning by nature through the internalisation of environmental costs into production and consumption patterns). A recent report by the United Nations Environment Programme (UNEP) defined a "green economy" as a low-carbon and resource-efficient economy, which significantly reduces environmental risks and ecological scarcities, prevents the loss of biodiversity and ecosystem services while improving human well-being and social equity (UNEP 2011). Hence the distinguishing characteristic of a green economy is that – through policy actions, appropriate regulations, institutions and structures – it acknowledges *nature* as an important source of ecosystem services with economic value that is indispensable for human well-being. The green economy accounts for the value of ecosystems in the design of production and consumption processes in order to enable their sustainability. In a similar vein, the distinguishing characteristic of a purple economy is that through a complementary set of policy actions, regulations, institutions and structures, it acknowledges *unpaid domestic labour* as an important source of care services with economic value that is indispensable for human well-being. The purple economy therefore accounts for the value of caring labour in the design of production and consumption processes to enable its sustainability. The green economy implies the need for an investment plan in an infrastructure of renewable energy and ecological production methods, and emphasises the employment generation potential of such green investments. The purple economy implies the need for an investment plan in social care infrastructure, and emphasises the employment generation potential of such purple investments. Hence both the green and purple economy concepts define what the distinguishing characteristics of a truly sustainable economic order need to be, while also putting forth a set of policy proposals for structural transformation.

This chapter draws upon recent empirical work on the employment generation potential of public investments in social care services to evaluate how a purple investment plan can contribute to equitable employment creation in Europe while improving gender equality and sustainability of caring labour.[1] To the extent that these recent empirical studies propose a demand-side economic rationale for public provisioning of social care services, they represent an important overlap with alternative post-Keynesian approaches to macroeconomic policy. In the context of wage-led versus profit-led growth, the post-Keynesian alternative solution to the global economic crisis has been to promote a wage-led recovery through public investments in physical as well as social infrastructure (see discussion by Onaran in this volume). This chapter points out the overlaps with a purple economy vision that calls for public investments in social care infrastructure as a primary area of government intervention for a gender-egalitarian sustainable economic order, which also has the potential to facilitate substantial job creation and a wage-led recovery.

This chapter is organised as follows. It first introduces the basic characteristics of a purple economy and discusses the overlaps with an equitable and inclusive employment generation strategy. An overview of recent applied studies on the impact of public investments in social care services on job generation, unemployment and poverty reduction is then provided. The final section draws conclusions and presents policy alternatives.

What is a purple economy?

The purple economy vision, developed in Ilkkaracan (2013), aims to extend the definition of a sustainable economy beyond that of the green economy with a focus on gender equality. As such there are a series of parallels between the green and purple economies. The green economy acknowledges the role of a healthy environment in determining human well-being, and hence the need for an economy that respects the integrity of ecosystems. The purple economy acknowledges dependence on caring labour as an indispensable component of well-being, and hence the need for an economy that accounts for the value of care work and enables its provisioning in a sustainable manner, without reverting to mechanisms that reproduce inequalities by gender, class and origin. The green economy calls for a reordering of priorities that places the nurturing of nature at the centre and a reorganisation and regulation of production and consumption patterns in harmony with the pace of renewal of natural resources. The purple economy builds on this and calls for a reordering of priorities that also places the nurturing of human beings at the centre and a reorganisation and regulation of production and consumption patterns in harmony with an equitable and sustainable system of reproduction of human beings.

Purple economic and social policies recognise, account for and redistribute the care burden through systemic internalisation of its costs. This is based on an economic philosophy that, first, acknowledges access to care as a basic human right. As such, Ilkkaracan (2013) pointed out that an important starting point for a purple economic order is the creation of an effective public social care infrastructure. A purple economy stands on four pillars, as detailed below.

The first pillar entails universal public provisioning of care services for children, the elderly, the disabled and the sick. This enables a reallocation of the costs of caring labour between households and the market through investment and spending on social care sectors. Obviously financing poses a serious challenge, particularly in a time of economic crisis. As discussed in a previous paper by the author (see Ilkkaracan 2013), a solution to the financing challenge may be the mobilisation of purple taxation and purple care finance schemes, based on an economic rationale that emphasises the potential of investments in labour-intensive social care sectors for alleviating the effects of the economic crisis through generation of "purple" jobs (see the discussion below on the findings of recent empirical work).

The second pillar complements the first through regulation of the labour market for work–life balance by creating equal incentives (and penalties) for men and women in undertaking care responsibilities. To this end, four areas of labour market regulation have been identified:

- the legal right to paid and unpaid care leave for child and dependent adult care;
- the shortening of labour market working hours within decent job standards;[2]
- the legal right to flexible work arrangements as per changing work–life balance needs over the life-cycle; and
- the regulation of the labour market to eliminate discriminatory practices in hiring, pay and promotions (most importantly equal pay for work of equal value) so that the costs of taking time out from employment in order to fulfil caring responsibilities are equalised for men and women.

The combined aim of these labour market regulatory policies would be a transformation of household structure from a single male breadwinner, female homemaker model (or a part-time female earner model), towards a dual-earner, dual-carer household model.

The third pillar of the purple economy entails public policies to address the special needs of rural communities for a sustainable and egalitarian care infrastructure. This applies more to developing economies of the South, where subsistence and small-scale family farming continues to provide livelihoods, rather than the developed economies of the North where agricultural production has been fully commodified and integrated into the market system. The nature of unpaid care work is distinct in less-developed rural settings from that of urban populations in middle- or high-income economies. Unpaid caring labour in less-developed rural settings includes a larger array of activities dependent on availability of natural resources, such as fetching water or firewood and growing food for self-consumption. Women (and men) engaged in small-scale and/or subsistence farming are in the status of unpaid family worker or self-employed. Hence the building of an efficient care infrastructure in these communities necessitates more than public provisioning of care services, and labour market regulation for the most part is tangentially relevant. The care infrastructure in these communities would need to be supported in a context of green investments in agriculture and rural infrastructure, green technology transfer programmes that build on women's local knowledge of ecosystems, targeted agricultural subsidies for women, employment programmes for landless women and men in green sectors such as organic farming, as well as (where necessary) employment guarantee programmes to facilitate women and men's equal employment opportunities in public works.[3]

The fourth and final pillar of a purple economy entails regulation of the macroeconomic environment for nature and nurture as the core objectives of macroeconomic policy. In order for the above three pillars to achieve their intended objectives, an enabling macroeconomic environment is a necessary precondition. This means that conventional macroeconomic policy thinking would need to undergo substantial transformation, so as to first shift its focus from GDP growth and efficiency to generation of decent jobs and ensuring sustainable livelihoods. Growth and efficiency need to be acknowledged as possible tools (amongst others) of macroeconomic policy in reaching its ultimate objectives of nature and nurture – but by no means are they indispensable tools. Employment generation based on decent jobs needs to become a core objective, not only as a solution to unemployment but also in acknowledgement of the gender gap in labour force participation. In other words, decent jobs are needed not only for the unemployed, but also for substantial numbers of "non-participant" women who are excluded from the labour market. It is necessary to note that such a prioritisation of employment generation in macro policy design could in fact be growth enhancing to the extent that the economy is embedded in a wage-led growth regime.[4]

In addition, a purple macroeconomic framework requires that policies are evaluated for their impact on (re)distribution of the unpaid care burden. Fiscal austerity, for instance, which has been a strong component of the conventional macroeconomic response to economic crises particularly in Europe, calls for reductions in social expenditures. There has been substantial research showing how this facilitates the shifting of caring labour from paid work to women's unpaid work, with negative results for lower-skilled women's labour market participation and time-use patterns. Hence taxation and public spending allocations would need to be evaluated in an analytical framework (such as gender budgeting) for their impact on distribution of the burden of unpaid caring labour and associated inequalities by gender, class and origin without presuming an infinite supply of female caring labour.

Based on these pillars, the purple economy entails an alternative to austerity policies through a number of mechanisms. It calls for an immediate and direct emphasis on employment generation rather than keeping it as one of the side objectives expected to be achieved indirectly and in the long run through austerity. A number of institutional characteristics of the purple economy facilitate employment creation in an organic manner through a reorganisation of the care economy: universal provisioning of social care services is a source of generation of "purple care jobs"; shortening labour market work hours to enable work–life balance for both men and women has the potential to distribute existing employment hours over a larger number of workers; and investment in green and purple rural infrastructure is a source of green and purple jobs.

The section below evaluates the employment creation potential of a purple economy, particularly through the first mechanism, i.e. public investments for provisioning of social care services.

How does the purple economy offer a policy alternative to the economic crisis and the jobs challenge?

Universal public provisioning of care services for children, the elderly, the disabled and the sick was introduced above as the first pillar of a purple economy. This is to act as a primary mechanism for redistribution of the costs of caring labour between the private and the public spheres. Social care expansion has indeed been one of the important policy items on the gender equality agenda of governmental and intergovernmental platforms such as the EU, OECD and the UN. Yet the issue has been approached for the most part via its supply-side effects through improvement of female labour force participation rates. Beyond gender equality, the socioeconomic equality-enhancing effects of childcare provisioning have also emerged as one of the primary motivations for policy design. A recent recommendation by the European Commission (EC) (2013) titled *Investing in Children: Breaking the Cycle of Disadvantage* pointed out two supply-side channels through which the equality-enhancing effects of access to early childcare services prevail. Such access supports equal opportunities for children from disadvantaged households, enhancing school success and adult earnings. The EC recommendation also pointed to the improved viability of dual-earner households under universal access to early childhood care, particularly for less-educated couples, and hence the poverty-alleviation and additional equality-improvement outcomes for children from disadvantaged households.

An expansion of social care service sectors necessitates increased investment and spending, inevitably pointing to fiscal expansion as a source of financing. The position vis-à-vis fiscal expansion will depend upon one's approach to the macroeconomics of crises. From a Keynesian perspective this is a necessary response to a recessionary turn of the economy.[5] A neoclassical approach, however, calls for the opposite solution of austerity. Even if fiscal expansion is removed as an option, the problem of financing could be addressed through a combination of reallocation of existing public spending and/or incentives for private investments in the care economy in the form of tax cuts or in-kind subsidies, such as allocation of facilities.

As mentioned above, an important economic rationale for an expansion or reallocation of public spending in a recessionary context with high unemployment rates is the employment creation potential of investments in the labour-intensive social care sectors. South Korean policy on social care services between the 1997 Asian and 2008 global economic crises sets a good example. One of the Korean government's strategies to address the unemployment problem during this period (along with the problem of low fertility rates) was public subsidies for the expansion of social care services focused largely on children and the elderly. In its evaluation of this policy, the South Korean Ministry of Labor underscores the multifaceted positive impact of this initiative:

> Creating social service jobs has boosted our economy's growth potential as it has helped the not economically active population, including housewives and the aged, to be brought into the economically active population. In particular, providing social services, such as child caring, housekeeping and patient caring, have liberated women from domestic work, which in turn, has increased employment. The project to create social service jobs has not only created jobs for vulnerable groups of workers ... [but] has also played the role of providing social services which are in short supply, thereby largely contributing to supplying social services for low-income lower middle classes who want to get such services but have little purchasing power. The project has a great significance in that it has opened up new horizons by creating jobs in the social service sector, which is often called the third sector beyond the private and public sectors and need to expand its share of employment, through cooperation between NGOs and the government.
>
> *(Peng 2011: 917)*

With the exception of South Korea, however, the research and policy debates on improving access to social care services has for the most part focused on the positive supply-side effects, such as boosting female labour supply or supporting child development, and reducing associated gender and socioeconomic inequalities through these supply-side interventions.[6] Nevertheless, there has been an increasing number of recent empirical studies that explore the *demand-side* effects of social care service sector expansion on employment generation and gender equality through changing sectoral and gender composition of employment.

One such study is by Andersen and Dahl in this volume (Ch.9), who explore the effects of public investment in childcare services on growth and employment creation through a macrosimulation of the Eurozone countries and the UK. The study points out that there is ample room for expanding and improving childcare facilities in Europe, particularly in Southern Europe, and that this implies not only generation of new jobs but also a substantial increase in the female participation rate. They report that a five-year "gendered investment plan" designed to expand public childcare services through public investments equivalent to 1–1.5% of GDP in 2014–18, would lead to 2.4% GDP growth through combined demand and supply effects.[7] A total of 4.8 million new jobs would be created in five years and more than half of these jobs (2.7 million) would be held by women. It is assumed that the improvement in childcare will gradually increase public employment by 0.5% by 2018 (0.75% for the Southern Eurozone countries), and that the improved framework will gradually increase the labour force over the next five years, resulting in a 1% increase in 2018. Taxes are assumed to increase in a balanced way, so that the total effect on the public budget is neutral.

A recent study on Austria approached the issue from a similar demand-side perspective and showed that investment in the provision of childcare could not only eliminate current deficits in terms of available places and quality but also generate considerable employment and budgetary effects (AK Europa 2013). The policy target in the simulation was the creation of 35,000 new places for small children (under three years old) and better operating hours for 70,000 existing kindergarten places. This was estimated to require an average annual financing of €200 million by the central and local governments over five years. The study found that 14,000 new jobs in childcare would be created, as well as another 2,300 in other sectors due to enhanced demand. Furthermore, it was estimated that 14,000–28,000 parents who could not participate in the labour market due to their care responsibilities could find employment. The study also showed that taxes from the new employment opportunities and the savings in unemployment benefits would create public revenue that would exceed the costs of the initiative beginning in the fifth year of the initial investment and continuing thereafter.

A study on the US by Warner and Liu (2006) also approached the issue from a demand-side perspective but used an input-output approach to compare the intersectoral linkages in a regional economy that would be triggered by childcare sector multipliers. The study found that only hospitals have larger employment and output multipliers than childcare centres. The authors attributed this finding to the short-term output and employment-enhancing effects of childcare expansion in the regional economy to its relatively large output and employment multipliers and to its higher backward linkages.

Finally, there have also been a series of country policy simulations by the Levy Economics Institute on South Africa (Antonopoulos and Kim 2008), the US

34 Ipek Ilkkaracan

(Antonopoulos et al. 2010) and Turkey (Ilkkaracan et al. 2015) that have assessed the likely outcome of public investments in social care services on job creation as well as income distributional effects by gender, education and household income group. These studies followed a two-tiered approach: first, they used input-output analysis to assess the macroeconomic effects of social care expansion at an aggregate level, namely the impact on direct and indirect employment generation and in some cases also on growth. Beyond such aggregate effects, these studies also adopted a microsimulation method to examine the distributional impacts of social care expansion in terms of gender, education/skills and household income. The simulations compared the impact of a certain amount of spending increase on social care services versus another reference sector, typically physical infrastructure (in the case of the US also green energy), and showed that a social care service sector expansion was the superior performer by all demand-side criteria. Not only did it have the potential for generating many more jobs than physical infrastructure, but the distribution of new jobs and income was significantly more favourable for women, the lower skilled and also poor households.

The South Africa study (Antonopoulos and Kim 2008) simulated a scenario whereby there was a hypothetical increase in spending on early childhood care services and home-based sick care services for HIV patients by 13.3 billion rand (in 2007 prices, equivalent to 3.5% of public expenditures and 1.1% of GDP). This was found to generate 772,000 new jobs, with 60% going to women and 89% going to unskilled workers. Furthermore, the national growth rate increased by 1.8%, and growth was shown to be pro-poor in that income of ultra-poor households increased by 9.2%, poor households by 5.6% and non-poor households by 1.3%. These results were far superior to those for physical infrastructure where an equivalent amount of spending was found to generate only about 400,000 new jobs, with 82% going to men and 79% going to unskilled workers.

The study on the US (Antonopoulos et al. 2010) simulated a hypothetical $50 billion investment in home-based healthcare for the elderly and the chronically ill, and early childhood development services. The study found that such an investment was likely to generate approximately 1.2 million jobs (over 90% going to women), versus 555,000 jobs created by an equivalent investment in physical infrastructure (88% going to men). The simulation also showed that almost half of the social care jobs would go to poor households below the fourth decile of the income distribution, while half of the jobs created in physical infrastructure would go to middle-income households.[8]

Finally, the study on Turkey simulated the possible effects of hypothetical public investments in early childhood care and pre-school education services, targeting OECD average enrolment rates. This was estimated to require an additional 20.7 billion TRY expenditure on childcare centres and pre-schools corresponding to approximately 1.1% of GDP in 2014. An expenditure of this magnitude on expansion of early childcare and pre-school education was found to generate 719,000 new direct and indirect jobs versus only 290,000 new direct and indirect jobs via spending a similar amount on a construction boom. While women were estimated to take up 73% of the new jobs created via childcare expansion, as little as 6% of the new jobs created via a construction boom would go to women. Nevertheless, the study pointed out that in terms of absolute numbers, childcare expansion still created a substantial number of jobs for men (195,000 jobs) – as much as 72% of the total number of male jobs created through construction (272,000 jobs). Childcare expansion was also found to create more jobs for the unemployed (253,000 jobs) than a construction boom of similar cost (242,000 jobs), besides creating a substantial number of jobs for "non-participant women" (394,000 female homemakers were estimated to enter the labour market).

The Turkish study also explored the quality of new job creation. It found that childcare expansion created more decent jobs than a construction boom. Of the childcare expansion-generated new jobs, 85% were estimated to come with social security benefits, versus 30.2% in the case of construction-generated new jobs. In the case of construction, the new jobs created were predominantly (64.1%) occasional jobs without a contract, 24.6% were permanent jobs with a contract of unlimited duration and 11.3% were temporary jobs with contracts of limited duration. These ratios were reversed for the childcare expansion scenario, where 84% of the new jobs were estimated to be permanent jobs with a contract of unlimited duration, 10.5% were temporary jobs with contracts of limited duration and only 6.1% were occasional jobs without a contract.

As for the impact on the poverty rate, the Turkish study found that, combining both demand- and supply-side effects, a childcare expansion targeting new labour demand towards prime-working-age poor mothers of small children had the potential to decrease the relative poverty rate by as much as 1.14 percentage points versus only a 0.35 percentage point reduction in the relative poverty rate through a construction boom. The study also explored the short-run fiscal sustainability of public expenditures and found that 77% of increased expenditures on childcare centres and pre-schools was likely to be recovered through increased government revenues by the end of the year, while for construction the same ratio stood at 52%.[9]

An interesting aspect of the results of these policy simulations on the demand-side impact of social care expansion versus an alternative sector such as construction is that the pro-women bias of the jobs generated via the former derives directly from the sectoral and occupational gender segregation observed in these various labour markets (South Africa, US, Turkey). The simulations were based on current labour market data, which reflected an unbalanced gender composition of employment in the social care versus the construction sectors. A purple economy, which aims at full gender equality in the economic sphere, would inevitably entail policies and actions that would eliminate such horizontal gender segregation across sectors and occupations. Hence employment generation through social care expansion would not necessarily have a pro-women bias in terms of who the jobs go to; yet it would sustain its superiority in terms of generating a substantially higher number of jobs, instigating a stronger impact on poverty reduction and carrying the additional positive externalities, such as supporting equal opportunities

36 Ipek Ilkkaracan

for children (and associated positive supply-side effects on human capital and productivity) and improving quality of life for the dependent elderly, disabled and the ill.

To summarise, these recent empirical studies have provided ample evidence that there is a strong demand-side economic rationale to expanding social care services particularly in times of crisis and high unemployment.

Conclusions

Austerity policies have often been criticised for their adverse impact on gender equality through their negative implications for labour market conditions, as well as cuts in public spending and provisioning of services. Gender critiques of austerity policies have pointed out that both are likely to result in gendered patterns. The negative labour market effects can have gender-segregated outcomes for increasing the probability of women falling out of the labour market back to traditional homemaker roles. This gendered impact is partly due to austerity measures instigating cuts in public employment where women are overrepresented; however, it is also due to the fact that generally slack labour demand is more likely to push women into their traditional secondary earner roles, particularly in contexts of higher social and political conservatism. Moreover, deteriorating labour market conditions (through higher unemployment levels) redistribute negotiating power to the disadvantage of workers, resulting in lower likelihood of worker claims on rights to care leave and shorter working hours. Austerity-related cuts in public spending on services such as childcare, education, health and social services, on the other hand, lead to higher unpaid work burdens on women.

This chapter has used the vision of the "purple economy" to move beyond these critiques to offer an alternative. It has explained why and how universal provisioning of social care services is a fundamental characteristic of a gender-egalitarian and sustainable purple economic order, and has presented ample evidence that investments in the social care service sector carry a strong potential for employment creation that is pro-women and pro-poor. Hence in a context of economic crisis, the purple economy carries important implications for fiscal policy – it reveals where to spend limited revenues for the most effective results. If the policy response to the crisis is a Keynesian fiscal stimulus, public investments and spending on social care service expansion are a must for such stimulatory spending promising to yield multiple returns. If the policy response is a more prudent one, the purple economy tells us where cuts should *not* be made and how to reallocate existing spending.

Proponents of austerity often acknowledge that, while it involves huge social costs, it is unavoidable when a country is said to have "lived beyond its means" and lost the confidence of creditors and investors. This chapter has tried to show that public spending on social care should be perceived as an investment that pays off not only in the long run through supply effects but also in the short run through demand effects. It is through such acknowledgement of the productive role of

A feminist alternative to austerity **37**

social policy that the debate on austerity measures might start to transform. This is particularly relevant for macroeconomic policy discussions in Europe for a number of reasons. Most importantly, high unemployment rates combined with unequal gender employment and pay gaps along with horizontal and vertical segregation continue to persist in most EU economies. A purple economy where caring labour is socialised to a large extent promises to generate jobs while eliminating a fundamental source of gender inequalities in the labour market. Moreover, given the demographic shift to ageing societies in Europe, a purple economy promises to address a fundamental problem of care for the elderly and the ill, while at the same time pointing towards a potential underdeveloped sector with ample capacity to contribute to economic growth and to reduce unemployment.

Finally, the above discussion also calls attention to the strong gender biases entailed in the composition of macro investment and stimulus packages. The EU 2008 stimulus plan adopted as a measure against the adverse effects of the global economic crisis entailed an investment plan where incentives were geared towards strategic investments in "energy efficiency to create jobs and save energy; investing in clean technologies to boost sectors like construction and automobiles in the low-carbon markets of the future; and investing in infrastructure and inter-connection to promote efficiency and innovation" (EU 2008). Similarly, the EU Infrastructure Investment Plan (also known as the Juncker Plan), adopted in 2015, points to green energy and technology sectors as well as R&D activities as priorities, while there is hardly any mention of social care infrastructure development. What the foregoing discussion has showed is that such macro-level interventions aimed at economic recovery and lower unemployment in Europe have the potential to be more effective if the focus on stimulus through green jobs for an environmentally sustainable recovery is complemented by stimulus via purple jobs for an economic recovery that ensures sustainability of caring labour through gender-equitable strategies.

Notes

1   Social care entails care services for children, the elderly, disabled and ill provided through public or private institutions such as childcare centres and pre-schools for young children, after-school care centres for school-age children, senior centres and active living centres providing day services for the elderly and disabled, elderly homes, hospitals and the like. Social care can also be provided as home-based services, yet what makes it "social" is that it is provided through the paid labour of trained professionals and service workers rather than through the unpaid domestic labour of family members.

2   Cross-country comparative studies point out the significant differences between the legal labour market working hours in the North and the South as an important source of divergence in work–family reconciliation environments. In a cross-country study of seven OECD countries, Ilkkaracan (2012) contrasted the French norm of a 35-hour work week and the Southern norm of a 48-hour work week (Mexico, South Korea, Turkey) as a significant difference with substantial impacts on gender inequalities in employment. As the norm for weekly working hours increases, the single male breadwinner, full-time female homemaker model imposes itself as the only possibility.

3 See Hirway (2008) for implementation of employment guarantee programmes for rural women in India.
4 Ilkkaracan (2013) pointed out the overlaps between a purple macroeconomic framework and the research on a wage-led versus profit-led growth regime; see also Onaran, Ch.3 in this volume.
5 For an assessment of a gendered-expansionary macroeconomic framework as an alternative to austerity policies, see Ch.8 in this volume by Bargawi and Cozzi and Ch.9 by Andersen and Dahl.
6 For the impact of improved access to childcare services on female labour supply, see e.g. cross-country studies by Del Boca and Pasqua (2005), Del Boca and Vuri (2007), and Apps and Rees (2004, 2005). On human capital impact of early childcare and pre-school education, see Heckman et al. (2010), Conti and Heckman (2012) and Heckman et al. (2013).
7 Southern Eurozone countries are investing 1.5% of GDP in 2014 and gradually increasing to 2.5% of GDP by 2018.
8 The US study also made comparisons to the green energy sector using findings from another empirical study by Pollin et al. (2009, referenced in Antonpoulos and Kim 2011). It found that an equivalent $50 billion investment in building a green energy infrastructure created 850,000 jobs and more than 52% of these jobs would go to high-skilled workers with college or higher education.
9 Antonopoulos et al. (2014) explored similar effects under a proposed job guarantee (JG) programme for Greece in which a substantial share of job creation is directed at social service provisioning. The study found a high multiplier impact such that for every €100 spent on the JG, roughly €230 would be added to the Greek economy; and for every 320 jobs directly created (JG positions), another 100 full-time jobs (mainly skilled) would be created in the private sector.

References

AK Europa. 2013. "Social Investment, Growth, Employment and Financial Sustainability: Economic and Fiscal Effects of Improving Childcare in Austria." AK Position Paper. Brussels and Vienna: AK Europa.

Antonopoulos, R. and K. Kim. 2008. "Impact of Employment Guarantee Programmes on Gender Equality and Pro-poor Economic Development." Policy Brief: Case Study on South Africa. Annandale-on-Hudson, NY: Levy Economics Institute of Bard College.

Antonpoulos, R. and K. Kim, 2011. "Public Job-creation Programs: The Economic Benefits of Investing in Social Care Case Studies in South Africa and the United States." Working Paper No. 671, Levy Economics Institute, New York.

Antonopoulos, R., K. Kim, T. Masterson and A. Zacharias. 2010. "Why President Obama Should Care about 'Care': An Effective and Equitable Investment Strategy for Job Creation." Public Policy Brief No.108. Annandale-on-Hudson, NY: Levy Economics Institute of Bard College.

Antonopoulos, R., S. Adam, K. Kim, T. Masterson and D.B. Papadimitriou. 2014. "Responding to the Unemployment Challenge: A Job Guarantee Proposal for Greece." Research Project Report. Annandale-on-Hudson, NY: Levy Economics Institute of Bard College.

Apps, P. and R. Rees. 2004. "Fertility, Taxation and Family Policy." *The Scandinavian Journal of Economics* 106(4): 745–763.

Apps, P. and R. Rees. 2005. "Time Use and the Costs of Children over the Life Cycle." In D. Hamermesh and G. Phann (eds). *The Economics of Time Use*. London: Elsevier.

Conti, G. and J. Heckman. 2012. "The Economics of Child Well-Being." IZA Discussion Paper No. 6930. Bonn: Institute for the Study of Labor.

Del Boca, D. and S. Pasqua. 2005. "Labour Supply and Fertility in Europe and the US." In T. Boeri, D. Del Boca and C. Pissarides (eds). *Women at Work: An Economic Perspective.* Oxford: Oxford University Press.

Del Boca, D. and D. Vuri. 2007. "The Mismatch between Labor Supply and Child Care." *Journal of Population Economics* 20(4): 805–32.

European Commission. 2013. Commission Recommendation of 20 February 2013 *Investing in Children: Breaking the Cycle of Disadvantage* (2013/112/EU), Official Journal of the European Union, .3.2013, L 59/5. http://eur-lex.europa.eu/legal-content/EN/TXT/PDF/?uri=CELEX:32013H0112&from=EN (accessed 26 April 2016).

European Union (EU). 2008. "A European Economic Recovery Plan." Brussels (26 November). http://eur-lex.europa.eu/legal-content/EN/ALL/?uri=CELEX:52008 DC0800 (accessed 6 January 2016).

Heckman, J., S.H. Moon, R. Pinto, P.A. Savelyev and A.Q. Yavitz. 2010. "Analyzing Social Experiments as Implemented: A Reexamination of the Evidence From the HighScope Perry Preschool Program." *Quantitative Economics* 1(1): 1–46.

Heckman, J., R. Pinto and P.A. Savelyev. 2013. "Understanding the Mechanisms through which an Influential Early Childhood Program Boosted Adult Outcomes." *American Economic Review* 103(6): 2052–86.

Hirway, I. 2008. "Impact of Employment Guarantee Programmes on Gender Equality and Pro-Poor Economic Development." Levy Economics Institute of Bard College, New York.

Ilkkaracan, I. 2012. "Work–Family Balance and Public Policy: A Cross-country Perspective." *Development*, 55(3): 325–32.

Ilkkaracan, I. 2013. "The Purple Economy: A Call for a New Economic Order beyond the Green Economy." In U. Röhr and C. van Heemstra (eds). *Green Economy and Green Growth: Who Cares?* Berlin: Life E.V. and German Ministry for the Environment.

Ilkkaracan, I., K. Kim and T. Kaya. 2015. "The Impact of Public Investment in Social Care Services on Employment, Gender Equality and Poverty." ITU WSC-SET, Levy Economics Institute, ILO, UNDP and UN Women, İstanbul.

Peng, I. 2011. "The Good, the Bad and the Confusing: The Political Economy of Social Care Expansion in South Korea." *Development and Change* 42(4): 905–23.

Pollin, R., J. Heintz and Heidi Garrett-Peltier. 2009. "The Economic Benefits of Investing in Clean Energy: How the Economic Stimulus Program and New Legislation Can Boost US Economic Growth and Employment." Amherst, MA: Department of Economics and Political Economy Research Institute.

United Nations Environmental Programme (UNEP). 2011. "Towards a Green Economy: Pathways to Sustainable Development and Poverty Eradication." UNEP. www.unep.org/greeneconomy (accessed 6 January 2016).

Warner, M. and Z. Liu. 2006. "The Importance of Childcare in Economic Development: A Comparative Analysis of Regional Economic Linkage." *Economic Development Quarterly*, 20(1): 97–103.

3

THE ROLE OF GENDER EQUALITY IN AN EQUALITY-LED SUSTAINABLE DEVELOPMENT STRATEGY

Özlem Onaran

Introduction

Mainstream economics continues to guide policy towards further wage moderation and austerity as two of the major responses to the Great Recession, in particular in Europe. These policies are deepening inequality in all dimensions and are having detrimental consequences for gender equality in regards to labour market outcomes, such as employment and pay, as well as the division of the unpaid and invisible work burden at home.

The austerity agenda since 2010 has aimed at reducing the size of the state, in particular social protection spending (as if the cause of the crisis in Europe was the generosity of the welfare state). In parallel to this there has been a remarkable change in employment and collective bargaining legislations. The erosion of the power of labour unions in the public sector, along with downsizing and pay freezes, have been implicit aims of the austerity agenda and have hit women on three fronts – as workers in the public sector, users of public services and as those mostly likely to make up for the absence of public services by their own unpaid labour.

The advocates of this dominant policy framework of austerity would argue that a fall in real wages, and a rise in inequality, is good for growth or at best is an unavoidable consequence of dealing with the crisis. Evidence shows that the dilemma of pay versus jobs is not empirically validated for a wage-led economy like Europe; austerity policies with detrimental effects on wage shares only bring further stagnation.

Among the critiques of this mainstream approach, there is an increasing consensus regarding the destabilising effects of rising inequality; however, there has not been sufficient attention paid to the interplay of different dimensions of inequality, and in particular gender inequality. The aim of this chapter is to examine a gendered macroeconomic model and outline the cornerstones of such a model in order to analyse the various channels through which gender equality can influence growth and employment outcomes.

This chapter is organised as follows. First, it introduces the basic Post-Keynesian/neo-Kaleckian demand-led growth model, and contrasts this with the mainstream neoclassical growth model. It then presents current contributions in feminist economics to gendering demand-led growth models, and suggests an extended model that incorporates gender-relevant categories in the behavioural functions that determine private aggregate demand (consumption, investment), and the role of the government in a model with endogenous changes in productivity and employment. The penultimate section discusses policy alternatives, before the final section concludes.

Demand-led growth model

Mainstream economic policy informed by the standard neoclassical growth model (i.e. the Solow growth model) emphasises the supply side rather than the demand side of the economy as the determinant of growth, and assumes that demand will follow supply. Typically, wages are treated merely as a component of cost. When the wage share falls and profit share increases this is expected to lead to a rise in both private investment due to higher profitability, and net exports due to lower unit labour costs, and thus higher international competitiveness. This thinking has guided policies promoting wage moderation in Europe. For example, the European Commission (EC) (2006) explicitly argued that wage moderation, i.e. real wage growth below productivity growth, was the key to international competitiveness, which is seen to be one of the most crucial policy tools to stimulate growth and jobs in a globalised economy. From this perspective, further deregulation in the labour markets would be seen as a positive development to ensure wage moderation.

However, this mainstream theory fails to explain why growth was lower in the post-1980s compared to the 1960s and 1970s despite a rise in the profit share, and why recovery is still so sluggish after the Great Recession of 2008. The standard neoclassical growth model, based on microeconomic decisions of optimising agents, assumes full employment and does not incorporate demand-side constraints and hence excess capacity and involuntary unemployment.

Post-Keynesian/neo-Kaleckian macroeconomic models

Heterodox Post-Keynesian/neo-Kaleckian macroeconomic models address this problem by integrating the dual role of wages both as a cost and a source of demand.[1] These models synthesise the ideas of Keynes, Kalecki and Marx, and while they accept the direct positive effects of higher profits on private investment and net exports as emphasised in mainstream models, they contrast these positive effects with the negative effects on consumption. Demand plays a central role in determining growth and employment; hence growth is demand-constrained as long as the economy is operating below full employment levels, and the distribution

42 Özlem Onaran

of income between workers and capitalists (wages and profits) has a crucial effect on demand.[2]

These models allow for involuntary unemployment, underemployment and excess capacity. Components of aggregate demand are determined by behavioural equations. Wages are an outcome of a bargaining process between employers and workers, as opposed to the neoclassical theory where they are determined by the marginal product of labour. Neoclassical labour supply is based on the choice between leisure and consumption. The difference in the demand-led models of growth and employment is that unemployment is involuntary: labour supply is inelastic and employment is demand-constrained in an economy where there is involuntary unemployment, and hence is not supply determined; leisure is not a choice but a residual.

On the demand side – first, consumption is expected to decrease when the wage share decreases, since workers consume more as a proportion of their income compared to the owners of capital. In technical terms, the marginal propensity to consume out of wage income is higher than that out of profit income. Secondly, higher profitability (i.e. a higher profit share and a lower wage share)[3] is expected to stimulate private investment for a given level of aggregate demand. Thirdly, net exports (exports minus imports), will depend negatively on unit labour costs, which are by definition closely related to the wage share, as well as the levels of domestic and foreign demand. Thus, the total effect of the decrease in the wage share on aggregate demand of the private sector (households and firms) depends on the relative size of the reactions of consumption, private investment and net exports to changes in income distribution. If the total effect is negative, the demand regime is called wage-led; otherwise the regime is profit-led.

Theoretically, both are possible scenarios, and whether the negative effect of lower wages on consumption, or the positive effect on investment and net exports, is larger in absolute value is an empirical question depending on the parameters of an economy. If consumption is highly sensitive to distribution (i.e. if the differences in the marginal propensity to consume out of wages and profits is very high), if investment is less sensitive to profits but responds more to demand, if domestic demand constitutes a more significant part of aggregate demand, and if net exports are not highly responsive to relative prices and the effect of labour costs on export prices are not very large – then the economy is more likely to be wage-led. If the responsiveness of investment to profits is strong and foreign trade is an important part of the economy (as is the case in small open economies) and is highly responsive to labour costs – then the economy is more likely to be profit-led. In a wage-led economy, a fall in the labour share would generate a decline in GDP; a higher wage share is required for growth. Pro-capital policies would generate more growth only if an economy is profit-led.

While Post-Keynesian/post-Kaleckian models offer a general theory that allows for different regimes and opposing effects of the wage share on growth, mainstream economic policy assumes that all economies are profit-led. Indeed the mainstream argument goes beyond that since the EC's policy of wage moderation is prescribed to all the countries in Europe – hence the EC implicitly assumes that Europe as a whole is profit-led. Similarly, these policies have been exported to the developing world through the IMF and the World Bank – hence the implicit assumption must be that the global economy is profit-led.

Empirical evidence

A wide body of empirical research in the tradition of Post-Keynesian/post-Kaleckian models challenge the assumption that all countries are profit-led (e.g. Onaran and Galanis 2014; Onaran et al. 2011; Stockhammer et al. 2009; Hein and Vogel 2008; Naastepad and Storm 2007; Stockhammer and Onaran 2004; Bowles and Boyer 1995). Germany, France and Italy as individual large members of the Eurozone are wage-led (Onaran and Obst 2015; Onaran and Galanis 2014; Hein and Vogel 2008), while small open economies in the Eurozone, such as Ireland and Austria, may be profit-led when analysed in isolation (Onaran and Obst 2015; Hein and Vogel 2008; Stockhammer and Ederer 2008). However, in the context of Europe, Onaran and Obst (2015), Stockhammer et al. (2009) and Onaran and Galanis (2014) have shown that demand in the Eurozone-12 taken together is wage-led. The Euro area as a whole is a rather closed economy with low extra-EU trade (albeit high intra-EU trade). Thus wage moderation, which keeps real wage growth below productivity and leads to a fall in the wage share in Europe, is likely to have only moderate effects on foreign trade but substantial effects on domestic demand. Further, if wages were to change simultaneously in all EU countries, the net export position of each country would change little because extra-EU trade is comparatively small. Thus, if all EU countries pursued "beggar thy neighbour" policies, i.e. wage moderation to gain a cost advantage in the global market, the international competitiveness effects would be minor, and the domestic effects would dominate the outcome.

A wage-led growth regime can be seen broadly as an equality-led growth regime, embracing all dimensions of equality. Redistribution from profits to wages as well as from the rich to the poor will lead to higher growth rates, as well as to greater income equality. Similarly, eliminating gender wage gaps as part of a process of an upward convergence in wages will contribute to greater equality and overall a higher wage share, which in turn, in a wage-led economy such as Europe, will lead to higher growth according to empirical evidence. However, a gendered approach to macroeconomic modelling should go beyond the effect of gender equality on aggregate income distribution (the wage share) and should incorporate gender-relevant categories in all behavioural components of the model.

Integrating gender in a demand-led growth model

A review of the literature on feminist macroeconomic models

The central role of inequality in Post-Keynesian/Kaleckian models provides a useful theoretical framework for analysing the impact of gender inequality on

44 Özlem Onaran

macroeconomic outcomes. Feminist economists have incorporated into this framework gender differences in income in order to analyse the effects of both inter-class and intra-class distribution as well as household dynamics and caring labour (see Seguino 2012a for a review). As opposed to conventional macroeconomic models, in feminist models labour is treated as a produced means of production: the reproduction of labour is carried out by both paid and unpaid work; and women have a disproportionate share of unpaid work relative to men. Furthermore, in the tradition of structuralist macroeconomics, the stylised structural features of economies (i.e. market structure, the structure of production and trade and resulting price elasticities, and balance of payments constraints to growth) play a crucial role in these macro models. In feminist structuralist macroeconomic models a country's economic structure (i.e. agricultural, semi-industrialised, post-industrial), macro-level policies that influence relations with the rest of the world (i.e. rules governing trade and cross-border investment and finance), the form and extent of gendered job segregation (e.g. women's association with paid care work) and the distribution of unpaid care labour between men and women have been incorporated.

Most of the feminist macroeconomics on the effects of gender inequality on growth have analysed the cases of developing economies (Seguino 2012a). Significant contributions include Ertürk and Çağatay (1995), Braunstein (2000), Blecker and Seguino (2002), Akram-Lodhi and Hanmer (2008), Seguino (2010, 2012b) and Braunstein et al. (2011). Seguino (2012b) and Braunstein et al. (2011) developed theoretical macro models based on the stylised structural features of a modern industrial economy with a large human services sector that primarily employs women. Braunstein (2013) offered a non-technical presentation of the model; however, the model is not empirically estimated.

The model by Braunstein et al. (2011) incorporates "investments in human capacities" by individuals and households. "Human capacities" include those that standard human capital measures such as skills and education attempt to capture, as well as broader aspects such as emotional maturity, patience and self-confidence. This "investment" first generates current aggregate demand directly. Second, it increases labour productivity both through the short-term, day-to-day aspects of reproduction and in the longer term, through creating future productive capacity and boosting economic growth; however, the latter is not incorporated in what is a short-run model. Investments in human capacities play a similar role to physical investments, unlike outside feminist economics, where investment in future human capacities tend not to be acknowledged as investment at all. Investments in human capacities are determined by expectations about future economic opportunities, which are directly related to higher wages as well as economic activity.

Braunstein et al.'s model defines "caring spirits" as the tendency to provide care, which determines the process through which expectations are transformed into actual investments in human capacities.[4] Caring spirits are determined by social norms, individual motivation, public preferences and the structure of the social welfare state. The model distinguishes between "strong/altruistic" versus "weak/individualistic" caring spirits as well as "caring" and "non-caring" states. Favourable

An equality-led sustainable development strategy **45**

opportunities translate into higher investment in human capacities in societies with "strong/altruistic" caring spirits than in individualistic ones. Strong caring spirits increase the likelihood of an economy being wage-led, because higher wages translate into a higher investment in human capacities. If the increase in human capacities investment is high enough, total investment in physical and human capacities could increase despite a lower profit share. Overall, Braunstein et al.'s model shows that higher female wages not only directly affect demand, but also could raise labour productivity and reduce unit labour costs via greater investment in "human capacities" at the household level. The net effect of higher female wages on profits and investment is ambiguous, and may be positive under certain parameters.

The model by Braunstein et al. (2011) is the most detailed theoretical model to integrate gender in a demand-led growth model. However, it does not explicitly model the government sector, employment, the effects of the gender distribution of income on consumption and the long-run supply-side (productivity) effects of social infrastructure on private investment.

The task ahead is to build in gender inequality in not only theoretical but also empirical models of demand-led growth. Furthermore, a model is needed that integrates both the short-run demand effects and the long-run productivity effects.

There are four important entry points in the Post-Keynesian/Kaleckian demand-led growth models for integrating gender. The first is via household spending: a higher degree of gender equality is expected to change the composition of household spending, e.g. more income in the hands of women is expected to increase the share of household spending that will benefit children – hence spending on human capacities, such as on education, is taken to be a positive function of gender equality at the household level.[5] Demand-led growth models traditionally model consumption as a function of wages and profits;[6] a gender-aware macro modelling strategy requires estimating consumption as a function of female and male wages and profits, and disaggregating consumption into household spending on human capacities and the rest.

The second entry point is via investment. In the standard demand-led growth models private investment by firms is simply a function of profitability and demand. However, private investment responds to infrastructure. In mainstream models, public spending on only physical infrastructure, such as transport or ITC infrastructure, has positive crowding-in effects on private investment. However, social infrastructure in terms of education and health plays a crucial role in the productivity and profitability of private investment. Hence, investment should be modelled as a function of both public and private spending that enhances human capacities and social infrastructure. Greater gender equality, e.g. a decrease in gender pay gap,[7] through changing not just the level but also the composition of consumption and increasing social infrastructure, will therefore have a further positive effect on private investment.

The third and fourth entry points are through integrating the role of the government and the impact of changes in distribution and spending on employment, as will be discussed in more detail below.

An extended gendered macro model

The aim of this chapter is to outline the cornerstones of a gendered macroeconomic model by integrating several different theoretical contributions in the literature, including: i) the effect of income distribution on growth (e.g. Bhaduri and Marglin 1990; Stockhammer et al. 2009; Onaran and Galanis 2014); ii) the effect of income distribution and growth on employment (Stockhammer and Onaran 2004); iii) the effect of government spending on demand and growth (Blecker 2002; Seguino 2012b); iv) the interaction of growth, income distribution and productivity (Hein and Tarassow 2010; Naastepad 2006); and v) the effects of changes in male and female wages in an economy with social reproduction (Braunstein et al. 2011).

For simplicity, a two-sector model is proposed for the market economy[8] – a "social" sector that provides the social infrastructure that includes the services such as care, health and education that contribute to building human capacities, and a remaining sector that represents the rest of the market economy. Social infrastructure is produced both in the market economy by the paid labour of men and women in the public and private sectors, and in the home economy by unpaid labour. The social sector typically employs more women than men. The rest of the economy includes physical infrastructure, among other things, and employment is predominantly male. Aggregate output is determined by demand, made up of private consumption (household spending), private investment, net exports and government spending. While the model acknowledges that unpaid labour contributes to the welfare of the society, its market value is zero, and it is not therefore part of aggregate output as measured by the conventional GDP figures.

Demand-led growth models traditionally model consumption by households only of those goods and services produced in the market economy by paid labour. A gender-aware macro modelling strategy first requires disaggregating consumption into two categories: household spending on social infrastructure (produced by both paid and unpaid labour), and consumption of goods and services produced by the rest of the economy. Secondly, while consumption is traditionally modelled as a function of aggregate wages and profits, a gender-aware approach has to address gender income differentials by modelling consumption (in both sectors) as a function of income from female waged employment, male waged employment and profits. For simplicity, wages are treated as exogenous, determined outside the model by bargaining and labour market institutions. (Employment as an endogenous variable is discussed in more detail below.) Hence, total female and male wage incomes, as well as wage and profit shares, are endogenous.

There is limited empirical research on the differences in propensities to consume by men and women, as well as the composition of consumption with respect to types of goods and services and their import content. There is empirical evidence that the marginal propensity to consume out of wages is higher than that out of profits (e.g. Onaran and Galanis 2014), and since female wage income in aggregate is lower than male wage income, the hypothesis here is that the marginal propensity to consume out of female wage income is higher than that out of male wage

An equality-led sustainable development strategy **47**

income. Hence, an increase in female wage rates or female employment, other things being equal, is expected to lead to higher consumption.

Another important empirical question to explore is how a higher degree of gender equality in wages or employment could change the composition of consumption. Braunstein (2013) theorised that the impact of income on human capacities depends not only on how much is earned and spent, but on what is purchased, and whether these commodities provide good substitutes or complements for unpaid care time. At first glance, women need to spend more of their income on social services to replace their unpaid reproductive labour, assuming these services are not freely provided by the public sector. Furthermore, it is expected that more income in the hands of women or the presence of an employed mother in the household will increase household spending on children and will lead to greater equality in the spending on boys and girls. Seguino (2012a) suggested that in developing countries, women are more likely to consume domestic goods, while men are more likely to consume a higher proportion of luxury and/or imported goods (such as cell phones, automobiles and televisions). Ertürk and Çağatay (1995) proposed that increases in the intensity of women's unpaid work in the household raises savings rates. Hence, a rise in female wage income may decrease unpaid work and increase the propensity to consume. However, interestingly Floro and Seguino (2002) found that, for a group of semi-industrialised countries, higher incomes and more bargaining power for women were associated with higher aggregate savings rates.

Most of the Post-Keynesian literature does not model the public sector (with the notable exceptions of Blecker (2002) and Seguino (2012b)). In the gendered framework presented here, the public sector has a crucial role to play in contributing to social infrastructure. Women do the majority of unpaid "reproductive" labour; therefore the development of the "social sector" in the market economy with services provided by paid labour in the public sector, as well as the private sector, will have profound effects on women as well as on aggregate macroeconomic outcomes. First, on the supply side, this will reduce the need for unpaid labour to provide care, education and health, and improve the chances of women to participate in the paid economy. Secondly, on the demand side, given the current rates of occupational segregation the new jobs generated in the social sector will be traditionally female jobs, and thereby increase the employment chances of women.[9] Thirdly, both the public supply of social services and increased paid employment opportunities could transform gender norms concerning divisions of labour both within the household and over paid versus unpaid work (Folbre and Nelson 2000). Hence, government spending should be introduced to the model in a similar disaggregated fashion as spending on social infrastructure, physical infrastructure and other public spending. Taxes are modelled as a function of wage and profit income. As an extension, consumption should also be modelled as a function of after tax wages of each gender and profits.

In the standard demand-led growth models private investment in physical capital is simply a function of profitability (the share of profits in national income) and demand. In a gendered macro model, in order to fully understand the importance of social infrastructure, the response of private investment to the business environment created by social as well as physical infrastructure in the short run and their positive effects on productivity in the long run also need to be included. Traditionally, public spending in physical infrastructure such as transport or ITC infrastructure is expected to generate positive crowding-in effects on private investment. However, social infrastructure in terms of education and health also plays a crucial role in the productivity and profitability of private investments. While we may expect to see positive effects on the "animal spirits" of firms even in the short run through an expected improvement in the business environment, longer-term effects of lagged public spending (or average values of the past five years) should be integrated into empirical estimations of private investment behaviour.

Net exports can be simply modelled as a function of aggregate demand and unit labour costs. Further, it could be assumed that social services are non-tradable and all net exports are in the rest of the economy.

To allow for the long-term effects of social infrastructure, the model should further integrate supply-side effects by modelling changes in labour productivity. Hein and Tarassow (2010) and Naastepad (2006) incorporated productivity into the standard (non-gendered) demand-led growth model. In our extended framework, productivity could be modelled as a function of investment disaggregated into private and public investment in social and physical infrastructure. Furthermore, following the Post-Keynesian literature on technological change, productivity is a positive function of demand and a negative function of the profit share. The latter is due to a higher wage share, i.e. a lower profit share, pushing firms to be more innovative. This is also consistent with efficiency wage effects in the new Keynesian labour economics literature. Overall, technological change is endogenous.

Finally, a gendered macroeconomic analysis should focus on outcomes beyond growth. As a measure of empowerment, the levels of employment of men and women may be a more direct indicator than the aggregate growth rate. Hence, a gendered macro model should also incorporate the effects on employment. In the standard demand-led growth models, Stockhammer and Onaran (2004) modelled employment in the context of an SVAR model. In this gendered framework, employment in social services and the rest of the economy can be modelled as a function of demand, labour productivity and labour costs. Using the latest figures about the share of female and male employment in each sector, and assuming these do not change, the total female and male employment in the economy for a given demand can be estimated.

The model can then be econometrically estimated and used to simulate the effects of changes in public spending in the social sector versus the rest of the economy on employment of men and women, as well as macroeconomic outcomes such as private investment, productivity, growth and the budget deficit. Other exogenous variables such as male and female wages or the gender composition of

An equality-led sustainable development strategy **49**

the sectors can also be changed to simulate effects on growth and employment. The ultimate aim is to have a model that can guide public spending policy and wage policy to achieve an equitable development strategy.

Expected outcomes and effects

Overall, a rise in female income may generate positive multiplier effects in the economy. With respect to the effects of public spending, although government spending in social infrastructure is expected to generate more female employment than male employment at the outset, the overall effects on male employment are also expected to be positive through aggregate multiplier effects. If women have a higher marginal propensity to consume, and if the import component of the inputs in the social infrastructure sector is lower as was found by Antonopoulos et al. (2010), public spending in the social sector is expected to have a larger multiplier effect on aggregate demand.

However, feminist economics emphasises the contradictory effects of increased female labour force participation on economic outcomes (Seguino 2012a). Under certain circumstances increased female labour force participation may stimulate output. However, if gender norms prevent a more equal distribution of unpaid care labour, in the absence of accessible public services for care, the increase in paid working hours by women may crowd out unpaid caring labour, which in turn would have a negative effect on the production of labour power and hence labour productivity (Ertürk and Darity 2000; Braunstein et al. 2011). In developed economies the supply of care services by the public or private sector may mediate the second effect; however, the effect will also depend on the wages and affordability of these services (Seguino 2012a). To develop the argument further, Braunstein et al. (2011) introduced a social reproduction function on the supply side with three types of inputs – non-market time, commodities and public infrastructure – which are combined to produce human capacities, including daily maintenance of the labour force as well as longer-term investments. Wage differentials between men and women and social norms lead to a higher share of female unpaid time input. Commodities include direct and indirect care services and capital goods financed by income from work or public and private transfers. Public infrastructure includes goods and services like roads, electricity, sanitation, water, nurseries, schools and nursing homes that increase the availability and accessibility of care commodities, or lower the required time for care work by women.

Braunstein (2013) distinguished between a "low-road" regime, where higher female labour force participation is associated with a decline in human capacities' production, and a "high-road" regime, where increased female labour force participation is associated with higher production of human capacities. An increase in economic activity and female labour force participation has both a negative (time) effect on the production of capacities through the increase in the opportunity cost of unpaid work and a positive (income) effect on the production of capacities through consumption of market care goods. However, the latter effect depends on the financial costs of reproduction, what care and capital commodities households ultimately decide to purchase, and the gender division of labour in unpaid care. If the time and financial burdens of social reproduction are spread among more contributors, increasing female labour force participation can be counterbalanced by supports in the family, community and the state. Braunstein (2013) called this the "gender egalitarian case". Smaller gender wage gaps with an upward convergence of female wages to male wages and public or private provision of care services are conducive to the high-road regime. In contrast, the low-road regime is characterised by the "feminization of responsibility and obligation" (Braunstein 2013). According to the theoretical framework of Braunstein et al. (2011), a wage-led economy with a high-road distribution of social reproduction and greater gender wage equality raises investment in human capacities and aggregate demand by more than it cuts into profits, and hence raises growth. Higher labour market participation among women induced by higher wages does lower the non-market time for human capacities production. However, gender egalitarian relations of reproduction and strong public support for care and the availability of care commodities lead to an increase in the production of human capacities thanks to higher incomes. This is the win-win scenario for the society, and the workers and carers.

While addressing the production and consumption of social services produced by unpaid labour is an integral part of feminist economics from a theoretical perspective, empirically pinning down these effects at the macroeconomic level runs against the constraints of data availability regarding unpaid labour; we need to know its composition as well as its precise contribution to human capacities, which necessarily includes abstract elements such as self-confidence. Time Use Surveys are not carried out frequently enough to provide sufficiently long historical data for time series analysis. Furthermore, the behavioural aspects of division of unpaid labour at the household level and labour supply decisions require a microeconometric analysis using individual data. Hence a full modelling of the labour supply behaviour and the incorporation of unpaid care labour requires an integrated microeconomic and macroeconomic model. Different from Braunstein et al. (2011), the model outlined here elaborates the demand side of the economy and employment in more detail, but is limited to an aggregate macroeconomic analysis excluding labour supply behaviour; therefore it assumes that labour market supply decisions of women are simply demand driven and women's unpaid labour is infinitely elastic. This simplification does not reflect the complete picture of the impact of changes in policies on the well-being of people as well as productivity in the future. Furthermore, Fontana (2014) emphasised that some unpaid household activities can be replaced with market services only to some extent, e.g. looking after children has a strong relational component and involves close emotional interaction. However, feminist economists have also emphasised that the use of market services does not rule out the presence of relational and emotional interaction (Folbre and Nelson 2000; Himmelweit 1999).

Policy implications for gender-aware policies as part of an equality-led and sustainable strategy in Europe

The push for wage-led/equality-led recovery could primarily come through a strengthening of the bargaining power of labour and bringing back the welfare state. Gender equality should be at the heart of the design, as well as the evaluation, of these policies. An equality-led development strategy requires policies targeting the top, middle and bottom of wage distribution, as well as systematic policies to close gender gaps, which would also work to correct the increased gap between productivity and wages in the last three decades. Strengthening the power of the labour unions via an improvement in union legislation, increasing the coverage of collective bargaining, increasing the social wage via public goods and social security, establishing sufficiently high minimum wages, eliminating the gender wage gap, eliminating discriminatory labour market practices, regulating high/executive pay and levelling the global playing field through international labour standards are the key elements of tipping the balance in favour of an equality-led recovery. It is also important to recognise the vital role of an independent feminist movement in not only influencing government policies towards promoting gender equality, but also in working to transform the labour unions to overcome any gender bias of their own.

However, the magnitude of the effects generated by a wage-led/equality-led recovery on growth and hence employment is likely to be modest, albeit positive. Wage-led growth is not a magic bullet to solve all the ills of our current economy. The neoliberal shift in macroeconomic policy away from a broad focus on full employment to a narrow focus on inflation targeting and tight fiscal and monetary policy in the post-1980s has been detrimental for growth, as well as labour's bargaining power and equality. Reorienting macroeconomic policies towards full employment, increasing the wage share and promoting gender equality is important for rebalancing not just power relations, but also the economy.

For sustainable and egalitarian development, all of the tools of economic policy and public spending need to be mobilised with the aim of achieving full employment, ecological sustainability, and equality between men and women. At this juncture, there is an important alliance between the agendas for green development and gender equality. The reconciliation of full employment and equality with a low-carbon economy requires a commitment to three policies: creating more labour-intensive jobs in social infrastructure; establishing shorter working hours with an emphasis on gender equality in care; and ecological investments. The first two policies are discussed below. These define a key role for the government regarding public spending and working hours' regulations.

First, public investment should fill the gaps in social infrastructure – i.e. in health, education, childcare and elderly care – which cannot be provided adequately by private investment based on profit motive, and is currently provided by unpaid invisible female labour. The need for social infrastructure is not sufficiently met under the present circumstances with inadequately low public spending in this

52 Özlem Onaran

field; private providers fill in the gap by supplying these services either at very low wages (to ensure an adequate profit) or as luxury services for the rich, and a large part is provided via invisible unpaid female labour within the gendered division of labour at home. To avoid this care deficit a rise in spending in social infrastructure by the state or by non-profit/community organisations is required.[10] Greater public provision of social infrastructure would create employment in labour-intensive social services, and be a vehicle for generating full employment with lower rates of growth – a target more consistent with low carbon emissions. This could also hit another target of increasing female labour force participation rates via socialising the invisible and unpaid care work done by women. Ilkkaracan (2013, and Ch.2 in this volume) has called these purple jobs. However, these jobs need to be made attractive to both men and women by improving pay and working conditions in these industries.

A new orientation of policies towards creating high-skilled, decent jobs in the social sector should be promoted instead of the current reliance on low-pay service jobs and weak labour unions. Such policies would put gender equality in pay and employment at the heart of a wage-led development strategy. However, if women are concentrated in the types of paid work where the prospect of higher wages does not exist, these policies may still be insufficient to significantly improve women's incomes. Wage policies should reflect the added value of social infrastructure for society, and should gradually target the problem of occupational segregation. This is a clear break from current policies and the imposing of pay freezes on public sector workers, who are predominantly women.

Secondly, a key policy measure to maintain full employment along with low carbon emissions and a more equal income distribution is a substantial shortening of working time in parallel with the historical growth in productivity. Reduction in weekly working hours should take place without loss of wages, in particular in the case of low and median wage earners, which means an increase in hourly wages as well as in the wage share. Again, this is not unrealistic given historical trends – compared to the 19th century we are all working part-time today. However, the shortening of working hours has slowed since the 1980s in most countries with the notable exception of France. More equal countries, such as Germany or the Netherlands, have shorter working hours (Schor 2010). The shortening of hours over the past decades has also been associated with higher hourly productivity (Bosch and Lehndorff 2001). Shorter working hours increase the job creation potential of a given rate of growth. The UK and the US have much longer hours than Germany and the Netherlands (Schor 2010). This means that an employer in the UK needs more additional demand than a German employer to create an additional full-time job, which is particularly problematic in the post-crisis era of high and persistent unemployment. The implications of shorter working hours for gender equality are twofold. First, shorter hours with wage compensation only for lower wage earners will imply a narrowing of gender wage gaps. Secondly, a proper shortening of the working hours should help address daily care responsibilities and enable a more equal work/life balance based on gender equality in the division

An equality-led sustainable development strategy **53**

of labour in the household, e.g. this requires shorter daily working hours as opposed to more holidays or longer weekends. Overall, shorter working time with wage compensation is likely to lead to a substantial restructuring of the economy.

Finally, for the purpose of ecological sustainability, there is need for a shift in the composition of aggregate demand towards long-term green investments, and this cannot be achieved without new strategic tasks for active public investment. Public investment in ecological maintenance and repair, renewable energy, public transport, insulation of the existing housing stock and the building of zero-energy houses can create jobs as well as a low-carbon economy. Furthermore, a larger proportion of the nation's time spent caring for each other is also a greener alternative, whether that is in paid or unpaid time.

Conclusion

This chapter has introduced the intuition behind a gendered macroeconomic model and outlined the cornerstones of a macroeconomic model to analyse the various channels through which gender equality can influence growth and employment outcomes. Understanding these channels is important in order not only to analyse the impact of austerity on men and women and gender equality, but also to understand the destabilising nature of inequality on the economy and society.

Most importantly, a gendered analysis of austerity is crucial in developing alternatives to it. The alternative presented above of an equality-led growth strategy that flows from a gendered macroeconomic analysis highlights the relevance of, as well as the complementarity between, the green and purple policy agendas to solving the multiple crises of inequality, care and climate change.

Notes

1 The theoretical models have been formally developed by Rowthorn (1981), Dutt (1984), Taylor (1985), Blecker (1989) and Bhaduri and Marglin (1990).
2 The distribution of income between wages and profits, i.e. labour and capital, reflects the "functional distribution of income" between different classes. The emphasis on personal income distribution in the mainstream debates on inequality, e.g. the share of the top 1%, neglects the change in the distribution of income between labour and capital. However, the latter has significant consequences for demand. Needless to say, this does not mean that the rise in top income shares is unimportant, but that the analysis of inequality should also incorporate the inequality between classes.
3 The wage share is by definition 1 – the profit share. The wage share is also the wage per employee divided by labour productivity. Higher productivity for a given wage rate (wage per employee) implies a lower wage share and higher profitability. The wage share is also identical to real unit labour costs, which is in return nominal unit labour costs deflated (divided) by the price index.
4 Braunstein et al. (2011) use the term "caring spirits" analogous to Keynes' animal spirits.
5 In the following we refer to household spending as consumption in line with the standard practice in macro models; but a note is in place here: household spending

54 Özlem Onaran

includes components that are beneficial to productivity, and part of that can be considered as spending in human capacity.

6 For simplicity, it is assumed that profits are not gendered (although there is a behavioural difference in the risk-taking of female versus male entrepreneurs, with implications for investment behaviour; given the low share of female entrepreneurs, this simplification is unlikely to affect outcomes).

7 There may be different mechanisms through which the gender pay gap can fall. E.g. if women's wages are predominantly below the living wage while men's wages are predominantly at least at the level of living wage or above, a rise of the statutory wage to the level of living wage will reduce the gender pay gap, increasing women's average wages while not affecting male wages. A rise in gender equality could also take the form of increases in the wages of both women and men, while at the same time closing the gender pay gap. Depending on the parameters of the economy, these will have different effects on growth and employment.

8 The non-market home economy provides goods and services produced by unpaid labour, predominantly supplied by women. In the rest of this chapter the model will focus on the market economy.

9 It is acknowledged that occupational segregation is an issue that needs to be tackled as well.

10 Governments can provide social infrastructure, e.g. care services, or it can directly or indirectly finance the private sector (for-profit or non-profits) to do so. Both direct provision and financing of these involve public spending and could count as public investment in care, but financing private for-profit provision can have the same problems of low wages and/or poor quality.

References

Akram-Lodhi, A.H. and L.C. Hanmer. 2008. "Ghosts in the Machine: A Post-Keynesian Analysis of Gender Relations, Households and Macroeconomics." In F. Bettio and A. Verashchagina (eds). *Frontiers in the Economics of Gender*. New York: Routledge.

Antonopoulos, R., K. Kim, T. Masterson and A. Zacharias. 2010. "Investing in Care: A Strategy for Effective and Equitable Job Creation." Working Paper No.610. Levy Economics Institute.

Bhaduri, A. and S. Marglin. 1990. "Unemployment and the Real Wage: The Economic Basis for Contesting Political Ideologies." *Cambridge Journal of Economics* 14: 375–93.

Blecker, R. 1989. "International Competition, Income Distribution and Economic Growth." *Cambridge Journal of Economics* 13: 395–412.

Blecker, R. 2002. "Distribution, Demand, and Growth in Neo-Kaleckian Macro Models." In M. Setterfield (ed.). *The Economics of Demand-Led Growth: Challenging the Supply-Side Vision of the Long Run*. Cheltenham (UK) and Northampton (MA, USA): Edward Elgar.

Blecker, R. and S. Seguino. 2002. "Macroeconomic Effects of Reducing Gender Wage Inequality in an Export-Oriented, Semi-industrialized Economy." *Review of Development Economics* 6(1): 103–19.

Bosch, G. and S. Lehndorff. 2001. "Working Time Reduction and Employment: Experiences in Europe and Economic Policy Recommendations." *Cambridge Journal of Economics* 25: 209–43.

Bowles, S. and R. Boyer. 1995. "Wages, Aggregate Demand, and Employment in an Open Economy: An Empirical Investigation" (pp.143–71). In G. Epstein and H. Gintis (eds). *Macroeconomic Policy after the Conservative Era. Studies in Investment, Saving and Finance*. Cambridge: Cambridge University Press.

Braunstein, E. 2000. "Engendering Foreign Direct Investment: Family Structure, Labor Markets and International Capital Mobility." *World Development* 28(7): 1157–72.

Braunstein, E. 2013. *Economic Growth and Social Reproduction: Gender Inequality as Cause and Consequence*. UN Women.

Braunstein, E., I. Stavaren and D. Tavani. 2011. "Embedding Care and Unpaid Work in Macroeconomic Modelling: A Structuralist Approach." *Feminist Economics* 17(4): 5–31.

Dutt, A. 1984. "Stagnation, Income Distribution and Monopoly Power." *Cambridge Journal of Economics* 8: 25–40.

Ertürk, K. and N. Çağatay. 1995. "Macroeconomic Consequences of Cyclical and Secular Changes in Feminization: An Experiment at Gendered Macromodelling." *World Development* 23(11): 1969–77.

Ertürk, K. and W.A. Darity. 2000. "Secular Changes in the Gender Composition of Employment and Growth Dynamics in the North and the South." *World Development* 28(7): 1231–38.

European Commission. 2006. "Time to Move up a Gear: The New Partnership for Jobs and Growth." http://ec.europa.eu/growthandjobs/pdf/illustrated-version_en.pdf (accessed 26 April 2016).

Floro, M.S. and S. Seguino. 2002. "Gender Effects on Aggregate Saving: Policy Research Report on Gender and Development." Working Paper Series. The World Bank.

Folbre, N. and J. Nelson. 2000. "For Love or Money – Or Both?" *Journal of Economic Perspectives* 14(4): 123–40.

Fontana. M. 2014. "Gender In Economy-Wide Modelling." In S. Rai, M. Shirin and G. Waylen (eds). *New Frontiers in Feminist Political Economy*. Oxford: Routledge.

Hein, E. and A. Tarassow. 2010. "Distribution, Aggregate Demand and Productivity Growth – Theory and Empirical Results for Six OECD Countries Based on a Post-Kaleckian Model." *Cambridge Journal of Economics* 34: 727–54.

Hein, E. and L. Vogel. 2008. "Distribution and Growth Reconsidered – Empirical Results for Six OECD Countries." *Cambridge Journal of Economics* 32: 479–511.

Himmelweit, S. 1999. "Emotional Labor in the Service Economy." *The Annals of the American Academy of Political and Social Science* 561: 27–38.

Ilkkaracan, I. 2013. "The Purple Economy: A Call for a New Economic Order beyond the Green." In U. Röhr and C. van Heemstra (eds). *Sustainable Economy and Green Growth: Who Cares?* Berlin: LIFE e.V. and German Federal Ministry for the Environment.

Naastepad, C.W.M. 2006. "Technology, Demand and Distribution: A Cumulative Growth Model with an Application to the Dutch Productivity Growth Slowdown." *Cambridge Journal of Economics* 30: 403–34.

Naastepad, C.W.M., and S. Storm (2007). "OECD demand regimes (1960–2000)." *Journal of Post-Keynesian Economics* 29: 213–48.

Onaran, Ö. and G. Galanis. 2014. "Income Distribution and Aggregate Demand: National and Global Effects." *Environment and Planning A* 46(10): 2489–513.

Onaran, Ö. and T. Obst. 2015. "Wage-led Growth in the EU15 Member States: The Effects of Income Distribution on Growth, Investment, Trade Balance, and Inflation." Greenwich Papers in Political Economy No.GPERC28. University of Greenwich.

Onaran, Ö, E Stockhammer and L. Grafl. 2011. "The Finance-dominated Growth Regime, Distribution, and Aggregate Demand in the US." *Cambridge Journal of Economics* 35(4): 637–61.

Rowthorn, R. 1981. "Demand, Real Wages and Economic Growth." *Thames Papers in Political Economy*, Autumn 1–39, reprinted in *Studi Economici* 1982 18: 3–54.

Schor, J. 2010. *Plenitude: The New Economics of True Wealth*. New York: The Penguin Press.

Seguino, S. 2010. "Gender, Distribution and the Balance of Payments: Constrained Growth in Developing Countries." *Review of Political Economy* 22(3): 373–404.

Seguino, S. 2012a. "From Micro-level Gender Relations to the Macro Economy and Back Again." In D. Figart and T. Warnecke (eds). *Handbook of Research on Gender and Economic Life*. Cheltenham: Edward Elgar.

Seguino, S. 2012b. "Macroeconomics, Human Development, and Distribution." *Journal of Human Development and Capabilities: A Multi-Disciplinary Journal for People-Centered Development* 13(1): 59–81.

Stockhammer, E. and S. Ederer. 2008. "Demand Effects of the Falling Wage Share in Austria." *Empirica* 35(5): 481–502.

Stockhammer, E. and Ö. Onaran. 2004. "Accumulation, Distribution and Employment: A Structural VAR Approach to a Kaleckian Macro Model." *Structural Change and Economic Dynamics* 15: 421–47.

Stockhammer, E., Ö. Onaran and S. Ederer. 2009. "Functional Income Distribution and Aggregate Demand in the Euro Area." *Cambridge Journal of Economics* 33(1): 139–59.

Taylor, L. 1985. "A Stagnationist Model of Economic Growth." *Cambridge Journal of Economics* 9: 383–403.

PART II

Case studies on the impact of austerity policies on women and men

4

CRISIS, POLICY RESPONSES AND GENDER

The Italian experience

Giovanna Vertova

Introduction

The subprime mortgage debacle in the Unites States has become the worse global crisis since the Great Crash. Not surprisingly, great attention has been focused on understanding the causes of the unfolding crisis in order to implement policy measures and recovery plans. However, despite the growing debate about the causes of the crisis, much less attention has been given to gender considerations. Feminist economists have long stated that the capitalist system is not gender neutral (Ferber and Nelson 1993; Picchio 2003); neither are its crises, nor the policy responses that follow. The aim of this chapter is to present a theoretical framework that can help us to understand the crisis, its implications and policy responses from a gender perspective. In order to do this, the gender and class dimensions must be examined simultaneously; to neglect either dimension gives rise to partial and odd explanations.

On the one hand, a "gender-without-class" explanation leads to the awkward idea that this is a "macho" crisis: if Lehman Brothers had been Lehman Sisters, run by women instead of men, the financial crisis might not have happened (or it might have been lighter). In February 2009, the World Economic Forum was animated by the discussion around machismo as a source of the crisis. The debate was immediately taken up by both international media and academic literature (Prügl 2012; Ruggieri 2010). The main argument was that, since the financial and banking sectors are dominated by men, who display more risk-taking behaviour, more women in leading roles might have lessened or even prevented the crisis, due to their more risk-averse conduct. Moreover, men's behaviour and their carelessness are believed to be due to testosterone and the "chromosome Y factor" (Apicella et al. 2008; Sapienza et al. 2009). In contrast, as stated by the gender-diversity management literature, prudent female behaviour is due to women's "natural"

60 Giovanna Vertova

characteristics, is good for business and, consequently, for capitalism (Luckerath-Rovers 2013; McKinsey & Co. 2007).

These types of explanations have some downsides. First, they tend to create and enforce a mythological idea of both sexes: the reckless man and the prudent woman. They ignore the longstanding feminist debate on the difference between "sex" and "gender" (Scott 1986), bringing back the old argument of biological determination, which assumes that differences in men's and women's behaviours are due to "natural" features of each sex, instead of social constructions. Secondly, they explain the crisis based on individual behaviours of a certain social group – male bankers and financial CEOs – thus diverting the attention from the capitalist system as a whole, as if the law of motion of capital depends upon the sex ruling it.

On the other hand, a "class-without-gender" explanation hides the economic and political impacts of the crisis on the social reproduction system, which has been proved to be crucial for capitalist accumulation. Despite different views, the 1970s feminist debate over domestic labour had the merit to draw attention to two important, and today taken-for-granted, insights: (i) capitalist production is not self-sufficient but depends on domestic labour, occurring outside capitalist relations; and (ii) men and women participate to the labour market in different ways due to their unequal domestic responsibilities (Dalla Costa and James 1972; Himmelweit and Mohun 1977; Benería 1979; Molyneux 1979). More recently, a number of feminist economists have extended the classical political macroeconomic approach in order to include the social reproduction system (Picchio 2003). This approach conceives well-being not in terms of individual choices, but as part of a structural framework that includes the material processes of production, distribution and exchange of wealth, as well as the process of social reproduction of the working class. Placing unpaid work within macroeconomic theory makes it possible to address the question of the quality and adequacy of living conditions and well-being of the working class not as a female responsibility but as a central and general problem of the capitalist system, thus redefining the traditional view in which the functioning of the system is reduced to monetary transactions. The point is not to reduce the work of social reproduction to an economic variable, but to find an approach that does not relegate it to the margin of the analysis of the system and its dynamics.

A comprehensive look at the impact and the policy response to the crisis must, therefore, consider the two dimensions of class and gender in tandem. To this end, this chapter proposes a theoretical framework for a class-based gender analysis. First, it presents a brief review of the literature before outlining the theoretical framework. It then presents the empirical investigation, applying the theoretical framework to the Italian case, and finally concludes with some general remarks.

A brief literature review

Early attention to gender considerations was given by some international organisations. The 53rd session of the Commission on the Status of Women of the

United Nations was entirely dedicated to "The Gender Perspective of the Financial Crisis" (Buvinic 2009; Eilor 2009; Fukuda-Parr 2009; Seguino 2009; Sirimanne 2009). The International Labour Organization grew immediately concerned about the impact of the crisis on the labour market (ILO 2009; Otobe 2011). These early concerns were more focused on women's conditions in developing countries, showing that women were more likely to be affected by the crisis in these areas (Antonopoulos 2009; Elson 2010; Espino 2013).

More recently, new studies have emerged. In 2013, *Feminist Economics* published a Special Issue about "Critical and Feminist Perspectives on Financial and Economic Crisis". Furthermore, in 2014, *Revue de l'OFCE* printed a Special Issue on "European Labour Market in Time of Crisis: A Gender Perspective". Some of these works have an empirically narrow approach, by focusing their attention only on the labour market (Eydoux 2014; Périvier 2014; Karamessini and Rubery 2014; Smith and Villa 2014; Weinkopf 2014); these studies are mainly concerned with *employment* and the way to assess whether the crisis hurt men more than women. Some of them briefly consider care work (Karamessini and Rubery 2014), employment policies (Eydoux 2014; Smith and Villa 2014; Weinkopf 2014) or material deprivation (Fodor and Nagy 2014). Overall, they show that in the first phase of the recession (i.e. the fall in GDP), job loss was higher for men than women, because male workers are greatly concentrated in critically sensitive industries, such as manufacturing and construction – occupational segregation therefore worked as a shield mechanism. In the second phase, characterised by a relative recovery (i.e. the rebound of GDP), male employment recovered faster than female employment; this was largely due to the gender blindness of the anti-crisis fiscal packages of national governments. Besides the public money used to bail out banks, policy responses targeted male-dominated sectors because these were hardest hit by the crisis (i.e. in most advanced countries, benefits were given to the automobile and construction industries). Finally, in the third phase of the crisis, the austerity period, when most countries, especially European ones, introduced fiscal consolidation plans, women were more likely to be affected due to their high concentration in public sectors – hence the shielding mechanism stopped working and became a liability. Therefore, a long-term analysis rightly identifies an initial "he-cession" and a following "she-austerity" (Karamessini and Rubery 2014).

These empirical analyses have the great merit to uncover the gender inequalities in labour markets. Yet analysing the impact of the crisis by concentrating mainly on headcount measurements of men's and women's employment neglects the impact on unpaid work in the private, domestic sphere. Moreover, this narrow approach overlooks the links between fiscal policy, unpaid work and female participation in the labour market (links that were brought to attention by the feminist debate of the 1970s, as recalled above).

Some other works have a wider approach, looking at both paid and unpaid work (Bahçe and Memiş 2013; Berik and Kongar 2013; Espino 2013; European Commission 2012; González 2014; McKay et al. 2013). Overall, economic welfare

62 Giovanna Vertova

is best investigated by looking at both types of work, where the links between conditions in the labour market and the burden of unpaid work, resulting also from governments' fiscal policies, and gender impacts of the crisis are explicitly taken into account. Documenting the different effects on men and women of the current recession requires a clear and explicit consideration of the gendered structure in which it takes place. Moreover, it must consider fiscal policy as a tool to enhance or harm the long and winding road towards gender equality.

It is here suggested that the full gender impact of the crisis and subsequent policy responses is only visible with a holistic, comprehensive, broad-based analysis where paid and unpaid work are both taken into consideration simultaneously. Therefore, this chapter belongs to this second group and has a twofold goal: first, it proposes a theoretical framework allowing gender considerations to be taken into account; and secondly, it empirically applies this framework to the Italian case, with the aim of filling the gap of this under-studied case (Tescari and Vaona 2014; Verashchagina and Capparucci 2013; Vertova 2014).

The theoretical framework

In order to have a class-and-gender approach for analysing the impact and responses to the crisis, the extended macroeconomic system must first be examined (Benería 1979; Ferber and Nelson 1993; Picchio 2003). A gender perspective must look at both the productive and the reproductive systems – individual as well as social well-being is given by the sum of these two sub-systems (see Table 4.1).

The *production system* (PS) – i.e. the provision of goods and services (i.e. commodities) through market transactions – is grounded on wage labour commanded by capital and productive value. The focus, here, is on the gender differences in the labour market. Disaggregated data by gender must give the most comprehensive picture possible about the conditions of men and women in the labour market. A gender decomposition of employment, by taking into account sectors, professions, types of contracts, working hours and salaries (where possible), and unemployment must be supplied. Moreover, inactivity must be taken into consideration, because unemployment statistics do not include discouraged workers. When there is increasing difficulty to balance paid and unpaid work, a person tends to pull back from the labour market. In this case, unemployment decreases, because the person is not counted as unemployed anymore but as inactive. This phenomenon tends to be very gendered.

A detailed gender analysis of the labour market could be a useful tool to uncover the prevailing effects: "added worker" versus "discouraged worker"; buffer versus substitute; segmentation versus segregation. The "added worker effect" occurs when a person enters the labour market when the head of the household is fired. In contrast, the "discouraged worker effect" happens when people opt to leave the labour market entirely when unemployment is high, thus resulting in a reduction of the unemployment rate in statistical terms. If the added worker effect prevails, activity increases due to women entering the labour market. Otherwise, inactivity increases.

The Italian experience **63**

TABLE 4.1 The theoretical framework

Dimensions	Characteristics	Variables
The production system (PS)	Goods/services through market transaction	Employment, unemployment, inactivity
	Wage labour productive of value	(Fiscal policy for public jobs)
The public SRS	Public goods/services through non-market activities	Fiscal policy that affects specific public goods/services
The familiar SRS	Unpaid work within the household (contribution of migrant women)	Time Use Survey
Patriarchy	Stereotypes, social and cultural beliefs	(Too many)

Based on the Marxian theory considering women as a labour reserve army, the "buffer effect" occurs when employers use the female labour force as a shock absorber of the change in demand – i.e. women are fired when demand slows down and are (re)hired when demand increases again. The opposite "substitute hypothesis" occurs when employers substitute women for men because, during a recession, pressure to lower labour costs intensifies, and female labour is usually cheaper.

Finally, the "segmentation hypothesis" states that the most important division is between primary and secondary jobs. Women are, generally, part of a secondary job market, together with many members of minorities. Since there is limited mobility between these two segments, the secondary market plays a buffer role in periods of crisis. In contrast, the "segregation hypothesis" affirms that female employment may be protected during a crisis, because women are segregated in jobs that are less affected by economic slowdown.

The *social reproduction system* (SRS) offers goods and services through non-market activities (i.e. public works or unpaid household labour) and, therefore, is not based on product value. The SRS can be split into two parts.

The *public SRS* is based on paid (but non-market) work in public sectors. Needless to say, not all public sectors are related to the SRS (e.g. military expenditure, political costs, etc.); however, some play a crucial role in the SRS (e.g. healthcare, pensions systems, etc.), while others contribute by taking a weight off the burden of family responsibilities (e.g. nursery schools, nursing homes, etc.). The public SRS allows the creation of those social infrastructures that are necessary, yet not sufficient, to balance paid and unpaid work. Moreover, the public SRS is a source of female employment – in general, these sectors are female-dominated. Hence, fiscal policy becomes a crucial element here, and has both direct effects on women's employment (cuts in public expenditures lead to reductions in female-dominated public jobs) and indirect effects (cuts in social public goods/services are likely to lead women to retreat from the labour market due to the increasing difficulties in balancing paid and unpaid work). Therefore, both the level and

64 Giovanna Vertova

composition of public expenditures are important sources of gender equity, and they must be investigated together. Naturally, not all public expenditures are relevant here, but only those relating to some specific public goods/services.

A useful instrument to analyse both the level and composition of public expenditures is the gender budget (Elson 1998; Rubin and Bartle 2005). Gender budgeting is a tool aimed at assessing the gender implications of government policies, thus challenging the assumption that they are gender neutral. It is worth mentioning that the gender budget is not the creation of separate budgets for men and women (as is commonly believed), but rather the breaking down of government budgets in order to see the different effects of public expenditures on men and women. Fiscal policy can have gendered impacts through the supply of public goods and services, public employment opportunities, income transfers and the system of taxation. The gender budget is both a practical feminist tool helping to question the role of the state as supporter of gender equality and a practical tool for government in making its own policies more effective. Within the framework proposed, gender budget analysis should be carried out on the fiscal stimulus packages and the austerity measures, in order to stress their gender effects.

The *familiar SRS* refers to the unpaid work carried out within households by family members. This kind of work includes service activities for today's generation (such as cooking, cleaning. etc.), for tomorrow's one (the care of children) and for the past one (the care of the elderly). It is not the aim of this chapter to review the "domestic labour debate" (Benaría 1979; Himmelweit and Mohun 1977; Molyneux 1979), but to remind readers that unequal domestic responsibilities are the major source of the different conditions under which men and women enter the labour market. A gender analysis of this type of unpaid work must also be carried out alongside that listed above. In this case, the Time Use Survey is a useful tool to reveal how men and women divide their time and how much of this time is dedicated to family responsibilities.

Splitting the SRS into two parts (the public and the familiar) allows us to draw attention to their negative relationship: the burden of unpaid labour increases when the supply of social public goods/services declines, with "familiar" welfare becoming a substitute for the lack of "public" welfare. Yet, while the reduction of social public goods/services is visible, recorded and accountable in a country's public budget, the increase in unpaid work is invisible and is not registered in any national accounts. For example, the reduction of a hospital stay – politically implemented in order to reduce the public expenditure of the National Health Service – immediately results in more work for the person who, within the family, takes care of the sick person. Hence, the "public" and the "familiar" part of the SRS are both affected by the government's fiscal policy, directly the former and indirectly the latter.

Finally, *patriarchal dimensions* must be taken into account. Gender norms can be defined as "social norms that constrain the choices of men and women, and their associated social sanctions, encouraging forms of behaviour that conform to the norms, and discouraging behaviour that does not" (Elson 2010: 203). Gender

The Italian experience **65**

norms are based on gender stereotypes and social and cultural beliefs, and can strongly influence male and female behaviour. These norms can also affect economic outcomes (Badgett and Folbre 1999). Examples of gender norms can be found across several spheres: in the education sphere (e.g. high professional qualification is considered to be important only for men); in the professional sphere (e.g. the workplace is not considered to be the primary area for women, therefore career and professional advancement are deemed unimportant for them); in the domestic sphere (e.g. housekeeping and childcare are considered to be the primary functions of women); and in decision-making processes (e.g. in the case of conflicts men have the last say, such as in the choice of place to live, the choice of school for children, and in household consumption and investment decisions). In a period of crisis, gender norms tend to change, thus increasing or reducing gender equality. For example, when jobs are scarce, it becomes socially and culturally acceptable to fire women first because it is thought that men have a family to support. In this case, gender norms work as a backlash mechanism, bringing back the traditional "male-breadwinner family model". Hence, gender norms must be taken into consideration in order to see whether new norms appear because of the crisis and how they can influence long-term gender equality.

The empirical investigation: the Italian case

This framework is now applied to the Italian case. In order to present the impact of the crisis and of policy responses, the analysis begins with a short introduction to the gender situation prior to the outbreak of the crisis. Following Périvier's approach (2014), three stages of the Italian economy are identified according to the change in the rate of growth of GDP:

- 2009 – the year of the recession phase itself, with a fall in GDP of -5.5%;
- 2010 and 2011 – the years of the relative recovery, when GDP rebounded by 1.7% and 0.6%, respectively; and
- 2012, 2013 and 2014 – the austerity phase, with a fall in GDP by -2.8%, -1.7% and -0.4%, respectively.[1]

Changes in the PS and SRS during these three periods are also examined.

The public SRS

Since fiscal policy can affect both the public SRS as well as the PS, as far as public jobs are concerned, the analysis begins here. Before the outbreak of the crisis, the public SRSs of most advanced countries were not in good shape. By going back to the British "Treasury view" of the 1920s and 1930s, neoliberalism proclaimed that the government needed a balanced budget. This approach entails a reshaping of state intervention in the economy, with the inevitable consequence of cutting social expenditure and turning the welfare state into a workfare (and sometime warfare) state. Privatisation, liberalisation and deregulation were tools to those ends. Moreover, neoliberalism became the inspiration of European integration, the Maastricht Treaty and its parameters. Hence, before entering the euro-zone, those countries with very high public deficits and debt, such as Italy, applied those same tools to meet the Maastricht criteria. Afterwards, they became the usual policy to keep public finance in balance. The Treasury view together with the shrinking of the welfare state led to an increased commodification of social public goods/services, with strong gender impacts. The neoliberal agenda was, therefore, highly gendered (Eisestein 2009). Within this trend, Italy presented some peculiarities. First, even during the Golden Age, the Italian welfare system has never functioned very well (Boeri 2000; Del Boca 2009). There were limited financial resources and Italian social benefits were more in cash than in kind, thus having limited impacts (Matsaganis 2013). Moreover, the Italian welfare system was (and still is) strongly geographically fragmented, due to the decentralisation of power to local and regional authorities that are responsible for providing local public services and goods.

During the recession phase, most advanced countries implemented fiscal boosts as part of their policy response to the crisis. Among OECD countries, stimulus packages were quantitatively very different (OECD 2009); yet, they did share a common feature: the neglect of any kind of gender considerations. "The majority of Member States characterised the interventions to the economic and financial downturn to date as being 'gender neutral', with only a select number of States reporting the carrying out of gender impact assessments when developing new policy" (European Commission 2009: 10). To be fair, what the European Commission called "gender neutrality" must, in fact, be renamed as "gender blindness": the inability to see that, what is supposed to be a neutral fiscal policy is indeed highly gendered. Most of these packages reflected the underlying gender-political conservatism of policy-makers, still clinging to the idea of the male-breadwinner family model. In general, stimulus packages targeted male-dominated sectors (e.g. the automobile industry and its suppliers, the construction and transport industries, etc.), because they were harder hit by the crisis. Contrary to what was done, fiscal stimulus packages should have been designed with the goal to achieve gender equality, as many female economists suggested (Antonopoulos 2009; Hartmann et al. 2010: Ruggieri 2010; Seguino 2009). As also highlighted in Ch.8 by Bargawi and Cozzi, the support to physical infrastructures (generally male-dominated sectors) should have been accompanied by the support to social infrastructures and services (generally female-dominated sectors). Moreover, since the public sector is an important source of female employment, governments should have avoided budget cuts.

The Italian case was rather peculiar among the OECD countries. In 2008 and 2009, under the Berlusconi Cabinet, the first Budgetary Laws dealing with the crisis were passed. Yet, they were not fiscal boosts – since the increase in public expenditure was compensated for by an increase in taxes, the net effect on the fiscal balance was zero (OECD 2009). It could have been possible to audit both the expenditure and the tax revenue; however, gender budgeting is not a common practice in Italy. The few Italian experiences focus on the budgets of local administrations (such as municipalities, provinces or regions), rather than the national one (Genova and Vincenti 2011). Hence, no gender considerations were taken into account.

The austerity period was characterised by the same gender blindness, both at the European and Italian level. This chapter does not discuss whether restrictive fiscal policy would have had expansionary results, but rather to understand its gender implications; however, if we grant for the sake of argument that fiscal austerity would indeed have the desired economic results, it is important to remember that the decision to cut some parts of the public budget and not others is (and perhaps is mostly) a political choice as well as an economic one. Like other advanced countries, Italy cut social expenditures: the national government cut money transfers to regional and local public authorities, which, in turn, cut social services and goods. A consequence of this policy was women's withdrawing from the labour market due to the increasing difficulties in balancing paid work and family responsibilities. This can be seen by measuring changes in inactivity and the number of discouraged workers (see Table 4.4, discussed below). The reduction of Italian women's inactivity (showing women's willingness to enter the labour market) must be linked to the increase of female discouraged workers. At the time of writing, the decrease in inactivity was outdoing the discouraged worker effect; however, the impact of austerity measures is yet to be seen.

The PS

The gender analysis of the Italian PS before the outbreak of the crisis is compared with those of the euro-zone (EA18) and the European Union (EU28) where possible, in order to give an idea of the situation of Italian women over time.

Even before the outbreak of the crisis, the labour markets of all advanced countries were characterised by strong gender inequalities and employment was still male-dominated. Despite the long-term trend of the feminisation of labour markets, Italian employment was still male-dominated, with a feminisation rate lower than those of the EA18 and EU28 (see Table 4.2).

Moreover, men and women were and continue to be employed in very different situations – occupational segregation (both horizontal and vertical), contractual inequalities, a gender pay gap and pension disparities are the most common gender inequalities experienced in Italy. Horizontal occupational segregation can be seen in the fact that female workers are concentrated in services where the feminisation rate is higher, in comparison to agriculture and manufacturing (see Table 4.2). By putting occupations in a hierarchical decreasing order according to the status of the profession (which is generally also linked to low levels of remuneration and bargaining power), it is possible to notice that, by going down the hierarchy, the presence of female workers increases, thus showing the so-called "glass ceiling" effect. Women are concentrated in the less-qualified professions (clerical support

68 Giovanna Vertova

TABLE 4.2 Feminisation rate* of employment, 2008

	Italy	EA18	EU28
Total employment	40.5	44.5	44.9
Employment in agriculture	31.0	32.5	36.5
Employment in manufacturing	28.5	28.3	30.4
Employment in services	48.9	53.4	53.5
Unemployment	51.7	49.5	48.3
Inactivity (15–64 years of age)	65.5	62.8	62.2
Inactivity not seeking**	66.3	65.2	63.5

Sources: Author's elaboration on Eurostat (variables: lfsa_egan, lfsa_egan2, lfsa_ugan, lfsa_igan, lfsa_igaww).

Note: * The feminisation rate measures the female share of the phenomenon under observation [F / (M+F)]. It has the great advantage of making the situation of both sexes visible with just one number. This measure allows us to take into account men and women together, as part of the same statistical population, thus enabling an inter-sex analysis.

** Inactive persons not seeking work can be used as a proxy for the discouraged worker phenomenon.

workers, services and sale workers), where the feminisation rate is higher (respectively 60.5% in the former and 58.0% in the latter in Italy; 67.7% and 68.7% in the EA18; and 69.7% and 68.9% in the EU28).[2] Occupational segregation is a common trend among European countries, yet Italy shows the worst.

Contractual inequality refers to the fact that men and women are employed under different types of contracts. The neoliberal political agenda with its pressure on labour pushed towards more flexibility in the labour market. Since the 1990s, in the European countries there has been a general tendency towards a decline in "secure" jobs, welfare protection and social security, and an increase of temporary positions, characterised by uncertainty, irregularity and interruption. While, on the one hand, temporary contracts are, more or less, equally distributed between men and women (with feminisation rates of roughly 50% for all three geographical areas[3]); on the other hand, part-time positions are very feminised (with a female share above 77% for all three geographical areas[4]). This situation is not surprising. Part-time contracts were implemented with the precise aim of increasing female participation in the labour market and, at the same time, to allow women to balance paid work and family responsibilities. Yet, quite recently, a debate on the shortcomings of part-time jobs, and their potential to increase occupational segregation, has emerged (Lambert et al. 1996; Watts and Rich 1991, 1992; Whittard 2003). The feminisation rate of involuntary part-time work (72.7% in Italy and 73.1% in the EU28 (OECD 2009)) can give an idea of the impact of this type of contract on women.

Since women are prevented from reaching top positions and are stuck in "typical" female jobs, which are generally low paid and have more part-time contracts, the gender pay gap is an obvious result. The lower Italian gender pay gap (4.9%) compared to the EU28 (17.4%)[5] is largely due to the levelling down of the whole salary scale. However, at the end of their working lives, women will have lower pensions due to their lower income and their more irregular presence in the labour market (resulting from maternity leave and care work, for example). In 2009, Italian men on average received higher pensions than women by 31%, lower than the gender gap in pensions at the EU28 level (39%) (European Commission 2012).

To give an overall picture of the Italian PS, unemployment and inactivity must also be taken into consideration. In 2008, before the outbreak of the crisis, unemployment was fairly equally distributed between the sexes; by contrast, inactivity is highly feminised, as well as the discouraged worker phenomenon (see Table 4.2).

The impact of these three stages on the PS depends on the gender composition of employment (see Table 4.3). During the recession stage, what happened in Italy is consistent with what happened at the European level and in other advanced countries (European Commission 2012; Hartmann et al. 2010). Men were hit harder by the crisis because they are more concentrated in pro-cyclical industries where employment can easily be adjusted to the volatile changes in demand occurring with economic expansion or contraction. In contrast, women are more concentrated in counter-cyclical industries, such as services and public jobs. Hence, occupational and sectoral segregation worked as a shielding mechanism. The relative recovery phase witnessed an increase of female employment, thus suggesting a substitution effect. What distanced Italy from the common trend of other advanced countries was that the increase of female employment continued also in

TABLE 4.3 The three stages of the Italian PS (absolute change, thousands)

	2009	2010–11	2012–14
Total employment (15–64 years of age)[a]	–375	–110	–406
M	–261	–203	–460
F	–114	93	54
Temporary employment[b]	–165	130	30
M	–88	111	60
F	–77	19	–30
Part-time employment[c]	–70	180	147
M	–37	70	242
F	–33	110	175
Involuntary part-time employment[c]	138	378	759
M	20	114	310
F	118	264	449

Sources: [a] Eurostat (variable: lfsa_egan); [b] Eurostat (variable: lfsa_etgaed); [c] OECD.

70 Giovanna Vertova

the austerity phase (at least at the time of writing and as shown in the 2014 data). For the Italian case, it is not possible to speak about a "he-cession" and a "sh(e)-austerity" (Karamessini and Rubery 2014). Yet, the impact of the austerity measures might have a time lag, and, therefore, it may not show up in the 2014 data – an examination of future data is necessary to follow potential gender differences during the austerity period, which is far from over.

After a first assessment of the trend in total employment, it is also important to understand the quality of employment created (or destroyed) during the three stages. Particular attention is, therefore, given to the so-called atypical jobs/contracts (i.e. temporary, part-time and involuntary part-time) (see Table 4.3).

During the recession stage, only involuntary part-time contracts witnessed a rise, with a strong gender difference – more women were obliged to accept part-time contracts. During both the relative recovery phase and the austerity phase only atypical employment increased, and, again, with strong gender differences. In both phases, male temporary employment increased more than the female level. By contrast, female employment grew thanks to part-time contracts, mostly involuntary.

The analysis of the PS concludes with a look at unemployment and inactivity (see Table 4.4). Common trends can be found during the crisis and the relative recovery: male unemployment and inactivity grew more than female; and female discouraged workers decreased more than male. These results confirm the "he-cession" hypothesis, with Italian men hit hardest. Moreover, the reduction of female discouraged workers shows a tendency for Italian women to start looking for jobs, thus corroborating a potential added worker effect. Italian women were willing to enter the labour market when their male partners were fired. During the austerity phase the situation changed as far as inactivity and discouraged workers were concerned. Female inactivity decreased more than the male level, thus

TABLE 4.4 The three stages of unemployment and inactivity (absolute change, thousands)

	2009	*2010–11*	*2012–14*
Unemployment[a]	243	155	1.175
M	173	108	658
F	70	47	517
Inactivity (15–64 years of age)[b]	328	158	-720
M	167	154	-130
F	161	4	-590
Discouraged workers[c]	-278	117	513
M	-16	133	220
F	-262	-16	293

Sources: [a] Eurostat (variable: lfsa_ugan); [b] Eurostat (variable: lfsa_igan); [c] Eurostat (variable: lfsa_igaww).

suggesting, again, Italian women's willingness to start looking for jobs. Nevertheless, female discouragement increased more than male. By looking only at women's situation, the decrease in inactivity is much higher (-590) than the increase in discouragement (+293), thus indicating that women are more willing than before to enter the labour market and, therefore, suggesting a potential added worker effect. If these results are combined with the employment results, it is not possible to speak about an Italian "sh(e)-cession".

The familiar SRS and gender norms

The Time Use Survey (TUS) is nowadays the most common tool used to identify the division of time by men and women, as well as to measure the time spent in unpaid work (although the TUS must be handled with caution) (Fleming and Spellerberg 1999; Budlender 2007). The TUS is helpful in making the unpaid work carried out within families visible. Before the crisis, the familiar SRS was as much gendered as the PS, despite significant national disparities. In Italy, those differences were quite strong, due also to persistent gender stereotypes assuming and accepting that women have a "natural" feel for domestic and care work. The latest available TUS, carried out in 2002–2003, showed that, on an average day, Italian women spent five hours and 20 minutes on unpaid work versus one hour and 35 minutes by Italian men (Istat 2008).

It is not yet possible to assess the impact of the fiscal stimulus packages and of austerity policies on the familiar SRS, as those effects will take time to be fully realised. Nevertheless, it is possible to make plausible assumptions. As mentioned above, in Italy as in other advanced countries, the fiscal boost did not include any kind of gender consideration. It is, therefore, reasonable to assume that, during the recovery stage, the Italian gender division of unpaid labour remained the same as before. In contrast, during the austerity phase, it is reasonable to assume that cuts in public social goods/services will increase the burden of unpaid work. Since in Italy most of this work is still carried out by women, austerity measures are very likely to have strong gender differences. Hence, today's situation confirms the existence of the paradox pointed out by Antonopoulos (2009): too little paid work for everybody and too much unpaid work for women. Austerity measures always have two kinds of costs: the visible economic ones (i.e. the reduction of public jobs or of public social goods/services); and the invisible ones (the increased time spent on unpaid work in order to compensate for the lack of public social goods/services). While this is a common trend within advanced countries, the Italian situation is generally worse. The gender blindness of Italian society is shown in the Italian public discourse and media: all agree that cuts in the welfare system are compensated for by the family system, but they neglect to mention that the latter is sustained mostly by women's unpaid work. Italian women are, thus, becoming the shock absorber for the crisis and austerity measures. Moreover, the socially acceptable idea of women functioning as shock absorber has the great risk of bringing back the male-breadwinner family model, thus endangering the path towards gender equality.

72 Giovanna Vertova

Conclusions

The theoretical framework proposed in this chapter is an attempt to offer a tool for a gender perspective on the impact of the crisis and policy responses. Only by examining both the productive and the reproductive systems is it possible to have an overall view of the gender implications of the crisis and its aftermath. The analysis must be carried out at the macroeconomic level, by looking at the "enlarged" capitalist system, where unpaid work is also taken into consideration. Also fiscal policy – the former anti-crisis packages and the latter austerity measures of some European countries – is revealed to be highly gendered variable. Expansionary fiscal policy must be assessed as to whether it is designed to protect women as well as men, while also examining the gender situation in public jobs. Austerity measurements must be assessed to see if their costs, in terms of cuts in public expenditures, will reduce (or increase) existing gender inequalities.

The feminist debate on productive and reproductive work has returned in this time of crisis, emphasising the gender-segregated labour market, the gender pay gap, and the unsolved issue of domestic unpaid work and of immigrant domestic labour. Despite years of feminist theory on women's invisible reproductive labour, the dominant economic and political thinking still does not afford it proper value. Most gender analysis proposes a reform of the financial architecture with more democratic control (Antonopoulos 2009; Elson 2002), and the need for a gendered economic view, which includes social reproduction as a basis for anti-crisis policies (i.e. sustainable livelihoods, decent work, gender equality and women's rights). Moreover, specific recommendations for fiscal policy usually include the gender budgeting of the fiscal stimulus packages and of the austerity measurements, where policy-makers recognise that the economic system includes paid as well as unpaid work.

Unfortunately, though the crisis has shaken the belief in the free market, it has not altered the theoretical, political and ideological foundations of the neoliberal agenda. So far, the only change is that nation states have temporarily reappeared as the vehicle to allocate national tax money to bankrupt firms and banks. Yet, burdening national budgets with these enormous debts will lead to further privatisation, and the additional rollback of welfare regimes will result in a worsening of women's standard of living. The only hope left is that the crisis will be an opportunity for putting the unsolved question of the social reproduction problem at the core of economic analysis (at the same level as the production system).

Notes

1 Source: Eurostat (variable: nama_10_gdp).
2 Author's elaborations on Eurostat (variable: lfsa_egan2).
3 Author's elaborations on Eurostat (variable: lfsa_etgead).
4 Author's elaborations on Eurostat (variable: lfsa_epgaed).
5 Eurostat.

References

Antonopoulos, R. 2009. "The Current Economic and Financial Crisis: A Gender Perspective." Working Paper No.562. The Levy Institute.

Apicella C.L., A. Dreber, B. Campbell, P.B. Gray, M. Hoffman and A.C. Little. 2008. "Testosterone and Financial Risk Preferences." *Evolution and Human Behavior* 29(6): 384–90.

Badgett, M.V.L. and N. Folbre. 1999. "Assigning Care: Gender Norms and Economic Outcomes." *International Labour Review* 138(3): 311–26.

Bahçe, S.A.K. and E. Memiş. 2013. "Estimating the Impact of 2008–09 Economic Crisis on Work Time in Turkey." *Feminist Economics* 19(3): 181–207.

Benaría, L. 1979. "Reproduction, Production and the Sexual Division of Labour." *Cambridge Journal of Economics* 3(3): 203–25.

Berik, G. and E. Kongar. 2013. "Time Allocation of Married Mothers and Fathers in Hard Times: The 2008–09 US Recession." *Feminist Economics* 19(3): 208–37.

Boeri, T. 2000. *Uno Stato Asociale: Perché è Fallito il Welfare in Italia*. Roma e Bari: Laterza.

Budlender, D. 2007. "A Critical Review of Selected Time Use Surveys." Gender and Development Programme Paper No. 2. United Nations Research Institute for Social Development.

Buvinic, M. 2009. "The Global Financial Crisis: Assessing the Vulnerability for Women and Children, Identifying Policy Responses." Written Statement (March). Division for the Advancement of Women Interactive Expert Panel on Gender Perspective of the Financial Crisis, 53rd Session of the Commission on the Status of Women, United Nations.

Dalla Costa, M. and S. James. 1972. *The Power of Women and the Subversion of the Community*. Bristol: Falling Wall Press.

Del Boca, D. 2009. *Famiglie Sole: Sopravvivere con un Welfare Inefficiente*. Bologna: Il Mulino.

Eilor, E. 2009. "Written Statement." (March.) Division for the Advancement of Women Interactive Expert Panel on Gender Perspective of the Financial Crisis, 53rd Session of the Commission on the Status of Women, United Nations.

Eisenstein, H. 2009. *Feminism Seduced. How Global Elites Used Women's Labor and Ideas to Exploit the World*. Boulder (CO): Paradigm.

Elson D. 1998. "Integrating Gender Issues into National Budgetary Policies and Procedures: Some Policy Options" *Journal of International Development* 10(7): 929–41.

Elson, D. 2002. "International Financial Architecture: A View from the Kitchen." *Femina Politica* 11(1): 26–37.

Elson, D. 2010. "Gender and the Global Economic Crisis in Developing Countries: A Framework for Analysis." *Gender & Development* 18(2): 201–12.

Espino, A. 2013. "Gender Dimensions of the Global Economic and Financial Crisis in Central America and the Dominican Republic." *Feminist Economics* 19(3): 267–88.

European Commission. 2009. "Opinion on the Gender Perspective on the Response to the Economic and Financial Crisis." Report of the European Commission.

European Commission. 2012. "The Impact of the Economic Crisis on the Situation of Women and Men and on Gender Equality Policies." Report of the European Commission.

Eydoux, A. 2014. "Women during Recession in France and Germany. The Gender Biases of Public Policies." *Revue de l'OFCE* 2(133): 153–88.

Ferber, M.A. and J.A. Nelson. 1993. *Beyond Economic Man: Feminist Theory and Economics*. Chicago: University of Chicago Press.

Fleming, R. and A. Spellerberg. 1999. "Using Time Use Data. A History of Time Use Surveys and Uses of Time Use Data." Report of Statistics New Zealand.

Fodor, E. and B. Nagy. 2014. "An Ebbing Tide Lowers All Boats: How the Great Recession of 2008 has Affected Men and Women in Central and Eastern Europe." *Revue de l'OFCE* 2(133): 121–51.

Fujuda-Parr, S. 2009. "Human Impact of the Global Economic Crisis: Gender and Human Right Perspectives." Written Statement (March). Division for the Advancement of Women Interactive Expert Panel on Gender Perspective of the Financial Crisis, 53rd Session of the Commission on the Status of Women, United Nations.

Genova, A. and A. Vincenti. 2011. *Bilancio sociale e bilancio di genere*. Roma: Carocci.

González, P. 2014. "Gender Issues of the Recent Crisis in Portugal." *Revue de l'OFCE* 2(133): 241–75.

Hartmann, H., A. English and J. Hayes. 2010. "Women and Men's Employment and Unemployment in the Great Recession." Briefing Paper C373. Institute for Women's Policy Research.

Himmelweit, S. and S. Mohun. 1977. "Domestic Labour and Capital." *Cambridge Journal of Economics* 1(1): 15–31.

ILO. 2009. *Maintaining Gains for Women in Job Crisis*. Geneva: ILO.

Istat. 2008. *Time Use in Daily Life*. Rome: Istat.

Karamessini, M. and J. Rubery. 2014. "The Challenge of Austerity for Equality. A Consideration of Eight European Countries in the Crisis." *Revue de l'OFCE* 2(133): 15–39.

Lambert, S., R. Petridis and J. Galea. 1996. "Occupational Segregation in Full-time and Part-time Employment." *Australian Bulletin of Labour* 22(3): 212–31.

Luckerath-Rovers, M. 2013. "Women on Board and Firm Performance." *Journal of Management and Governance* 17(2): 491–509.

Matsaganis, M. 2013. "Benefits in Kind and in Cash." In B. Greve (ed.). *The Routledge Handbook of the Welfare State*. London and New York: Routledge.

McKay A., J. Campbell, E. Thomson and S. Ross. 2013. "Economic Recession and Recovery in the UK: What's Gender Got to do With It?" *Feminist Economics* 19(3): 108–23.

McKinsey & Co. 2007. "Women Matter: Gender Diversity, a Corporate Performance Driver." Report of McKinsey & Co.

Molyneux, M. 1979. "Beyond the Domestic Labour Debate." *New Left Review* 116: 3–27.

OECD. 2009. *Fiscal Packages across OECD Countries: Overview and Details*. Paris: OECD.

Otobe, N. 2011. "Global Economic Crisis, Gender and Employment: The Impact of Policy Response." Employment Working Paper No.74. ILO.

Périvier, H. 2014. "Men and Women during the Economic Crisis." *Revue de l'OFCE* 2(133): 41–84.

Picchio, A. (ed.). 2003. *Unpaid Work and the Economy: A Gender Analysis of the Standards of Living*. London and New York: Routledge.

Prügl, E. 2012. "'If Lehman Brothers had been Lehman Sisters…': Gender and Myth in the Aftermath of the Crisis." *International Political Sociology* 6(1): 21–35.

Rubin, M.M. and J.R. Bartle. 2005. "Integrating Gender into Government Budget: A New Perspective." *Public Administration Review* 65(3): 259–72.

Ruggieri, D. 2010. "Gender Perspectives on the Financial and Economic Crisis." *International Journal of Green Economics* 4(3): 217–30.

Sapienza, P., L. Zingales and D. Maestripieri. 2009. "Gender Differences in Financial Risk Aversion and Career Choices are Affected by Testosterone." *Proceedings of the National Academy of Science of the United States of America* 106(36): 15268–73.

Scott, J. 1986. "Gender: A Useful Category of Historical Analysis." *The American Historical Review* 91(5): 1053–75.

Seguino, S. 2009. "The Global Economic Crisis, its Gender Implications, and Policy Responses." Written Statement (March). Division for the Advancement of Women Interactive Expert Panel on Gender Perspective of the Financial Crisis, 53rd Session of the Commission on the Status of Women, United Nations.

Sirimanne, S. 2009. "Written Statement." (March.) Division for the Advancement of Women Interactive Expert Panel on Gender Perspective of the Financial Crisis, 53rd Session of the Commission on the Status of Women, United Nations.

Smith, M. and P. Villa. 2014. "The Long Tail of the Great Recession." *Revue de l'OFCE* 2(133): 85–119.

Tescari, A. and A. Vaona. 2014. "Gender Employment Disparities, Financialization, and Profitability Dynamics on the Eve of Italy's Post-2008 Crisis." *Feminist Economics* 20(3): 191–209.

Verashchagina, A. and M. Capparucci. 2013. "Living through the Crisis in Italy: The Labour Market Experience of Men and Women." In M. Karamessini and J. Rubery (eds). *Women and Austerity. The Economic Crisis and the Future of Gender Equality*. London and New York: Routledge.

Vertova, G. 2014. "What's Gender got to do with the Great Recession: The Italian Case." In R. Bellofiore and G. Vertova (eds). *The Great Recession and the Contradictions of Contemporary Capitalism*. Cheltenham (UK) and Northampton (MA, USA): Elgar.

Watts, M. and J. Rich. 1991. "Equal Employment Opportunity in Australia? The Role of Part-time Employment in Occupational Sex Segregation." *Australian Bulletin of Labour* 17(2): 160–79.

Watts, M. and J. Rich. 1992. "Occupational Sex Segregation in the UK 1979–1989: The Role of Part-time Employment." *International Review of Applied Economics* 6(3): 286–308.

Weinkopf, C. 2014. "Women's Employment in Germany." *Revue de l'OFCE* 2(133): 189–214.

Whittard, J. 2003. "Training and Career Experiences of Women Part-time Workers in a Finance Sector Organisation: Persistent Remnant of the 'Reserve Army'?" *Australian Journal of Labour Economics* 6(4): 537–57.

5

GENDER EQUALITY AND ECONOMIC CRISIS

Ireland and the EU

Ursula Barry

Introduction

This chapter explores the common gender dimensions to the austerity policies that have been pursued across the EU as a response to the 2008 economic crisis, looking specifically at the Irish experience (Barry and Conroy 2013). While emphasis is placed on the Irish case, it also presents a comparative study, drawing on analyses of core policies at the EU level in order to explore the gender patterns evident in the way in which economic and social policies have been developed and implemented, and their resulting consequences, from a gender equality perspective (Rubery and Karamessini 2013; ENEGE 2013; Oxfam 2013; UNAIDS 2012).

Changing EU policies towards gender equality

There was clear evidence at the EU level of an increased emphasis on gender equality in the decade prior to 2007, particularly in employment policy through the development of a European Employment Strategy (EES). Villa and Smith (2013) identify four phases in the implementation of the EES. Phase 1 (1998–2002) saw gender equality designated as a core EU priority and it was defined as one of the four pillars that made up the framework for employment policy (a policy based on 22 guidelines, five of which came under the gender equality pillar). During this period a new concept of "gender mainstreaming" was introduced with the stated aim of establishing gender equality as a "horizontal principle" across all policy areas, not just in employment policy. Further, the EU Council of Ministers in 2000 set down a target for the female employment rate of 60% and for an overall employment rate of 70%, to be reached by 2010. Throughout this period, the clear focus was on increasing employment rates, and women were seen as central to achieving that objective.

New changes were introduced in Phase 2 (2003–05), which coincided with the enlargement of the EU from 15 to 25 Member States, resulting in a redefinition of the EES to incorporate three overarching objectives and ten guidelines – only one of which was a gender equality guideline; however, the EES continued to include the stated objective of mainstreaming gender equality across all policy areas. Within another few years, further changes to the EES took place and two new Member States were incorporated into the EU. Phase 3 (2005–09) was characterised by the introduction of the Broad Economic Policy Guidelines and the setting down of a framework made up of 24 integrated policy guidelines, eight of which were related to employment. This time there was no gender equality guideline, just a statement in the preamble on the importance of gender equality, combating discrimination and gender mainstreaming. Phase 4 (2010–20) was developed in the aftermath of the crisis and saw a continuation of this process with ten integrated policy guidelines, four employment-specific guidelines and three EU objectives. Yet again, there was no gender equality guideline, only a simple statement in the preamble to the EES that "visible gender equality is important in all relevant policy areas". Villa and Smith (2013: 278) argued:

> The fourth phase was marked by the end of the Lisbon process in 2010 and the beginning of the formulation of a new strategy to take the EU to 2020. The new Europe 2020 strategy further marginalises gender equality with none of the ten integrated guidelines related specifically to equal opportunities and only four related to employment. Moreover, gender mainstreaming is not mentioned. Furthermore this reformulation occurred in the middle of the crisis, when policy makers' attention was focused on its immediate impact on male employment, a context in which the gains made in raising female employment during the Lisbon process were quickly overlooked.

As can be seen in Table 5.1, employment rates changed dramatically during the crisis years, effectively reversing over a very short period of time the gains made in reaching the Lisbon targets. And while the gender gap in employment rates between women and men appears to have narrowed, this does not reflect a positive change towards greater gender equality but rather the deteriorating employment situation of men across the EU, particularly during the first stage of the crisis.

The negative impact of these changes in employment at the EU level resulted in a significant policy shift – policy moved from supporting targeted gender equality initiatives, to an initial process of mainstreaming gender equality across the policy-making process, to a crisis period that lacked any definite support for gender equality. As Pfister (2008: 523) states: "The loss of a specific guideline on gender equality, combined with the greater emphasis on creating more jobs, was a significant blow to the status of gender equality."

A recent report on the economic crisis – the 2013 ENEGE Report (carried out by the EU Network of Experts on Gender Equality) – argued that there are specific austerity measures that have been widely applied in different countries, and are

78 Ursula Barry

TABLE 5.1 EU falling employment rates

| Stage | Change in employment rates (15–64 years) | | Gender gap |
	Women	Men	
2008–10	60% to 56%	76% to 64%	15 to 8 points
2010–14	56% to 55%	64% to 62%	8 to 7 points

Source: Bettio et al. (2012).

Note: Employment rates are calculated from the percentage of those between the ages of 15 and 64 years in paid employment across EU-27 countries.

having a particularly negative impact on gender equality. These include cutbacks in public sector employment levels and conditions of employment – the public sector is hugely important to women's employment as it has traditionally offered more flexible and more secure employment with better career development opportunities. Increased charges for public services, reduction in care and other supports to low-income households have also had disproportionately negative impacts on women, who make up the majority of carers and also those on low incomes. The box below lists more of the policy changes that have negatively impacted women, as well as how many EU countries have adopted these policies.

POLICY CHANGES WITH NEGATIVE IMPACTS ON GENDER EQUALITY

- Public sector cuts, including wage freezes or wage cuts (applied in ten EU countries).
- Ban on public sector recruitment (applied in ten EU countries).
- Pension cuts and changes in eligibility requirements (applied in ten EU countries).
- Staffing freezes or personnel cuts in the public sector (applied in nine EU countries).
- Pension reforms – postponing retirement (applied in eight EU countries).
- Reductions and restrictions in care supports and family-related benefits (applied in eight EU countries).
- Reduction of housing benefits or family benefits (applied in six EU countries).
- Restrictions on eligibility criteria for unemployment payments (applied in five EU countries).
- Increased charges for publicly subsidised services (applied in eight EU countries).

(Bettio et al. 2012)

Changes to employment

There are interesting employment patterns evident in the midst of the crisis across the EU, including in Ireland. One of the arguments, for which there is strong supporting evidence, is that the labour market behaviour of women during this particular crisis has taken on a different character to that of previous crises. Women who have lost paid jobs have maintained a strong attachment to the labour force, holding on to a self-definition as "unemployed" and thereby refusing to retreat into the self-definition of "engaged on home duties" (traditionally used in EU labour force surveys). The traditional view that women act as a reserve labour force – i.e. women are brought into paid employment at significant levels only when demand increases, and subsequently dumped back into unpaid work when demand levels contract (Gune 1980) – is not supported by the evidence documenting the experience of this crisis. The composition of the reserve labour force has changed and is made up of both women and men who are on the margins of the formal labour market. As the 2013 ENEGE Report on this recent crisis highlighted, the contemporary reserve labour force – those most vulnerable due to a lack of employment protection – are most likely to be young men and women on temporary, short-term employment contracts and migrant workers. This report also highlighted new evidence of a change in women's economic role across the EU. For example, where double-income/dual-earner couples have been displaced from the workforce, this has been almost exclusively due to female breadwinner couples, which have increased their share of the paid workforce by almost 10% (ENEGE Report 2013: 64).

Another gendered trend across the EU that can be seen throughout the crisis years and the following period of austerity is the rise in cases of discrimination against pregnant women in paid employment. The rights of pregnant women to maternity leave and benefits (such as provision for time off for attendance at antenatal classes and for breastfeeding on returning to work) have been curtailed, and increased levels of discrimination against pregnant women have been documented in case law in many countries (including Ireland). A recent report published by the Crisis Pregnancy Agency in Ireland revealed that "one-third of mothers who work during pregnancy said they had experienced 'unfair treatment'... five per cent of the women surveyed said they were dismissed, made redundant or treated so badly they had to leave their job" (Russell et al. 2011: 23).

A similar report concerning the UK revealed that discrimination cases involving pregnancy and maternity leave have increased dramatically over this period:

> In 2005, three years before the global financial crisis of late 2008 and subsequent economic recession, a landmark study by the Equal Opportunities Commission (since merged with other bodies to become the Equalities and Human Rights Commission) found that half of all pregnant women suffered a related disadvantage at work, and that each

year 30,000 were forced out of their job. Eight years on, the available evidence suggests that figure has ballooned to some 60,000. Since 2008, as many as 250,000 women have been forced out of their job simply for being pregnant or taking maternity leave.

(Maternity Action 2014: 3)

Another conclusion from the ENEGE Report that relates to the gender impact of the crisis was that "household expenditure went down in most European countries for the consumption of items for which women's unpaid work is acting as a substitute" (2013: 108) What is evident from this research is that cuts in services, particularly around care, are being replaced at the household and community level by unpaid labour, most likely carried out by women. The European Women's Lobby (EWL 2012) highlighted the gendered implications of cut-backs in public sector employment in a context in which women constitute 69% of public sector workers across the EU. This report analysed how during the early years of the crisis it was a "private sector crisis" that impacted more on the male-dominated sectors of the economy; in the latter years of austerity, however, it became a "public sector crisis" in which the negative consequences were felt more by women. The EWL Report showed how cuts have hit the female-dominated sectors of health and education hardest, giving an example from Latvia where a teacher's minimum salary was cut by 30% to €6,000 per year and the gender pay gap increased from 13.4% to 17.6%. Significant lay-offs among public sector workers are also detailed: 25% of public sector workers were laid-off in Greece; 20% in the UK; 10% in Romania; and 10% in Latvia. As the crisis intensified, wage cuts or freezes were recorded in at least 13 countries and increases in poverty rates (between 2009 and 2012) were recorded at especially high rates in Iceland, Latvia, Lithuania, Malta, Spain and Ireland for both men and women. A Eurobarometer survey conducted in December 2011 revealed that 58% of citizens in all countries felt threatened by, and vulnerable to, poverty (Eurobarometer 2012).

A 2013 European Parliament (EP) report on the austerity response to the crisis highlighted the gender equality measures that were cancelled or delayed, and stated that potential future cuts in public budgets would have a negative effect on female employment and on the promotion of equality. The report argued that the economic downturn should not have been used as an excuse to slow progress on work/life policies and to cut budgets allocated to care services for dependents and leave arrangements, affecting in particular women's access to the labour market. It argued that cuts in education, childcare and care services have pushed women to work shorter hours or part-time, thereby reducing not only their income but their pensions as well. In a further crisis impact analysis, the report stated that as well as the effect on women of employment changes and reduction in care services, studies have also shown that violence against women intensifies when men experience displacement and dispossession as a result of economic crisis (European Parliament 2013).

A global perspective

Lethbridge's 2012 report, *Global Context: Specific Impacts of Austerity on Women*, published by the Public Services International Research Unit (PSIRU), explored the global context of the crisis, including the impact on poorer countries, and came to a number of key conclusions that confirm EU-based research. Women workers and their children, in both the public and private sectors, have borne the brunt of cuts in vital public services. As women globally make up the majority of public sector workers, they have lost more jobs, while wage freezes and cuts have reduced the incomes and mobility of women who were already among the lowest paid. Lethbridge argued that more and more women are working in insecure jobs with long hours, low pay and poor working conditions to support their families and the gender pay gap has widened at a global level. She also argued that reductions in public services, including the closure of shelters for victims of domestic violence, and reduced levels of women's income will have long-term effects on the health, well-being and future opportunities of their children. In Lethbridge's view, the long struggle for equality has been set back by closure or cuts in funding for public institutions and services that promote equality for women at work and in society.

Lethbridge's work argued that those who are most vulnerable are being hurt the most and the report put forward the example in poorer countries of girls dropping out of school to care for other family members while their mothers seek work. Lethbridge also highlighted that often households have had to sell assets – a contributing factor to chronic poverty – and concluded that the economic crisis has reduced demand for exports from developing countries in sectors where most workers are female. At the same time, austerity responses by governments have brought about reduced access to health and education for women and girls – policy decisions that Lethbridge argued would have long-term effects on their position in gendered societies. The effects of an economic crisis will be felt for many years and will likely slow improvements in gender equality in the long run. Changes in the position of women in the labour market show different trends because of the crisis, the report argued, which has pushed more women into a deteriorating labour market to make up household income because of the rising rates of male unemployment. Lethbridge also concluded that women are having to work harder and often have to take on degrading activities (Lethbridge 2012).

The case of Ireland

Ireland was the first EU country to declare itself officially "in recession" in August 2008. It was also the second Eurozone country to have a structural adjustment programme imposed on it by the International Monetary Fund (IMF)/the European Central Bank (ECB)/EU (known as "the troika") and the first of the "bail-out" countries to exit the programme. The turnaround of the Irish economy in just a few short years was dramatic – from one with the highest levels of GDP and employment growth in the decade to 2007, to among those with the highest

82 Ursula Barry

unemployment, emigration and debt levels across the EU during the crisis. Ireland's economic policy throughout the "boom decade" from 1998–2007 was based on a neoliberal low-tax strategy and the consequences of this shaped the particular way in which the recession unfolded and its enormous negative impact on Irish public finances. Key characteristics of the Irish economic crisis included: first, the overreliance on declining taxation income from an overblown property and construction sector; and secondly, the high level of public subsidy that was made available to a crisis-ridden Irish banking sector.

A wide range of policy measures were implemented in Ireland over Stage 1 (2008–10) and Stage 2 (2011–14) of the crisis with the stated aim of reducing the gap between government revenue and expenditure. The collapse in taxation revenue from the property sector, high levels of unemployment, a drop in domestic demand and the drain on public funds caused by the decision to rescue the private banking sector, together generated a significant deficit in public finances. Stage 1 focused on reducing the public sector bill primarily through reducing public sector pay and pensions and freezing recruitment, as well as through significant cut-backs in social protection expenditure. Stage 2 continued these policies but with a focus on austerity measures, including increased taxation, significantly reducing the incomes of middle and lower income groups, and a further reduction of welfare payments (particularly those to lone parents). In addition, because of its unplanned nature and uneven take-up, the implementation of an early retirement scheme in the public sector led to gaps in critical areas, e.g. specialised nursing care. From a gender equality perspective, many of these measures have had an unacknowledged yet significant negative impact.

Recession and new austerity measures

Irish employment policy mirrored the changes happening at the EU level. Ireland had in fact reached the Lisbon employment targets by 2007 as women's employment rates had increased dramatically during the decade prior to the deep recession that engulfed the country. The Irish Development Plan 2000–06 had adopted gender mainstreaming as a horizontal principle and almost all measures funded under that plan had to be assessed from a gender equality perspective, reflecting EU policy at that time. While the gender impact assessment was limited in practice, it did reflect a greater recognition of gender equality in the policy-making process (McGauran 2009; Barry 2013). However, once the crisis hit, employment policy priorities shifted. Gender equality was no longer specified as a core aspect of Irish employment policy and the crisis and austerity years saw a move away from the objective of increasing the supply of labour through gender equality policies that promote women's access to the paid labour market. As male unemployment levels surged, policies aimed at reducing male unemployment and increasing demand took priority. Gender equality was marginalised and treated as a luxury that, due to the crisis, was rendered unattainable.

During the early years of the crisis in Ireland, the collapse of the construction industry – which was based on a hugely over-inflated property market – drove male unemployment to an extremely high level. Young men who had been lured onto the labour market during the so-called "Celtic Tiger" years found themselves moving into situations of long-term unemployment – many without the second-level educational or training qualifications that would have made emigration an option; for those that had those qualifications, emigration became the *only* option. During this first stage, Ireland experienced a dismantling of key elements of the equality infrastructure that had been hard won over the preceding two decades, the absence of which meant that resources to investigate and interrogate policy developments and discourses were scarce. Budgets of key agencies that were focused on women, equality, poverty and racism were slashed and important organisations closed down or denied their independence by being absorbed into government departments (Barry and Conroy 2013).

As the austerity response to the crisis took hold in Ireland another gender dimension became evident. Job losses and pay reductions were imposed across the public sector, which had over the past two decades become a key source of employment for women as it combined job security with some flexibility and provided for career development opportunities – a rarity in Ireland's heavily segregated labour market. This was combined with a number of specific policy measures that had severe negative consequences for lone parents (predominantly women), low-income households and disadvantaged minorities, including a reduction in the "earnings disregard" (this allowed lone parents to earn up to a threshold amount of income without loss of benefits) and the imposition of a new and regressive income tax (the Universal Social Charge (USC), discussed below). Alongside these new measures were other changes in policy that were small in scale but, in many cases, had a devastating effect, such as the abolition of the traditional double social welfare payment at Christmas and the loss of the "respite grant" for those caring for disabled children in their own homes (a grant that enabled households to access one or two weeks of subsidised care during which they could take a much needed holiday or break from their role as primary carers). Poverty levels and homelessness increased, debt levels reached new heights and disadvantaged minorities such as travellers had whole programmes closed down. Youth unemployment was staggeringly high and over 200,000 young people and young families emigrated (out of a labour force of 1.4 million), of whom nearly 15% were unemployed in 2011 at the height of the crisis. Household debt levels increased dramatically and measures to address this were slow to be introduced and limited in their effect (Harvey 2013; Barry and Conroy 2013).

What has become evident in the data on Ireland, in common with many other EU countries (as seen in the EU employment rate data), is that while gender gaps have narrowed in employment, wages and poverty over the course of the crisis this does not reflect progress towards greater gender equality. Rather, while economic conditions deteriorated across the board, gender gaps narrowed as the economic position of men – which had started from a significantly higher level – deteriorated at a faster rate than that of women. This was partially due to the fact that a proportion of men were forced into marginal sections of low-paid employment,

84 Ursula Barry

previously occupied by women. However, there is also new evidence that in Ireland, as the country has begun to show signs of a fragile recovery, male unemployment rates have begun to fall faster, reestablishing the traditionally wider gender gap (Rubery and Karamessini 2013; ENEGE Report 2013; Barry 2014).

Stage 1 (2008–10): impact of the crisis

A series of measures introduced at the onset of the crisis with the stated objective of reducing the public deficit by €6 billion included a combination of cuts in the public sector pay bill and a reduction in the level of social transfers. Direct pay cuts in the public sector and a reduction in future pension entitlements created a new scheme for all entrants to the public service from 2010 onwards, who would have a significantly lower level of entitlements than their colleagues. This resulted in a two-tier public sector based on a hierarchical intergenerational structure – new and younger entrants, to teaching for example, work alongside older-age colleagues who have significantly higher pay levels and pension entitlements; some estimates put the differential as high as 30% (Flynn 2012).

The Irish case supports the argument that low-value flexible workers, such as those on zero-hours contracts – or "the precariat" (Standing 2009) – have become even more widespread over the crisis years, particularly in the retail and hospitality sectors. This new precariat in Ireland is made up predominantly of women of different ages, young male and female workers and migrants (similar to the situation across the EU). Part-time employment, which has in the past been disproportionately dominated by women (and this continues to be the case), became, during the crisis and austerity years, the situation also for a small but growing proportion of men. For most men, and for many women, this increase in part-time work is based on high levels of involuntary part-time employment – a pattern again evident across the EU (Standing 2009; Mandate 2013; Barry and Conroy 2013; ENEGE Report 2013).

As these changes have been implemented they have impacted differently on women and men. During this stage, the public sector suffered relatively high pay cuts on relatively low levels of pay, with the severest cut of 10% imposed on those earning (in the Irish context) middle incomes (€55,000 per annum). The public sector is a significant employer of women in Ireland, partly because there are better conditions of work, including greater job flexibility; women make up 47% of those employed in public administration and defence, and around 75% of those employed in education and health sectors. Wage rates are higher and the gender pay gap is generally lower in the public sector. Consequently, the reduction in pay levels is having a negative impact on large numbers of women employees and, combined with the cut-backs in employment levels and a freeze on recruitment (until the end of 2016), there are higher job losses and fewer job opportunities for women as a result. Latest data show a 9% drop in public sector employment between 2009 and 2011, and a further 8% drop between 2011 and 2014 (CSO 2014a).

The austerity years have seen an increase in low-income taxes, introduced through a reduction in personal tax credits and a range of welfare cuts that were established over the course of the 2011–14 budgets. Unemployment and welfare payments were cut by approximately 10% per week, with greater cuts imposed on youth claimants; child benefits (paid directly to women, particularly in low-income and one-parent households) and carers allowance (claimed mainly by middle- to older-aged women looking after elderly or disabled relatives) were reduced; and disability payments, blind pensions and the level of emergency welfare relief were all cut back. In addition to the reduced level of welfare expenditure and social transfers that these cut-backs represent, reductions in general departmental spending also had a major impact on services delivered at the community and household level. Some 79% of carers are women in Ireland. Women, the elderly and lone parents experience the highest risk of poverty and are disproportionately affected by these changes. When these diverse cuts are looked at closely it is also evident that payments to young, unemployed, large families and specific minorities have been hard hit.

Pressure on government towards the end of Stage 1 led to a commitment under a new programme to maintain "headline" or basic social welfare rates and, under the current "social partnership" agreement (known as the "Croke Park Agreement"), the incoming government stated that taxes would not be raised, public sector pay rates would not be reduced and there would be no compulsory redundancies in the public sector. This agreement dominated the industrial relations landscape throughout this period of the crisis; however, it did not mitigate the serious consequences on low-income households resulting from key measures already introduced in 2011 and whose effects were ongoing. It also failed to prevent a series of additional reductions in welfare allowances, benefits and support programmes, such as fuel vouchers, double Christmas payments, fuel and telephone allowances for pensioners, funding for traveller support programmes and back-to-school allowances.

Stage 2 (2011–14): austerity years

The second stage of the crisis was characterised across the EU by austerity measures and in Ireland it has become increasingly evident that those on low incomes, the majority of whom are women, have been negatively affected by such policies to a disproportionate extent. The most current national data on poverty in Ireland can be found in the EU Study of Income and Living Conditions (EU SILC) data for 2013, which has confirmed the consequences for the lowest income groups of the crisis and the austerity measures that were imposed. The EU SILC data used a poverty line set at 60% of median income, and revealed that 16% of the Irish population were defined as "at risk of poverty" in 2013 (an increase from 14% in 2009); those in "consistent poverty" increased from 5.5% in 2009 to 7.7% in 2013. Children are the most vulnerable to poverty in Ireland, and in 2013 more than one in five children were at risk of poverty – double that of 2008 (CSO 2015). This data also revealed a systematic increase in the "enforced deprivation rate"[1] from 11.8% in 2009 to 22.6% in 2010, 24.5% in 2011, 26.9% in 2012 and 30.5% in

86 Ursula Barry

2013. The deprivation rate among lone parents was extremely high at 63% in 2013 – the highest of all the different social sectors. The particular vulnerability of lone parents is confirmed by new data, which highlights that lone-parent households are burdened with more debt than all other types of households (CSO 2015).

The gendered nature of poverty is also evident in recent figures from the Economic and Social Research Institute (ESRI) that show women in couples experienced a 14% drop in income compared with 9% for men during the recession years (CSO 2015; ESRI 2014). Lone parents, large families, unemployed households, travellers and people with disabilities are particularly at risk of combined rates of poverty and deprivation. Low pay and low incomes often go hand-in-hand in Ireland where an increasing proportion of those living in poverty are "working poor" – it is estimated that 20% of those households in poverty have an adult in paid employment. Clearly, paid employment is no guarantee of exiting from poverty. With the recession and accompanying austerity measures, the indebtedness of private households has risen. Tens of thousands are unable to pay the mortgage loans they have taken out to buy their houses and the interest payments on those loans, with some estimates putting the proportion of mortgage holders that are "in difficulties" as high as 30%. The proportion of those at risk of poverty in arrears with household bill payments increased from 20% to 34% over the crisis and austerity years (CSO 2014a; Barry and Conroy 2013).

An important turning point towards austerity was the 2011 budget. In an interesting analysis of this budget from a gender perspective, the Think Tank on Social Change (TASC) carried out a survey financed by the EU Progress Programme that demonstrated clearly the extent to which women and children were disproportionately affected by the negative changes to policy. The audit, entitled *Winners and Losers? Equality Lessons for Budget 2012*, was based on a sample of over 7,000 households and revealed that low-income and lone-parent households experienced the most adverse effects as gross average income fell by 5% as a result of this one budget in 2011:

> Overall, those on the lowest incomes were hardest hit by the measured budgetary changes. They were adversely affected by the cuts to social transfers and by changes to taxation, specifically the introduction of the Universal Social Charge, widening of tax bands and reductions in tax credits. As women are concentrated in lower income groups, they suffered a disproportionate impact.
>
> *(TASC 2011: 4)*

Additional policy measures were implemented during Stage 2 that had, and continue to have, negative impacts on the living conditions among specific vulnerable sectors. These include reduced funding for community development programmes, reductions in special needs assistants to children with disabilities in education, fewer language assistants and educational supports for travellers, reductions in community-based childcare, and reductions in home help services for the elderly and those with disabilities (Barry and Conroy 2013). The two significant changes highlighted below – the USC, and the targeting of low-income and lone-parent households – were introduced in January 2011. The USC openly challenged the social partner agreement, calling the new deduction from peoples' pay packets a "charge" rather than what it is – a severe form of new and additional taxation.

The Universal Social Charge (USC)

The USC – a new and highly regressive tax/levy paid on all gross incomes above an exemption threshold – was introduced in 2011 and estimated to raise €4 billion in government revenue. Staggered tax rates were applied to different income levels, although the highest rate (currently 5.5%) was paid once a person's income level reached only just above €18,000. Recent budgets have seen significant reforms of the USC, raising the entry point threshold and reducing rates levied on lower income households.[2] However, despite these reforms, the regressive aspect of this tax is still evident in that the exemption limit continues to operate at just barely over the at-rate-of-poverty income level, the tax is paid on gross incomes and the highest rate continues to come into effect only marginally below the National Minimum Wage (currently estimated at €17,000 per annum).

Targeting lone parents and low-income households

The second significant set of austerity measures were targeted at lone parents on welfare. The critical "earnings disregard" (i.e. the amount of income that could be earned without affecting benefits payments) which enabled many lone parents (the vast majority of whom are women) to reattach to paid employment was significantly lowered. As a consequence, lone parents who had been in a position to take up part-time (mainly low-paid) employment and to retain their One Parent Family Payment (OPFP) were no longer able to do so, thus creating new and deeper poverty traps.

A recent research report explored the extent to which the high costs of childcare act as a barrier to accessing paid employment in all low-income households (including lone parents) in Ireland. The report by Indecon Economic Consultants was released in December 2013 and concluded that 25% of parents were prevented from accessing paid employment due to the high costs of childcare, including 56% of parents in low-income households. Indecon estimated the cost of full-time childcare to be €16,500 per annum in a two-child household, putting the cost of childcare in Ireland, as a percentage of average wages, as the second highest in the OECD. Unless the availability and cost of childcare are addressed then these policy changes affecting lone-parent and low-income households will continue to have a hugely negative impact on women's income, particularly in low-income households, and undermine the potential for women to increase their participation in paid employment (Indecon 2013).

88 Ursula Barry

Also affecting low- to middle-income households is a new property tax introduced in January 2013, which takes no account of mortgage debt on houses and is based solely on the market value of the property. For example, two households pay the same property tax despite the fact that one has no mortgage and the other has a mortgage of hundreds of thousands of euros (the average house price in Ireland is €250,000). New water charges were also introduced in 2015, despite a widespread and effective campaign of non-payment. Without carrying out the net property valuation and the necessary water metering, these taxes and charges are seen as regressive, negatively impacting low-income households in which women are the majority.

Commenting critically on the negative impact of these cut-backs combined with the loss of funding to many significant community-based programmes, the report by the UN High Commissioner on Extreme Poverty on her visit to Ireland in 2011 stated:

> The impact of these measures will be exacerbated by funding reductions for a number of social services which are essential for the same vulnerable people, including disability, community and voluntary services, Travellers supports, drug outreach initiatives, rural development schemes, the Revitalising Areas by Planning, Investment and Development (RAPID) programme and Youthreach. By adopting these measures, Ireland runs a high risk of excluding those most in need of support and ignoring the needs of the most vulnerable. In particular, due to multiple forms of entrenched discrimination, women are especially vulnerable to the detrimental effects of reductions in social services and benefits.
>
> *(UN 2011: 9)*

Conclusion

The crisis and austerity years have seen successive Irish governments pursuing fiscal policies that have already made a significant impact on the public or "sovereign" deficit by reducing the budget deficit. However, the choices that have been made, and the nature of the policy measures that have been introduced, have been at a huge cost. The cost of turning private banking debt into public debt will circumscribe public expenditure on social, health and education expenditure for decades to come and the austerity measures that have been imposed have clearly had severe negative impacts on low-income and vulnerable groups, the majority of whom are women. It has been argued by many that the impact of central government austerity policies severely depressed demand, thereby creating conditions for continued unacceptably high levels of unemployment, poverty, inequality and emigration. From a gender equality perspective, many of the policy measures introduced have had an unacknowledged yet very significant negative impact.

What is evident when examining the policy-making process throughout the crisis years is that gender and equality impact analysis informed neither policy

Ireland and the EU **89**

design nor policy implementation, including at the EU level, and policy measures have not been assessed from a gender perspective in the vast majority of cases. One of the results of the dismantling of equality infrastructure at the national level and the lower commitment to gender equality evident at EU level is that gender equality has lost critical support in public policy-making. The consequences of these decisions can clearly be seen in the analysis within this chapter of the policies of austerity pursued in Ireland since the crisis years and their consequences for gender equality and social inequality.

Notes

1   A set of deprivation indicators are used by Eurostat to measure "enforced deprivation" in EU SILC data, which encompasses poverty data for EU28, including Ireland. These indicators are: owning two pairs of strong shoes; owning a warm waterproof overcoat; in a position to buy new (not second-hand) clothes; eat meals with meat, chicken, fish (or vegetarian equivalent) every second day; have a roast joint or its equivalent once a week; have not had to go without heating during the last fortnight; have family or friends for a drink or meal once a month; have a morning, afternoon or evening out in the last fortnight, for entertainment.
2   The exemption limit has been raised to €13,000 (from €10,000) and incomes over €13,000 will pay the 1% rate on gross incomes (down from 1.5%); the 3% rate (down from 3.5%) will be applied on incomes up to €18,688; the 5.5% (down from 7.0%) will be applied on incomes from €18,668 up to €70,044; the 8% rate will be applied to any PAYE income over €100,000; and the 11% rate will be applied to self-employed people with an income in excess of €100,000.

References

Barry, U. 2013. "Gender Perspective on Employment Policy and National Reform Programme." Irish Report. ENEGE, Equality Office EU Commission and FGB (Italy).
Barry, U. 2014. *Gender Perspective on Irish Employment Policy.* Irish Report to ENEGE, Equality Office EU Commission; FGB, Italy.
Barry, U. and P. Conroy. 2013. "Ireland in Crisis – Gender, Inequality and Austerity." In J. Rubery and M. Karamessini (eds). *Women and Austerity – The Economic Crisis and the Future for Gender Equality.* London: Routledge.
Bettio, F., M. Corsi, C. D'Ippoliti, A. Lyberaki, M. Samek Lodovici and A. Verashchagina. 2012. "The Impact of the Economic Crisis on the Situation of Women and Men and on Gender Equality Policies." Synthesis Report. FGB, IRS and ENEGE. www.ingenere. it/sites/default/files/ricerche/crisis%20report-def-7web.pdf (accessed 16 December 2015).
Central Statistics Office (CSO). 2014a. *Quarterly National Household Survey.* Dublin: CSO.
Central Statistics Office (CSO). 2014b. *Population and Migration Estimates.* Dublin: CSO.
Central Statistics Office (CSO). 2015. *Survey of Incomes and Living Standards SILC 2012.* Dublin: CSO.
ENEGE. 2013. "The Impact of the Economic Crisis on the Situation of Women and Men and on Gender Equality Policies." ENEGE. Brussels.
ESRI. 2014. "The Gender Impact of Tax and Benefit Change: A Microsimulation Approach." Dublin: ESRI.

Eurobarometer. 2012. "Monitoring the Social Impact of the Crisis: Public Perceptions in the European Union." Brussels. Eurobarometer.

European Parliament. 2013. "On the Impact of the Economic Crisis on Gender Equality and Women's Rights." www.europarl.europa.eu/sides/getDoc.do?pubRef=-//EP//TEXT+REPORT+A7-2013-0048+0+DOC+XML+V0//EN (accessed 16 December 2015).

European Women's Lobby. 2012. "The Price of Austerity – the Impact on Women's Rights and Gender Equality Issues." www.womenlobby.org/The-Price-of-Austerity-The-Impact-on-Women-s-Rights-and-Gender-Equality-in (accessed 16 December 2015).

Flynn, Sean. 2012. "Pay for New Teachers Down 30% since 2010." (28 August) *The Irish Times*. Dublin.

Gune, S. 1980. *Feminist Knowledge Critique and Construct.* London: Routledge.

Harvey, B. 2013. *Travelling with Austerity – Impacts of Cuts on Travellers, Traveller Projects and Services*. Dublin: Pavee Point.

Indecon. 2013. "Indecon Report on Support for Childcare for Working Families and Implications for Employment." Donegal, Ireland.

Lethbridge, J. 2012. *Global Context: Specific Impacts of Austerity on Women*. University of Greenwich, London: Public Services International Research Unit (PSIRU).

Mandate. 2013. "Decent Work? The Impact of the Recession on Low Paid Workers." Mandate. Dublin.

Maternity Action. 2014. "Overdue: A Plan of Action to Tackle Pregnancy Discrimination Now." Maternity Action UK.

McGauran, A.-M. 2009. "The Experience of Gender Mainstreaming the National Development Plan." *Administration* 53(2): 24–44.

Oxfam. 2013. *The True Cost of Austerity and Inequality Ireland Case Study*. Oxford: Oxfam G.B.

Pfister, T. 2008. "Mainstreamed Away? Assessing the Gender Equality Dimension of the European Employment Strategy." *Policy and Politics* 36(4): 521–538.

Rubery, J. and M. Karamessini. 2013. *Women and Austerity – The Economic Crisis and the Future of Gender Equality*. London: Routledge.

Russell, H., D. Watson and J. Banks. 2011. *Pregnancy at Work: A National Survey*. Equality Authority and Health Service Executive Crisis Pregnancy Programme.

Standing, G. 2009. *The Precariat – the New Dangerous Class*. London and New York: Bloomsbury.

TASC. 2011. *Winners and Losers – Equality Lessons for Budget 2012*. Dublin: TASC.

UN. 2011. "Report of the Independent Expert on the Question of Human Rights and Extreme Poverty, Magdalena Sepúlveda Carmona, Mission to Ireland in January 2011." General Assembly, Human Rights Council, 17th Session Agenda, Item 3.

UNAIDS. 2012 "Impact of the Global Economic Crisis on Women, Girls and Gender Equality." UNAIDS. Geneva.

Villa, P. and M. Smith. 2013. "Policy in a Time of Crisis – Employment Policy and Gender Equality in Europe." In J. Rubery and M. Karamessini (eds). *Women and Austerity – The Economic Crisis and the Future for Gender Equality*. London: Routledge.

6

THE EFFECTS OF THE ECONOMIC CRISIS AND AUSTERITY ON GENDER EQUALITY IN SPAIN AND THE SPANISH REGIONS

Elvira González Gago

Introduction

The effects of the international financial crisis that started in the US in 2007 have added to Spain's already existing economic imbalances, among them the construction bubble, which had underpinned the country's previous strong economic and employment growth. The international financial crisis accelerated the bursting of the bubble with devastating effects, destroying jobs and increasing unemployment and the risk of poverty. Later, the adoption of some structural reforms, the management of the sovereign debt crisis and the austerity policies adopted have added to rather than resolved these difficulties. In spite of these policies, an incipient economic recovery started in 2014, with a GDP growth of 1.4%, which is expected to accelerate to 3.1% in 2015 (Funcas 2015).

The crisis initially hit men harder than women, so that a downwards convergence in gender gaps in employment and unemployment emerged. This was due to a worsening situation for men, rather than improved conditions for women. Later, the impact of the crisis on male employment in construction and manufacturing activities softened but spread to female dominated activities in the services sector. All in all, taking the long view of the crisis, women have been and continue to be worse off as regards the main indicators of the labour market, with lower employment and higher unemployment rates. This chapter will analyse how the gendered components of the economic crisis, subsequent structural reforms, austerity policies and the dismantling of gender infrastructure have seriously damaged equality, not only as regards the unequal situation of women and men, but – even more worrisome – the political importance granted to equality issues, policies and institutions.

Spain is a highly decentralized country in which autonomous communities (administratively devolved regions) have devolved competences for managing the

92 Elvira González Gago

bulk of public policies, such as active labour market policies (ALMP), education, health, social services (including childcare and long-term care, gender equality), housing, etc. In the framework of nationwide regulations, they implement them according to their needs and political will. Across the autonomous communities the outcomes of the crisis have differed substantially; this chapter will show that responses to the crisis have affected women and men differently.

This chapter is structured as follows: first, it outlines the main macroeconomic features of the crisis, with a brief mention of the regional impact. Second, it discusses in more detail the policy response given by the country and the regions. Finally, the third section analyses the gender impacts of both the crisis and the policy response before concluding with some final reflections.

The Spanish crisis

After many years of uninterrupted growth rates of around 4% since the mid-1990s, GDP grew in Spain by a low 1.1% in 2008 before falling -3.7% during 2009. Over the next two years GDP stagnated, then fell again -2.1% and -1.2% in 2012 and 2013 respectively. The astonishing employment growth and declining unemployment in the years prior to the crisis were too reliant on an enormous housing bubble that multiplied by two the weight of the construction sector in GDP and employment,[1] fuelled by too-low interest rates and an increasing trade deficit after Spain's entry into the European Monetary Union (EMU). Since then, in 23 consecutive quarters of negative annual employment growth, the Spanish economy has lost virtually all of the previous employment gains, so that the lowest employment level, reached at the beginning of 2014, was similar to that of 2002 (Figure 6.1).

Public finances have drastically deteriorated. The much praised fiscal surplus of 2.2% GDP in 2007, coupled with a very manageable low public debt (36% of GDP), turned sharply negative and reached in 2009 a fiscal deficit of 11.0% of GDP followed by ratios of 9.4% in 2010 and 2011, even after the adoption of a severe austerity package that started in May 2010. The Spanish public debt started its own upwards trend, whereas private debt was three times as large as the public one and represented over 220% of GDP in 2008. The high-risk activities engaged in by banks during the economic boom, particularly in activities linked to the housing bubble and construction, lie behind these developments. The failure of several financial market reforms led the markets to anticipate the conversion of this private into public debt, increasing the country risk premium and the financing cost. In June 2012 Spain was forced to ask for financial aid from its European Union partners to support the recapitalization of the financial system, thus socializing private heavy losses of the bank system. The final total amount injected into the system has been €61.5 billion (approximately 6% of GDP). As a consequence of diminishing public revenues resulting from reduced economic activity and employment, and in spite of huge austerity efforts, the fiscal deficit has not been brought to sustainable levels and the public debt has kept on rising, reaching at

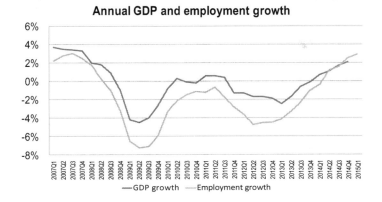

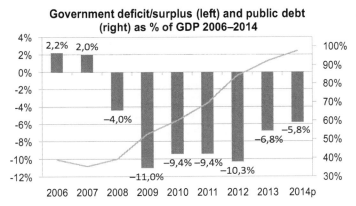

FIGURE 6.1 The Spanish economic crisis: evolution of main macroeconomic variables
Source: National Statistics Institute (INE), Labour Force Survey, and Eurostat, national accounts (both deficit and public debt data include bank rescue)

present 99.6% of GDP in August 2015. The exigency of bringing down the public deficit was somehow eased in 2013, after implicit acknowledgement that the reduction of public expenditure had been excessive and had suffocated economic growth. Austerity had pushed the economy into a spiral of recession, decreasing public revenues, reducing public expenditure (yet not able to counteract increasing interest paid for the public debt) and diminishing economic activity.

The regional dimension of this crisis has been unequal (Peña Sánchez et al. 2013; Chasco Lafuente 2014) with some Spanish regions having lost around 2% of GDP in the period 2008 to 2014 (accumulated terms) and others losing around 8–10% of their initial GDP levels. These large differences can also be found in the evolution of employment, which shows a wider variation range of -12% to -25% in the case of male employment and +4% to -13% in the case of female employment (Figure 6.2). Indeed, as will be shown later, one of the results of the crisis is the increased inequalities among regions in some variables.

94 Elvira González Gago

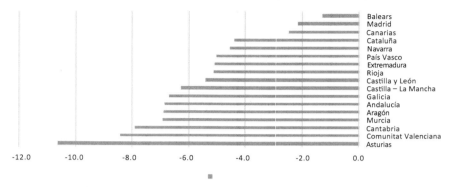

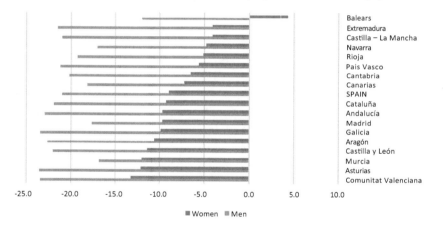

FIGURE 6.2 Evolution of regional economic indicators

The policy response

The policy response to the economic imbalances following the international and the domestic crises has been twofold, focusing on fiscal consolidation, i.e. austerity measures, on the one hand and on so-called structural reforms on the other (González et al. 2011; González and Segales Kirzner 2014). This section follows with a description of the most relevant austerity measures and their impact on gender equality; it is worth mentioning that many of these measures were decided upon by the central government, but implemented necessarily by the regions, with the intensity and direction they have been able and willing to give. Among the structural reforms are: fiscal reforms to increase tax revenues (income and corporate tax, VAT); financial reforms to restructure and support the banking system; and minor liberalization measures to open up some professional activities to the markets. Two reforms will be analysed in detail in this section because of their gender impact: the pensions reform of 2011 and the labour market reform of 2012.

Main fiscal consolidation measures

The initial policy response to the international financial crisis and to the bursting of the construction bubble was counter-cyclical, with expansive measures adopted to cushion the negative effects of the economic downturn, particularly in the male-dominated construction, financial and automotive sectors. An investment of €13 billion was made to slow down the loss of jobs in 2009–2010. After a while, however, the Spanish government faced pressure from EU institutions and the financial markets to implement orthodox fiscal consolidation packages together with a set of equally orthodox structural reforms, which started in 2010 and were strengthened in 2012. A somewhat irrational, disordered set of varied measures were rapidly adopted, with the immediate aim of appeasing EU and international lenders, and with little regard for the foreseeable impacts on gender, on inequalities, on poverty, etc. The climate of urgency led to far-reaching reforms that have eroded some of the most important institutions and policies, and their capacity to improve the situation of many people.

One of the first reforms was a fatal attack to gender equality policies with the elimination of the Equality Ministry, established only in 2008 and closed on 20 October 2010 to save money. This was part of a broader process in which gender institutions in some regions were withdrawn, in theory, for cost reasons. However, given the relatively small savings, these developments simply sent an austerity 'morality' message, which is that striving for gender equality is a waste of money we can no longer afford. There are both practical and symbolic consequences of downgrading the importance of equality policies: it decreases the consideration of gender problems in public policy making and hampers the coordination of multi-ministerial, multi-level and territorial equality policies among the diverse public administrations (González Gago and Segales Kirzner 2014; García-Serrano and Arranz 2013). More recently, the Women's Institute, established in 1897 as an autonomous body and with the mission of promoting gender equality, has been changed into the Women's Institute and Equal Opportunities,[2] thereby losing its exclusive goal of gender equality and eroding its political independence.

Together with the elimination and modifications of gender equality structures, the suspension of further development of the long-term care system is the most significant regression of policies that support gender equality. The so-called Dependency Law (*Ley de Dependencia*)[3] was passed in 2006 as an acknowledgement of the need for women to be supported in their access to the labour market; of the need for the labour market and the economy to recognize the importance of women to promote economic growth and equality; of the economic and social profitability of such an investment. The Dependency Law divides the dependent population into three classifications according to their dependency level: moderate, severe and great. These needs would be addressed gradually, starting with the dependants whose needs are classified as "great". When the local and/or regional administrations cannot provide the care services outlined in the law (domiciliary care, home help services, day care centres, etc.), beneficiaries are entitled to monetary benefits that can be used to pay somebody (including a member of the family) to care for them. The social security contributions of these informal carers (*ciudadores informales*) were to be paid by the State.

The gradual implementation of the law came to a stop in 2010, and now only great and severe dependants are covered. In 2012 the system was reformed to enable a cut of €2.2 billion until 2014, which meant a reduction in the number of persons entitled by 150,000 and the number of persons cared for by 40,000 (Barriga Martín et al. 2015).[4] In November 2012, the State suddenly ended the payment of social security contributions for informal carers, the vast majority of them women. As a consequence, the number of informal carers paying social security contributions has diminished by 93.4%; at the end of 2011 the figure stood at 173,000 persons, while at present only 11,000 persons opt to pay their social security contributions.[5] The other informal carers are no longer in the social security system.

The public long-term care system has been a great achievement but the constraints it now faces are damaging the lives of many; its effective implementation has not transformed social gender roles regarding care activities and family structures. The lack of social recognition of care workers, the inadequate and diminishing coverage of the care system and the drastic budgetary cuts hinder support for both women in need of long-term care (two out of three beneficiaries of the system) and women who care (almost 95% of professional and non-professional care givers).

Children's care facilities have also been a victim of austerity. The 'Educa3 Plan' was set up in 2008 with the objective of supporting the construction of pre-primary school infrastructure for under-three-year-olds. In 2012 the Plan was cancelled, having built a record 72,548 new additional places in the four years it lasted, covering 3.92% additional children aged 0–3 (Parliament Session's Diary 2014). It was paid for from a €100 million central administration budget, to be complemented with similar amounts by regional authorities. Although the use of formal 0–3 childcare services is higher in Spain than in the EU28 average (35% and 27% respectively in 2013, according to EU-SILC Eurostat), it decreased by four percentage points during the crisis from 39% in 2007. As this analysis will later show, women have remained in the labour market during the crisis, all the while the burden of their family responsibilities has increased.

Another disappointing initiative from a gender perspective was the postponement of the extension of paternity leave, apparently *sine die*. The extension from 13 days to 28 was adopted in January 2011 but its effective implementation has been repeatedly postponed every year until now, again because of its cost. The cost of this extension has been estimated at €136 million a year, an increase of 15% with respect to the existing budget (López-Ibor et al. 2013). The discriminatory situation between maternity and paternity leave and the lack of action in this regard does not contribute to achieving an equality model. Besides, since the current design of parental leave allows the mother to decide whether or not to transfer part of the maternity leave to the father, the model does not foster co-responsibility, and reinforces gender stereotypes. This is another example of how the measure was adopted without comparing its costs (€136 million) to the potential financial benefits of gender equality and more women (re)entering the labour market.

Public enterprises and, in general, civil servants have become one of the targets of the austerity measures in what could be understood as a broader strategy to downgrade their working conditions, their public image and reputation, and, more importantly, the very idea of the welfare state. Public enterprises that fail an objective utility test and public services unable to prove 'profitability' are to be cut, as if public services must be subject to private sector criteria. In this context, in May 2010, public servants' wages were cut by 5% on average, with higher wages reduced more than lower ones; in 2012 one monthly extra wage pay was eliminated.[6] Although these cuts have slightly improved the gender pay gap within the public administration as women's average salaries are lower than men's,[7] this is again a levelling-down convergence and the cuts constitute a regressive measure from a gender perspective, since women are more affected due to their higher participation in public employment. Moreover, they have presumably contributed to the increased gender pay gap of the whole economy, as is shown below. According to the Labour Force Survey of 2012, women represented 55% of civil servants and were overrepresented in the areas most affected by the austerity measures (67% in education, 73% in health and 87% in long-term care). Real wages of female and male public servants have diminished, but women are undoubtedly more affected. Moreover, civil servants' working time has been increased up to 37.5 weekly hours.

Only in 2014 have GDP and employment started to recover, with a long way to go before employment and unemployment reach acceptable levels. One may argue that this recovery is the fortunate result of the needed, if painful, reforms and austerity, as the government and some analysts claim now (Schwartz 2015); it is equally arguable that this was the only way and that the damage to gender equality is an affordable price to pay; it is also arguable that the recession of 2012–2013 could have been avoided, that the additional one million jobs lost between mid-2012 until mid-2014 were not inevitable. The socialization of the large losses incurred by the banks has cost €61.5 billion, plus the associated interest; as a comparison, the cut in the public budget devoted to welfare policies has amounted to €19 billion (-6%) between 2011 and 2013.[8] Whether the restructuring of the bank system and the associated costs were inevitable is not an easy question to answer; whether or not the counterpart had to be this austerity is clearer.

As mentioned in these pages, the Spanish regions have devolved competences across the most important public services, such as social, employment, health, education or housing policies. Aspects of the described implementation of austerity policies have been managed by the regions, which can be clearly observed through the evolution of the budgetary means devoted in each region to welfare policies. As

98 Elvira González Gago

can be seen in Table 6.1, there have been and are still large regional disparities in Spain as regards the budget devoted to welfare policies.[9] Before the crisis and the austerity policies, the highest per capita budget (€5,033 per capita) was double the one in the region with the lowest ratio (€2,212 per capita); six years later, this difference remains almost unchanged. On average, the accumulated reduction of the nominal per capita welfare budget amounts to -10.4%, which finds a regional maximum at -20.5% and a minimum at +7.6%. In absolute terms, the reduction between 2008 and 2014 equals to €10.8 billion (-9.2%), and has been most intense across "social protection and promotion policies" worth €2.7 billion (-14.8%): within this, the budget devoted to housing policies has collapsed by -59.3% and active labour market policies by -31.8%, whereas social services, particularly the regional minimum income schemes, have experienced an increase of +7.2%. On the other side, departments covering "public services" (health, education and culture) have seen their regional budget diminished by €8.5 billion (-8.8%, with health policies -5.6%, education -9.6% and culture -56.7%). The counterpart is the public debt service, which has multiplied by more than four times (+432%) and absorbed €25 billion more in 2014 than in 2008, offsetting by far the savings of €10.8 billion in regional social policies.

The labour market reform

A comprehensive and profound labour market reform was passed in 2012.[10] After several attempts in recent years, this one intended again to reduce the secular segmentation of the Spanish labour market between much protected permanent workers and temporary workers with lower employment protection levels (Hernánz and Jimeno 2013): this aims to ease and make cheaper the firing of permanent workers (external flexibility), so as to narrow the gap with the firing costs of temporary workers, with the ultimate goal being to promote open-ended contracts and create stable employment. The reform also aims to increase internal flexibility that arguably contributes to the internal devaluation, i.e. lower wages, mainly through a very important reform of the collective bargaining (Infante 2015). Changes affect three main features:

- employers can effectively suspend the application of collective agreements in their companies on economic, technical or organizational grounds, so that collective agreements at firm level are given priority over other levels (provincial, sectoral, national, etc.);
- employers can modify substantial working conditions (wage, number and distribution of working hours) without any significant possibility of reply by workers;
- wages are no longer linked to the evolution of prices, to avoid price-wage spirals, but to productivity.

Although the reform is meant to ease companies' internal flexibility rather than resorting to individual and collective dismissals in recessionary contexts, in fact it

TABLE 6.1 Evolution 2008-2014 of regional budget devoted to welfare policies (%)

ANDALUCÍA	Welfare policy pc 2014	Welfare policy pc 2008	Evolution welfare policy pc 2008–14 (%)	(A)+(B) Evolution total welfare policy budget (%)	(A) Evolution "social protection and promotion" budget (%)★	(B) Evolution "public services (health, education, culture)" budget (%)★★
ARAGÓN	2,151	2,464	-12.7	-10.6	-20.9	-11.3
ASTURIAS	2,269	2,598	-12.7	-12.8	-10.7	-13.5
C. VALENCIANA	2,532	2,533	0.0	-1.7	-4.1	-1.2
CANARIAS	2,071	2,212	-6.4	-6.9	-17.8	-5.5
CANTABRIA	2,504	2,828	-11.5	-10.2	-34.7	-10.2
CSTILLA Y LEÓN	2,732	2,734	0.0	1.1	13.7	-1.5
CASTILLA LA MANCHA	2,423	2,688	-9.9	-12.1	-20.0	-10.0
CATALUÑA	2,209	2,781	-20.5	-19.2	-30.9	-16.2
EXTREMADURA	2,174	2,482	-12.4	-10.5	6.7	-12.8
GALICIA	2,716	3,181	-14.6	-14.5	-19.8	-12.9
BALEARES	2,332	2,648	-11.9	-13.1	-29.2	-10.3
MADRID	2,149	2,239	-4.0	-1.3	-13.1	-2.6
MURCIA	2,046	2,295	-10.9	-8.3	-20.9	-5.7
NAVARRA	2,201	2,476	-11.1	-8.5	-11.8	-8.1
PAÍS VASCO	4,139	5,033	-17.8	-15.1	-37.9	-7.7
RIOJA	3,192	2,968	7.6	9.2	47.8	4.7
TOTAL	2,520	2,820	-10.6	-10.2	-3.8	-11.6
	2,280	2,544	-10.4	-9.2	-14.8	-8.8

Source: Ministry of Finance and Public Administrations (Public Budgets 2008-2014) and INE (population statistics). Own calculations.

★ Following the classification made by the Ministry of Finance and Public Administration, "Social protection and promotion" in the regions include social services, promotion of employment, housing. ★★ "Public services" include health, education and culture.

led to a new peak in job losses in 2012 of -4.3% (3.0% women and 5.4% men). It moreover entails an unbalanced transformation of labour relations in favour of the employers that will arguably affect the weakest workers with less bargaining power most. This will eventually lead to specific groups, particularly mothers or fathers, lacking protection when they need to conciliate their personal, family and professional lives.

As reported by trade unions (Herranz Sainz-Ezquerra and Brunel Aranda 2014; Unión General de Trabajadores 2015) the severity of the situation relegates gender equality to the category of a luxury that workers can no longer afford, as perceived by both working women and men. However, collective bargaining, with much room for improvement,[11] is an important tool for achieving equal opportunities within firms, specifically through the Equality Plans, compulsory in Spain for firms employing more than 250 workers,[12] an area in which trade unions are actively engaged. The crisis and the labour market reform have erased equality issues from the agenda of firms' strategies: workers are afraid of being dismissed, so they do not demand that Equality Plans be implemented; firms allege too high costs as a reason for not doing so (Bodelón et al. 2012). More generally, the lack of gender perspective in labour market reform is impacting negatively on female participation and labour conditions, as will be seen later.

The pensions reform

Especially damaging for women's economic and social situation is the pension system reform passed in 2011 (Law 27/2011), in force since January 2013 and agreed upon and signed by the government and its social partners. Acknowledging the need to address the challenges of an ageing population and to guarantee the sustainability of the system, the reform was considered essential to fiscal consolidation as non-contributory pensions are financed by the general state budget. However, it cannot be considered a full reform that redistributes resources according to a more sustainable structure, but rather a partial reform of the eligibility criteria for retirement pensions with the sole aim of reducing the total payroll (González and Segales Kirzner 2011).

The most controversial measure in the public debate was the raising of the retirement age from 65 to 67 for men and women. Moreover, the entitlement to receive the full pension now requires paying contributions for 38.5 years instead of 35 years, regardless of the pensioner's age, which, given women's more sporadic labour market participation, affects a larger number of women than men (González Gago and Segales Kirzner 2012). Furthermore, the pension calculation basis was also tightened to take into account the last 25 years of working life, 10 more than the previous 15 years. The minimum contributory period required for having a right to a contributory pension remains 15 years, too high for many women.

More than three years were devoted to analysis and debate of the pensions reform, but substantial and far-reaching debates concerning its gender effects were almost absent. The earnings base depends on wages, which are lower for women

Spain and the Spanish regions **101**

throughout their working life, so when they do contribute and are entitled to contributory pensions (not so frequent for the eldest cohorts of women), they are significantly lower (Bettio et al. 2013). Certainly, women work for fewer years, amounting to less time in total and, although they retire one year later than men on average (at the age of 64.9 compared to 63.9 years for men (Villate 2015)), they receive less money: women's average general retirement pension amounted to 60% of that of men's in 2013.[13]

Acknowledging that women are worse off with the tightening of access and quantity conditions, the period spent out of the labour market caring for children (unpaid childcare leave) is computed as a contributory period up to a maximum of three years, one year more than before the reform.[14] Similarly, the period of reduced working time and salary due to childcare[15] is considered the same as full contribution, to avoid the negative impact on the future pension of reduced contributions. The limit for this allowance is two years' contribution, which has not been changed by the reform.

In any case, these two or three years can hardly compensate for the amount of time actually spent by women out of the labour market caring for their children. These measures may mitigate the asymmetric effect on women of child caring, but they do not reduce the cause of these situations. It actually increases the incentive of carers, most of them women, to leave the labour market instead of the opposite, because the detrimental effects of working less on their future pensions are mitigated to some extent, that is, the economic cost of caring for their children seems to diminish. However, the correct incentive should be that women stay in the labour market and do not have to face or compensate for any income loss, that family responsibilities and costs are equally shared by men and women and that quality and affordable childcare services are available.

Strangely enough, the pension reform does not assume a more equal participation of women in the labour market and society. The reform fails to recognize the potential of more women in employment, such as more equality and a more sustainable pension system, and whether a sustainable pension system in fact requires more and better participation of women. The reforms pay no attention either to the effect on the system of an eventual increase of children cared for by fathers, as co-responsibility requires.

The gender effects of the crisis and the policy responses

The labour market responded with its traditional high elasticity to GDP growth, so that real GDP has diminished by 6.7% and total employment by 15.3%, that is by 3.1 million workers, between 2008 and 2014.[16] Men have absorbed 75.6% of this employment loss (20% fall), due to the concentration of net employment losses in construction and manufacturing activities. As in other countries, the sectoral segregation of women (particularly their concentration in public services such as education, health and social work) has protected female employment, which has diminished by 8.8% over the period. However, the situation reversed in 2014 and so did the impact on women's employment: more than half a million jobs were created in 2014 and the first quarter of 2015, of which 70% have been absorbed by men. Industry and construction activities have led the growth with 6.2% and 12.6% rates respectively, compared to 2.3% on average.

In terms of the employment and unemployment rates, the effects of the crisis have closed the existing gender gaps by 10 and 20 percentage points respectively until 2013 (Figure 6.3). This cannot be seen as a success for gender equality, since it has not been based on an improvement of the female rates but on the deterioration of the male ones (Bettio et al. 2012). Moreover, the most recent evolution has brought the gaps again to 10.5 and 2.8 percentage points in 2015, which is indeed worrying. It evidences that the recovery of the economy and growing employment is favouring more men than women, so that new divergences are already appearing.

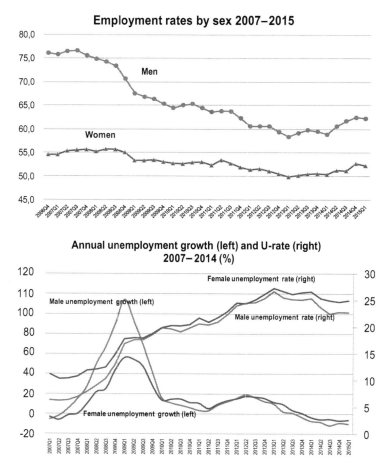

FIGURE 6.3 Evolution of employment and unemployment rates by sex
Source: Eurostat (LFS)

The household and individual strategies adopted to cope with the economic downturn reveal some interesting patterns worthy of further analysis. Whereas men have reacted to their massive job losses in part by retiring from the labour market (more than 800,000 men, 6.2%, have become inactive since the second quarter of 2008) almost 700,000 women (6.9%) have in contrast entered the labour market to counteract family income losses caused by higher male unemployment. In the case of women, however, this process reversed in 2013, after which they began to leave the labour market. Prior to 2013 1.5 million women aged over 35 took the lead and became active, increasing the amount of active women by +26%, and more than compensating for the loss of 0.5 million younger women who quit the labour market. However, from 2013 on only 300,000 women over 40 increased their activity, and this is no longer enough to compensate for the loss among 400,000 younger ones. The total female activity rate has diminished from 53.98% in 2012 to 53.67% in 2014, after having increased three percentage points between 2008 and 2012.

While higher education levels have deterred men from leaving the labour market (the highly educated maintaining their activity rate compared to -3.4 percentage points among the low qualified in 2008–2014), the opposite has occurred among women, who have become more active the lower their education level (7 percentage points increase among the low qualified and only 2.6 percentage points among the higher educated).

The *labour market has become more precarious*, which in Spain means temporary, involuntary part-time and low wages, features that very often go together (García-Serrano and Arranz 2013; Fundación 1° de Mayo 2013; Conde-Ruiz and Gorjón 2015). Whereas one of the declared aims of the labour market reform of 2012 was to reduce the high share of temporary jobs in Spain, according to the LFS this percentage has even increased among men since the approval of the reform (+1.5 percentage points, hovering at 23.5% in 1Q2015) and has decreased only by one percentage point among women, down to 23.7%. Although the most feminized sectors suffer from high rates of temporary employment, the concentration of job losses in construction and manufacturing has resulted in many more men on fixed-term contracts being affected and thus a convergence of temporary employment rates, which used to be around three to five percentage points higher among women. On the other hand, in contrast to the general trend, part-time employment has increased sharply (16.5% between 2Q2008 and 1Q2015) during the crisis, seven times faster among men (52% compared to 7% for women in the period). In 2008 and 2009 working time reduction was promoted as an alternative to dismissals in collective redundancy procedures. Later, part-time hiring was made flexible and promoted with economic incentives. Still, it constitutes a minor share of men's jobs (9% in 2015), and women are still the vast majority of total part-timers (73%). Part-time can hardly be considered a refuge for employment since 68% of men and 59% of women (1Q2015) work part-time because they cannot find a full-time job and these numbers have greatly increased. Children and other dependents to care for, and

104 Elvira González Gago

other family responsibilities are the reasons given by 18% of women and 2.8% of men for working part-time; it is worth mentioning that this reason has almost halved both for women (31% in 2008 to 18% in 2015) and for men (4.6% and 2.8%).[17] Diminishing family income due to involuntary part-time and the urgency of the situation in many families have displaced the rank of the reasons.

In terms of salaries, the measures adopted have led to so-called internal devaluation, i.e. lower real salaries, but again not equally for everyone (Ayala 2013; Davia 2014; García-Serrano and Arranz, 2013). The S80/S20 income quintile ratio has increased from 5.7 in 2008 to 6.3 in 2013, which places Spain in the sixth worst position among the EU28 countries and depicts the worst evolution in recent years. Similar conclusions can be drawn from the Gini coefficient, which has increased from 31.9 in 2008 to 33.7 in 2013, so that Spain occupies the seventh position and shows one of the worst performances during the crisis.[18] Indeed, the crisis and the policies adopted have not resulted in more equality but less; and the recovery is not showing better prospects. Whereas in 2013 the wages received by the 50 best paid directors of the companies listed in Ibex35 were 75 times the average wage in their respective companies, in 2014 this ratio was 104 times. And while it may be a dubious indicator of success, there are only two women among these 50 directors.[19] As a matter of fact, the gender pay gap has increased in the period from 16.1% in 2008 to 19.3% in 2013, according to the last data available.[20]

As analysed above, the *Spanish regions* have experienced the impact of the crisis and of austerity policies very differently, with mixed results in terms of disparities in the regional labour markets. In the period 2008–2014, the employment rate of women aged 16–64 diminished by 4.4 percentage points and the male rate by 14 percentage points with large regional differences (Table 6.2).

- With some exceptions, the regions performing better before the crisis (higher employment rates) have performed proportionally better during the crisis (their employment rates diminishing less), so that inequalities in terms of employment rates have widened, more among male rates than female ones,[21] but regional inequalities are still larger for female employment rates.
- With some exceptions as well, the performance of the regions as regards male employment rates is strongly correlated with the performance in female rates,[22] which would point to regional economic, social and sectoral structures, dynamics and policies that affect both women and men in the respective region (Peña Sánchez et al. 2013). However, the impact of the crisis on regional female employment rates has been far more unequal than the impact on regional male employment rates,[23] suggesting that the mentioned regional economic, social and sectoral structures, dynamics and policies affect women and men differently.
- In general, regions with larger gender employment rate gaps before the crisis have performed worse in terms of the gap so that they have still larger than average gaps in 2015. As a consequence, the regional disparities have significantly increased.[24]

TABLE 6.2 Evolution of female and male regional employment rates

Evolution of male and female regional employment rates (16–64 years old), 2008–2014 and 2015

	Men		Women		Gender gap (pp)		Evolution 2008–2014 (pp)		Evolution 2014–2015 (pp)	
	2015Q2	2008Q2	2015Q2	2008Q2	2015Q2	Women 2008Q2	Men	Women	Men	Women
SPAIN	63.9	75.4	53.5	56.5	10.5	18.9	-13.9	-4.5	2.4	1.4
Andalucía	56.4	68.7	44.1	46.4	12.2	22.4	-16.0	-5.0	3.6	2.7
Aragón	71.4	80.7	56.2	61.2	15.1	19.5	-14.7	-5.4	5.4	0.4
Asturias	56.2	71.5	53.2	55.3	3.0	16.2	-13.6	-3.7	-1.7	1.6
Balears	71.1	79.7	63.8	62.7	7.3	17.0	-11.5	-0.3	2.9	1.4
Canarias	56.2	67.7	47.4	50.6	8.8	17.1	-13.8	-5.8	2.3	2.6
Cantabria	65.0	76.0	53.3	56.6	11.7	19.4	-13.3	-2.4	2.3	-0.9
Castilla – La Mancha	66.7	76.2	53.9	52.8	12.9	23.4	-12.4	0.0	3.0	1.0
Castilla y León	62.3	76.8	44.5	51.3	17.8	25.5	-16.5	-6.5	1.9	-0.4
Cataluña	68.5	79.8	59.8	65.0	8.7	14.8	-13.8	-5.1	2.5	-0.2
Comunitat Valenciana	62.5	75.6	53.1	56.1	9.4	19.5	-14.9	-6.3	1.9	3.3
Extremadura	57.8	72.1	41.7	44.3	16.1	27.8	-15.7	-2.0	1.5	-0.6
Galicia	61.8	74.3	54.7	56.8	7.1	17.5	-14.8	-3.1	2.3	0.9
Madrid	70.9	78.8	61.7	63.6	9.1	15.3	-10.7	-4.7	2.7	2.9
Murcia	64.7	74.0	45.5	55.8	19.2	18.3	-11.4	-7.4	2.2	-2.9
Navarra	69.7	80.1	60.9	61.8	8.8	18.3	-11.3	-2.9	1.0	2.0
País Vasco	66.1	78.6	59.7	60.0	6.4	18.6	-12.3	-0.5	-0.2	0.3
Rioja	71.1	79.3	58.7	59.1	12.4	20.2	-9.4	-1.4	1.2	1.0
Variation Coeff	0.08	0.05	0.12	0.10	0.38	0.18	-0.15	-0.61	0.73	1.75

Source: INE (LFS), own calculations

106 Elvira González Gago

The employment recovery experienced in 2014–2015 is still more unequally distributed among the regions than during the crisis period. Employment has grown by 3.4% among men, with only two regions still losing male employment; female employment in contrast has increased by only 2.4%, with six regions further losing female employment. Due attention should be paid to recent diverging and backwards trends in female employment rates in regions with lower rates and worse performance in 2014–2015, such as Murcia, Cantabria or Extremadura.

A similar analysis can be carried out for the impact of the crisis and austerity policies on regional unemployment rates. With large initial regional differences in unemployment rates in 2008, these disparities have decreased notably during the crisis,[25] especially in 2008–2012, because, on average, regions with better starting positions in 2008 (i.e. lower unemployment rates) have performed proportionally worse than regions lagging behind. The regions that performed worse in 2008–2014 in terms of male unemployment rates also performed worse in terms of female employment rate.[26] However, the gender gap, which was almost closed in 2012 (0.1 percentage point), has reached again the pre-crisis level of 3.1 percentage points in 2015, and shows large and increasing regional differences. Indeed, the regions with the largest gaps in 2008 show still larger gaps in 2015 (the region of Murcia is a notable exception because of the rapid increase of its gap). The recent improvement in the unemployment rate has led to a rapid increase in the unemployment gender gap in some regions by about five percentage points in only one year (2014–2015), such as Murcia, Aragón, Balearic Islands or Cantabria (Table 6.3).

Some concluding remarks: beyond austerity

Seven years of crisis *and* gender-blind political responses have levelled down gender gaps in employment and unemployment, not because of better conditions for women, but due to a worse situation for men. Still, Spanish women continue to be worse off as regards the main indicators of the labour market and worryingly divergences are reappearing together with the economic recovery. The austerity packages have increased precariousness and the risk that they may leave the labour market as a consequence of less childcare and long-term care support services. The crisis hit initially men, but austerity has hit women and gender equality. The savings made in early education and long-term care will have to be paid for in future with reduced female employment and more precariousness. Moreover, the unequal regional distribution of the impacts of the crisis has enlarged regional disparities and risks advancements made in the past as regards female employment and equality: inequalities have increased in female employment rates, and due attention should be paid to some poorly performing regions in the past (with lower female employment levels) that are performing worse, thus enlarging the differences with the rest.

The grounding has been laid for an unbalanced growth and, unsurprisingly, the incipient recovery is already leading to more inequality. The gender mainstreaming

TABLE 6.3 Evolution of regional female and male unemployment rates

Evolution of male and female regional unemployment rates 2008–2014 and 2015

	Men		Women		Gender gap (pp)		Evolution 2008–2014 (pp)		Evolution 2014–2015 (pp)	
	2015Q2	*2008Q2*	*2015Q2*	*2008Q2*	*2015Q2*	*2008Q2*	*Men*	*Women*	*Men*	*Women*
SPAIN	21.0	9.1	24.0	12.1	–3.1	–3.0	14.6	13.3	–2.7	–1.4
Andalucía	28.7	13.9	33.8	19.4	–5.1	–5.5	19.0	17.6	–4.3	–3.2
Aragón	13.5	5.7	21.2	8.7	–7.7	–3.0	14.1	13.5	–6.3	–0.9
Asturias	21.4	6.6	18.8	9.4	2.7	–2.8	13.6	12.6	1.3	–3.2
Balears	15.3	7.6	17.8	9.5	–2.5	–1.9	13.0	7.8	–5.3	0.5
Canarias	29.5	15.3	31.3	16.8	–1.8	–1.6	16.4	17.0	–2.2	–2.6
Cantabria	16.1	5.4	20.5	9.3	–4.4	–3.9	14.4	9.2	–3.8	2.0
Castilla – La Mancha	16.1	6.3	21.4	13.6	–5.2	–7.3	13.8	8.8	–4.0	–1.1
Castilla y León	22.6	7.7	32.8	15.0	–10.2	–7.3	18.0	17.5	–3.2	0.3
Cataluña	18.2	7.7	20.1	7.2	–1.9	0.4	12.7	12.8	–2.2	0.0
Comunitat Valenciana	22.3	10.3	23.9	12.9	–1.5	–2.6	15.2	14.2	–3.1	–3.3
Extremadura	26.3	9.4	33.8	21.1	–7.5	–11.7	17.7	11.3	–0.9	1.4
Galicia	19.5	6.4	20.6	10.6	–1.2	–4.2	15.7	12.0	–2.6	–2.0
Madrid	17.0	7.7	18.4	9.8	–1.5	–2.1	10.5	10.1	–1.3	–1.5
Murcia	20.3	10.6	30.5	12.3	–10.2	–1.8	12.2	15.8	–2.4	2.4
Navarra	11.9	4.8	13.3	7.1	–1.4	–2.3	10.7	9.2	–3.6	–3.0
País Vasco	16.5	4.5	15.4	7.4	1.1	–2.8	12.3	8.0	–0.3	0.0
Rioja	14.1	5.9	19.1	8.3	–5.0	–2.4	9.4	12.1	–1.3	–1.3
Variation Coeff	0.26	0.37	0.28	0.36	–0.95	–0.76	0.19	0.26	–0.68	–1.99

Source: INE (LFS), own calculations

infrastructures, the sensitivity to gender issues and the role of the welfare state in promoting equality have all been seriously damaged. The Spanish experience shows that what was believed to be a strong infrastructure achieving impressive progress in gender equality in the past has been too easily eroded. The Women's Institute, the Law for Gender Equality and the Ministry of Equality were all able to promote important normative changes, such as the Law for Gender Based Violence; the law setting up the long-term care system; the reform of the former abortion law; the law allowing marriage between persons of the same sex. Austerity and lack of funding have been too easy an excuse to downgrade equality policies.

Austerity, and the way it has been deployed, is definitely not a good idea. The recovery cannot be attributed to austerity, the same as gender equality and the welfare state cannot be blamed for the crisis. The moral connotation of the concept of austerity suggests a fair punishment for former excesses that is not acceptable. To conflate any amount of money with gender equality suggests that equality is a cost, whereby, as the Law for Equality guarantees, gender equality is a right that must be promoted and defended by public administrations, institutions, companies and society at large. Certainly, it could be argued that this is not only narrow-minded, but even illegal in Spain.

Austerity cannot be a guiding principle for designing policy any longer. Policies have to respond to and be aligned with the strategies and objectives they intend to achieve, within the given budgetary constraints, whatever these are. However, the reality in recent years has been that austerity and the budgetary cuts have become the strategy and the objectives themselves, relegating the specific policy objectives to mere context, particularly in the case of equality and related policies. In this context, the role played by the EU has made the situation worse, as it failed to use gender mainstreaming principles in its policies and strategies. Unfortunately, the European Commission and the Council have widely promoted the idea that fiscal consolidation policies were contradictory to policies attending to the social effects of the crisis, particularly from a gender point of view, especially in the period 2010–2012. They have also neglected the pre-assessment of the multiple impacts – both desired and undesired – of the measures they forced Member States to adopt (Smith and Vila 2010). The EU institutions should, on the contrary, ensure the adoption of gender mainstreaming in the design and assessment of public policies, starting at home and then in the Member States.

There are proven sound and rigorous assessment tools that guarantee that policies are designed to be more gender equitable. In Spain, the Law for Equality obliges impact assessment with respect to all relevant policy changes. This was completely neglected in the creation of the austerity programme, with the only exception being the yearly gender assessments of the General State Budget and a few regional budgets. Should this assessment have been made, then the gender impacts detailed in these pages could have been predicted and mitigated, as well as the impacts on poverty, on the youth (girls and boys) or on inequalities. It is high time that all relevant legislative acts and measures include a proper and serious assessment of the gender impact, an obligation already enshrined in the Organic

Law 3/2007 for the Effective Equality among women and men. "The pursuit of gender equality needs to be considered as part of the solution to the crisis and not treated as luxury policy to be pursued only once growth has returned" (Karamessini and Rubery 2013).

Notes

1 According to the Labour Force Survey (LFS), the share of workers in the construction sector was 12.4% of all employment in 2008, compared to 5.6% in 2014.
2 Law 15/2014, 16 September of the Head of State. For the rationalization of the public sector and other administrative reforms (*de racionalización del Sector Público y otras medidas de reforma administrativa*).
3 Law 39/2006, 14 December of the Head of State. For the promotion of personal autonomy and attention to dependent people (*Promoción de la Autonomía Personal y Atención a las personas en situación de dependencia*).
4 RD 8/2010 and RD 20/2011 aimed to limit the fiscal deficit and modified thus the implementation pathway as foreseen in Law 39/2006, to save money. Later, RDL 20/2012, changed several articles of Law 39/2006 to allow for further reductions in public financing of the system, by reducing the number of persons entitled to care services as well as the services offered and co-payments requested.
5 Source: Social Security: Statistics of Affiliation to the Social Security Regimes. Data refers to the period between November 2011 and November 2015.
6 It is usual in Spain that workers, in this case, civil servants, receive 12 monthly payments and two additional so-called extra-payments in July and December. In 2012, one of these two extra-payments was eliminated.
7 The gender pay gap decreased from 12% to 10.1% in 2008–2013 in the economic activity of "Public administration, defence and compulsory social security". Source: Eurostat
8 Own calculations using the data on public budgets of the state, regional and local administrations offered by the Ministry of Finance and Public Administrations. The figures refer to the consolidated budgets (central administration, regions and municipalities) for "Social protection and promotion" (*Actuaciones de Protección y Promoción Social*), which include pensions; other economic benefits; social services and social promotion; promotion of employment; unemployment benefits; housing; management of social security. Additionally, the budgets for the so-called "Public preferential goods" (Producción de bienes públicos de carácter preferente), education, health and culture, have been added. The amount in 2011 was €316 billion and in 2013 €297 billion.
9 Again, the classification used by the Ministry of Finance and Public Administrations monitoring regional and national budgets is followed: social, employment and housing policies are broadly named in this context "social protection and promotion"; and health, education and culture policies are grouped in "public services".
10 Law 3/2012 of 6 July of the Ministry for Employment and Social Security. For urgent measures for the reform of the labour market.
11 Trade unions get the third worst mark, only after the government and political parties, as regards the citizens' perception. Source: Centre for Sociological Research, Barometer 2014.
12 As included in the Organic Law 03/2007 of the Head of State, for the effective equality among women and men, known as the Law for Equality or Equality Law.
13 Own calculation based on date of the Statistical Yearbook of the Ministry for Employment and Social Security.
14 Law 21/2011 of 1 August of the Head of State. For the updating, adequacy and modernization of the social security system.

110 Elvira González Gago

15 Workers have the right to reduce their working time and salary, proportionally, until their children are eight years old.
16 Source: National Statistics Institute (LFS, annual data, and National Accounts).
17 Source: National Statistics Institute (LFS).
18 Source: Eurostat, S80/S20 and Gini coefficient of equivalent disposable income.
19 Source: data presented by the Ibex35 companies to the National Stock Exchange Commission, as published by El País, 3 May 2015.
20 Source: Eurostat, gender pay gap (GPG) in unadjusted form (%). Industry, construction and services, except public administration, defence, compulsory social security. In contrast, the GPG would have diminished from 12% in 2008 to 10.1% in 2013 in public administration, defence, compulsory social security.
21 The Coefficient of Variation (100*Standard deviation/mean) is a measure of the dispersion of a distribution and allows for comparison between distribution with different means; it can be expressed as a proportion of one or in percentage terms. Accordingly, inequalities of the regional employment rates have increased from 7% to 10% of the mean during the period 2008–2014, especially in 2008–2010. The disparities are lower among male employment rates, but have increased more (from 5% to 8%); the disparities are larger among women, but have increased less (from 10% to 12%).
22 The correlation between evolution of regional female and male employment between 2008 and 2014 is positive and high ($R^2=0.44$).
23 In this case, the Coefficient of Variation of the impact on female employment rates in 2008–2014 (in percentage points) is 61% of the mean, whereas the Coefficient equals 15% of the mean in the impact on male employment rates.
24 The correlation between gender employment gap in 2008 and 2015 is significant and positive ($R^2=0.43$). The Coefficient of Variation of the gender employment gap was 18% in 2008 and increased to 38% of the mean in 2015.
25 The Coefficient of Variation of the female regional unemployment rate was 36% of the mean in 2008 and diminished to 27% in 2014; the evolution was from 37% to 22% in male unemployment rate during the same period (Table 6.3). In spite of this reduction, the disparities remain very large: as a comparison, note that the respective ratios in 2014 for the employment rate were 12% (female) and 9% (male).
26 The correlation between the evolution in 2008–2014 of the male and female unemployment rates is significant and positive ($R^2=0.32$). The Coefficient of Variation of the gender employment gap was 18% in 2008 and increased to 38% of the mean in 2015.

References

Albert López-Ibor, R., J.A. Fernández Cornej C. and Poza Lara. 2013. "Paternity leave and gender inequality in Spain. Reform proposals for Spain (El permiso de paternidad y la desigualdad de género. Propuestas de reforma para el caso de España)." Economic Analysis Working Papers. Volume 7 – No. 13.
Ayala, L. 2013. "Economic crisis and income distribution: a compared perspective (Crisis económica y distribución de la renta: una perspectiva comparada)." *Papeles de Economía Española* 135: 2–19.
Barriga Martín, L.A., M.J. Brezmes Nieto, G.A. García Herrero and J.M. Ramírez Navarro. 2015. "XIV Report on the National Dependency System". Association of Directors of Public Social Services Centres. http://issuu.com/directorasgerentes/docs/xiv_dictamen_del_observatorio__1_?e=7134924/11409398 (accessed 1 April 2015).
Bettio F., M. Corsi, C. D'Ippoliti, A. Lyberaki, M. Samek, M.S. Lodovici and A. Verashchagina. 2012. "The economic crisis on the situation of women and men and on gender equality policies." Synthesis report. European Commission, Directorate-General

for Justice. http://www.ingenere.it/sites/default/files/ricerche/crisis%20report-def-7web.pdf (accessed 15 June 2015).

Bettio, F., G. Betti and P. Tinios. 2013. "The Gender Gap in Pensions in the EU." European Commission, Directorate-General for Justice. http://ec.europa.eu/justice/gender-equality/files/documents/130530_pensions_en.pdf (accessed 15 June 2015).

Bodelón, E., R. Rodríguez Luna, M. Barcons Campmajó, L. Garrido Jiménez, F. Puigpelat Marti, P. Giménez Alcover, G. Casa Vila and S. Ruiz. 2012. "The impact of Equality Plans on companies (El impacto de los planes de igualdad en las empresas)." Spanish Women's Institute. www.inmujer.gob.es/areasTematicas/estudios/estudioslinea2014/docs/El_impacto_planes_Igualdad_empresas.pdf (accessed 15 June 2015).

Castro García, C. 2013. "How do the crisis and austerity policies affect women's rights and equality? (¿Cómo afecta la crisis y las políticas de austeridad a los derechos de las mujeres y a la igualdad?)". In L. Vicent, C. Castro, A. Agenjo and Y. Herrero, *The unequal impact of the crisis on women (El desigual impacto de la crisis sobre las mujeres)*. Ed FUHEM Ecosocial. Madrid. FUHEM Ecosocial.

Chasco Lafuente, P. and B. Sánchez Reyes. 2014. "Regional analysis of the impact of the economic crisis (Análisis regional del impacto de la crisis económica)." *Revista Investigación y Marketing* 125: 16–21.

Conde-Ruiz, J.I. and I. Gorjón. 2015. "Precariousness (Precariedad)." Nada es Gratis blog post (5 February) http://nadaesgratis.es/j-ignacio-conde-ruiz/precariedad (accessed 15 October 2015).

Davia, M.A. 2014. "Evolution of low wage employment in Spain (Evolución del empleo de bajos salarios en España)." Working paper 4.2. VII Informe FOESSA, Fundación FOESSA.

FUNCAS. 2015. "Forecast panel for the Spanish economy, 30 November 2015 (Panel de previsiones de la economía española)." Spanish Foundation of Saving Banks www.funcas.es/Indicadores/ (accessed 30 November 2015).

Fundación 1° de Mayo. 2013. "Crisis, austerity policies and decent work (Crisis, políticas de austeridad y trabajo decente)." Colección Estudios 71.

García-Serrano, C. and J.M. Arranz. 2013. "Economic crisis and wage inequalities (Crisis económica y desigualdad salarial)." *Papeles de Economía Española* 135: 247–265.

González Gago, E. and M. Segales Kirzner. 2011. "The socioeconomic impact of pensions systems on the respective situations of women and men and the effects of recent trends in pension reforms. National Report, Spain." In C. Crepaldi, M. Samek and M. Corsi, "The socioeconomic impact of pension systems on the respective situations of women and men and the effects of recent trends in pension reforms. Synthesis Report." EGGSI (Expert Group on Gender Equality, Social Inclusion, Health and Long-term Care Issues). http://ec.europa.eu/justice/gender-equality/files/equal_economic_independence/pensions_report_en.pdf (accessed 15 June 2015).

González Gago, E. and M. Segales Kirzner. 2012. "The impact of the crisis on the situation of women and men and on gender equality policies. National report, Spain." In F. Bettio, M. Corsi, C. D'Ippoliti, A. Lyberaki, M. Samek and A. Verashchagina, "The impact of the economic crisis on the situation of women and men and on gender equality policies. Synthesis report," ed. European Commission, Directorate-General for Justice. Luxembourg, Publications Office of the European Union. www.ingenere.it/sites/default/files/ricerche/crisis%20report-def-7web.pdf (accessed 15 July 2015).

González Gago, E. and M. Segales Kirzner. 2014. "Women, gender equality and the economic crisis in Spain." In M. Karamessini and J. Rubery (eds). *Women and Austerity: The Economic Crisis and the Future for Gender Equality*. London: Routledge.

Hernánz, V. and J.F. Jimeno. 2013. "Labour segmentation and dual hiring in Spain: post-humous conversations with Luis Toharia." *Revista de Economía Laboral* 10(1): 135–149.

Herranz Sainz-Ezquerra, A. and S. Brunel Aranda. 2014. "Trade Unions' action against the gender pay gap." Madrid: Confederal Secretariat for Women and Equality of Trade Union CCOO.

Karamessini, M. and J. Rubery (eds). 2013. *Women and Austerity: The Economic Crisis and the Future for Gender Equality*. London: Routledge.

Parliament's Session's Diary. 2014. "Question on the non-legislative motion presented by the government on the Family Responsible Company mark". Spanish Parliament (Cortes Generales), n° 691, pp. 7, 19 November. www.congreso.es/public_oficiales/L10/CONG/DS/CO/DSCD-10-CO-691.PDF (accessed 15 June 2015).

Peña Sánchez, A., M. Jiménez García, and J. Ruiz Chico. 2013. "Sectoral analysis: the impact of the crisis on the Spanish regions (Análisis sectorial : el impacto de la crisis en las regiones españolas)." Working Document No. 1 Ed. Centre for Andalusian Studies, Department of Presidency of the Andalusian Government.

Pérez Infante, J.I. 2015. "Labour market reforms during the economic crisis: their economic impact (Las reformas laborales en la crisis económica: su impacto económico)." *Ekonomiaz* 87: 246–281. www.ogasun.ejgv.euskadi.net/r51-k86aekon/es/k86aEkonomiazWar/ekonomiaz/abrirArticulo?idpubl=83&registro=1 (accessed 15 October 2015).

Schwartz, P. 2015. "Economic growth thanks to austerity (Crecimiento económico gracias a la austeridad)." *Expansión* (14 May). www.pedroschwartz.com/dynamicdata/flash/2015-05-14_Expansion-Crecimiento-Economico-gracias-a-la-austeridad.pdf (accessed 15 October 2015).

Smith M. and P. Villa P. 2010. "The ever-declining role of gender equality in the European Employment Strategy." *Industrial Relations Journal* 41: 6, 526–554.

Unión General de Trabajadores. 2015. "Taking stock of the four year term 2011–2015. Four years of social and economic regression." Comisión Ejecutiva Confederal de UGT.

Villate, B. 2014. "Consequences of gender gaps on pensions (Consecuencias de la brecha de género en las pensiones)." In A. Herranz Sainz-Ezquerra and S. Brunel Aranda (eds), "Trade Unions' action against the gender pay gap." Confederal Secretariat for Women and Equality of the Trade Union CCOO. www2.ccoo.es/comunes/recursos/1/1968520-La_accion_sindical_frente_a_la_brecha_salarial__impacto_y_repercusion_de_genero_.pdf (accessed 15 June 2015).

7

THE GENDER IMPACT OF AUSTERITY IN THE UK UNDER THE CONSERVATIVE–LIBERAL DEMOCRAT COALITION GOVERNMENT, 2010–15

Howard Reed

Introduction

Following the 2008 financial crash, the perceived need for austerity rapidly assumed a dominant position in the political agenda in the United Kingdom as the public finances deteriorated sharply. In May 2010 the Labour Party was voted out of office after a 13-year period of government, replaced by a Conservative–Liberal Democrat Coalition Government, which pledged to eliminate the budget deficit (which then stood at around £75 billion cyclically adjusted, or around 5% of UK GDP) within four years. This chapter looks at the distributional impact of the policies that the Coalition Government implemented in its (mostly unsuccessful) attempt to close the budget deficit by 2015.[1] The chapter begins by analysing the amount of fiscal consolidation that took place over the 2010–15 Parliament and the balance between reductions in public spending and increases in tax in the austerity programme. Next, the Landman Economics tax-benefit model is used to analyse the distributional impact of the tax and social security reforms that took place over the 2010–15 Parliament, assessing impacts across the income distribution and by household demographic type, with a particular focus on impacts by gender. The chapter also models the distributional impact of cuts to spending on public services other than transfer payments (e.g. spending on health, social care, education, public transport and so on). To show the overall effect of the Coalition Government's fiscal programme on living standards, the results for the distributional impact of spending cuts are then combined with the results on the distributional impact of tax and social security measures. The chapter ends with some conclusions for policymakers and researchers in the context of current austerity policies in the UK and in Europe more generally.

The composition of austerity: tax increases vs spending cuts

The Coalition Government's original June 2010 plans for closing the deficit by 2014–15 involved a mixture of approximately 79% spending cuts and 21% tax rises, starting from 2009–10 (the year the deficit was at its highest).[2] The forecast plans for closing the deficit in the government's March 2015 Budget show that by 2015–16 increases in tax as a share of GDP had contributed less than 7% towards closing the deficit – around £8 billion of tax rises (in 2015–16 prices) compared with £117 billion of spending cuts. After 2015–16 tax was forecast to rise slightly as a share of GDP (from 35.5% to 36.2%), but this would still have meant that tax rises would have contributed less than 11% to the total deficit reduction process by 2018–19.

The distributional impact of tax and benefit changes

The Appendix to this chapter gives a detailed description of the tax and benefit changes introduced by the Coalition Government.[3] In brief, the main reforms included:

- above-inflation increases in the personal allowance for income tax;
- the reduction of the highest marginal rate of income tax (payable by individuals with gross incomes of more than £150,000 per year) from 50% to 45%;
- increases in the rates of employee, employer and self-employed National Insurance Contributions;
- an increase in the standard rate of Value Added Tax from 17.5% to 20%;
- real-terms reductions in the rate of excise duty on motor fuels;
- a freeze in the nominal rates of Council Tax;
- a switch from indexation using the Retail Price Index to the less generous Consumer Price Index for most benefits and tax credits;
- increased taper rates and the removal of several premiums for tax credits;
- Child Benefit frozen in nominal terms for three years from 2011–12;
- uprating of most working age benefits and tax credits by only 1% per year for 2013, 2014 and 2015 (resulting in a significant cut in real terms);
- the introduction of a maximum limit on the amount of benefit paid to out-of-work working age households (the 'benefit cap'); and
- state pension uprated by a 'triple lock' formula more generous than that used for most other benefits.

Between 2010 and 2015 Parliament also introduced Universal Credit as a replacement for the existing tax credit system and most means-tested working age benefits in the UK. However, by the end of the Parliament in May 2015, very few families had been moved on to Universal Credit and so its impact has not been included in the analysis in this chapter.[4] The analysis also excludes changes to taxes that do not directly impact household incomes (such as Inheritance Tax, Capital Gains Tax and Stamp Duty) and changes to corporate taxation.

Data sources and assumptions

The Landman Economics tax-benefit model uses data from two UK household datasets: the UK Family Resources Survey (FRS) to model the impact of the direct tax and social security changes, and the Living Costs and Food Survey (LCF) to model the impact of indirect taxes. These datasets collect information about gross earnings and incomes from other sources for each adult in the households surveyed, which can be used to help us understand the gender impact of tax and benefit reforms.

The distributional analysis compares modelled net incomes for each household in these datasets under a 'base' scenario (if the tax-benefit system in place in May 2010 had simply been uprated by inflation for five years up to May 2015, using the rules that were in place just before the 2010 election) with a 'reform' scenario (the actual tax-benefit system for the 2015–16 tax year as it stood in May 2015, at the end of the Coalition Government's period of office). Results are uprated to the April 2015 price level.

Analysis by household income decile

Figure 7.1 presents the distributional impact of tax and social security reforms over the 2010–15 Parliament in cash terms across the household income distribution. Households are ranked by poorest to highest by net household income (adjusted for family size using OECD equivalence scales) and split into ten equally sized groups or 'deciles'. Figure 7.1 shows the average impact of the reforms for each decile group. Figure 7.2 presents the same results but expressed as a percentage of household net income rather than in cash terms.

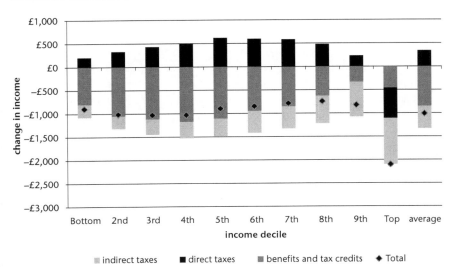

FIGURE 7.1 Cumulative impact of tax and social security reforms between 2010 and 2015 in cash terms

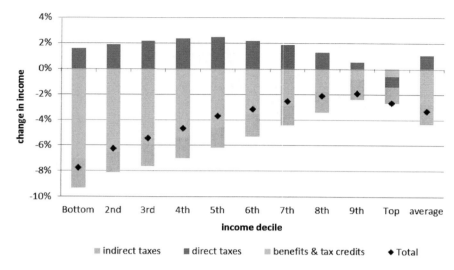

FIGURE 7.2 Cumulative impact of tax and social security reforms between 2010 and 2015 as a percentage of net income

Figure 7.1 shows that in cash terms, net losses are largest at the top decile at an average of £2,000 per year. For the other nine deciles losses are roughly even.

Figure 7.2 shows that as a percentage of disposable income the tax and welfare changes are regressive across the lowest nine-tenths of the income distribution. Average losses in the lowest decile are around 8%, four times larger than the losses in the ninth decile. Average losses in the top decile are slightly larger than in the ninth.

The biggest proportion of the losses for low-to-middle income households is reductions in benefits and tax credits; this is not surprising as the Coalition Government enacted reforms which reduced social security spending by over £20 billion across its term of office. Indirect tax increases, most importantly the increase in the standard rate of VAT from 17.5% to 20% in 2011, also impact negatively across the income distribution. Households in the bottom nine-tenths of the income distribution gain on average from the changes to direct taxation (most importantly the increase in the value of the tax-free personal allowance for income tax) but these gains are not large enough to offset the losses from the cuts to benefits and tax credits, and the increase in indirect taxes.

Analysis by gendered household type

This section shows distributional impacts of the tax, benefit and tax credit changes by household demographic type, dividing households into nine different types according to the number, gender and age of adults, and the presence or absence of children in the household, as follows:

1. working age single women with no children;[5]
2. working age single men with no children;
3. female single parents;
4. male single parents;[6]
5. working age couples with no children;
6. working age couples with children;
7. female single pensioners;
8. male single pensioners; and
9. couple pensioners.[7]

This classification enables analysis of the extent to which the distributional effect of tax and social security reforms differs across men and women, according to the presence or absence of children in the household, for pensioners compared to working age adults, and for single adult households compared to couples. Figures 7.3 and 7.4 show the distributional impact of tax and social security changes between 2010 and 2015 according to this classification, in cash terms and as a proportion of net income respectively.

Figure 7.3 shows that the cash impact of the tax and social security changes between 2010 and 2015 is greatest for the household types containing children – lone parents (both male and female) and couples with children. This pattern is largely driven by reductions in benefit and tax credit receipts for these groups, which is mainly a consequence of the fact that a substantial proportion of benefit

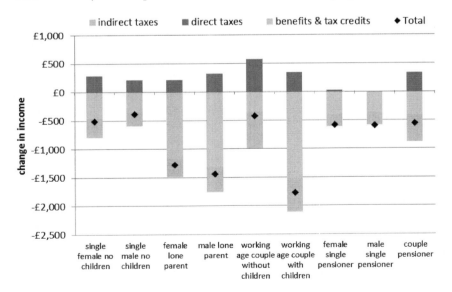

FIGURE 7.3 Distributional impact of tax, benefit and tax credit changes, 2010–2015, in cash terms by gendered household type

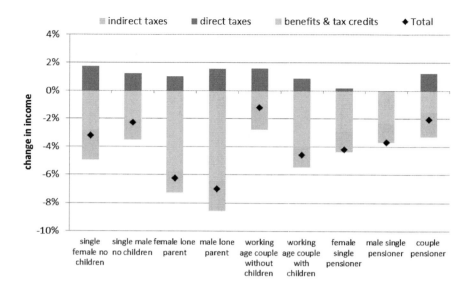

FIGURE 7.4 Distributional impact of tax, benefit and tax credit changes, 2010–2015, as a percentage of net income by gendered household type

and tax credit expenditure for working age families comprises transfer payments for children. Therefore, reductions in these transfer payments hit these family types hardest. Looking at Figure 7.4, as a percentage of income, it is lone parents who lose out the most of any group, partly because lone parent households have relatively low net incomes on average compared with couples with children and multiple benefit unit households. Couples with children and single pensioners experience the next largest falls in net incomes in percentage terms. The results also show that women in single-person childless households are being hit worse in percentage terms than men – this is the case both for working age single adults without children and for pensioners and is driven by the fact that net incomes are lower for women than for men in each of these groups. For lone parents, men lose slightly more in percentage terms than women.

Looking at the individual impact of each element of the tax reforms, working age couples without children benefit most on average in cash terms from the reductions in direct taxes. This is largely because the UK tax system is assessed mostly on an individual basis, and working age couples without children are more likely to have two adults in work than any other types of couple household (single adult households can only have a maximum of one adult in work by definition, and couples with children and pensioner couples are less likely to have two adults in work than working age couples without children). This means that working age couples without children are most likely to enjoy a double gain from the income tax reductions.[8] On average, single pensioners received almost no increase in net income from the direct tax changes because tax-free personal allowances for pensioners were reduced in generosity in real terms at the same time as the personal allowance for working age adults was reduced.[9] The increases in indirect taxes result in bigger losses for couple adult families than single adult families because these households have higher expenditure on goods and services subject to VAT. Lone parent households also have larger cash losses from indirect tax increases than single working age men and women without children, and single pensioners. As a percentage of net income, losses from indirect taxes are more even across the distribution of household types.

Individual-level analysis of gender impacts of tax and benefit reforms within families

In comparison to analysing distributional impacts by family unit within households, which is relatively straightforward, analysing impacts by individuals involves making some additional assumptions about how to allocate income that is jointly received by couples. The analysis in this chapter uses the FRS and assumes the following rules for the allocation of income within couples:

- Incomes from earnings, income from self-employment, investment income, private pension incomes and incomes from other non-state sources such as property income are allocated to individuals in the FRS data, net of direct taxes (income taxes and National Insurance contributions), which are levied on an individual rather than a joint basis for couples in the UK. This procedure is relatively straightforward as the source of each of these incomes is specified in the FRS data.
- Benefits and tax credits received by couples (with the exception of the State Pension) are allocated according to which adult records receipt of the benefit in the FRS data. If neither couple actually records receipt in the data (which happens in situations where a couple is assessed as eligible for a means-tested benefit or tax credit, but no actual receipt is recorded in the data) then the benefit or tax credit is split 50/50 between the couple. If both members of a couple report separate receipt of a benefit (which can happen with certain benefits such as Disability Living Allowance) then the amount of benefit is allocated to each person according to the actual amounts which they are recorded as receiving in the FRS data.
- If the FRS data specifically indicate that State Pension is being received on behalf of a couple then the pension amount is shared equally between the couple. On the other hand, if two adults in a couple are receiving separate amounts of State Pension in their own right then the pension is allocated separately to each partner as specified in the data.

Figures 7.5 and 7.6 present a selection of results from the individual analysis broken down by gender and by household income decile to show what the distribution of

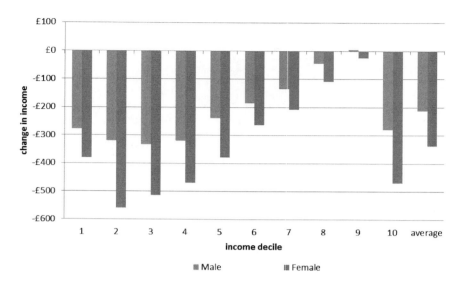

FIGURE 7.5 Distributional impact of changes to direct taxes and social security at the individual level in cash terms: men and women by household income decile

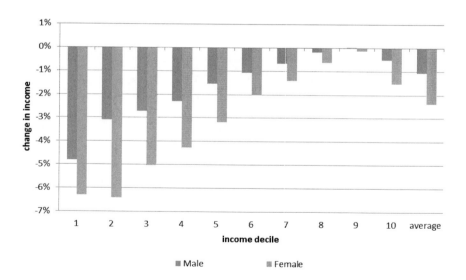

FIGURE 7.6 Distributional impact of changes to direct taxes and social security at the individual level as a percentage of net income: men and women by household income decile

changes in net income looks like using this methodology. These figures include both single adults and those in couples.

Figure 7.5 shows that, on average, women's losses from the tax, benefit and tax credit changes between 2010 and 2015 are larger than men's (women lose £338 per year on average compared with £213 for men). This is mainly to do with the fact that women receive a larger proportion of benefits and tax credits relating to children, and these comprise a large proportion of the reforms to social security between 2010 and 2015. The second, third and top deciles have the largest average losses for women relative to men. Because women also have lower gross earnings, and lower gross income from investments, than men on average, women's average losses in percentage terms are bigger relative to men than their average losses in cash terms relative to men. Figure 7.6 demonstrates this: as a proportion of net individual incomes, women's average losses are twice as large as men's.

The distributional impact of spending cuts

This section assesses the distributional effect of the spending cuts to public services such as health, education, social care, social housing and public transport which the Coalition Government implemented during the 2010–15 Parliament. These results are combined with estimates of the impact of tax, benefit and tax credit changes over the same period from the Landman Economics tax-benefit model to derive an overall estimate of the impact of fiscal measures over the 2010–15 Parliament.

The extent of the cuts

When assessing the size of the spending cuts over the 2010–15 Parliament it is important to have a benchmark for how large the cuts are. Relative to the Consumer Price Index measure of inflation, spending was around £41 billion lower in 2015–16 than in 2010–11 (just under 3% of GDP lower). If the Retail Price Index (the UK Government's preferred measure of inflation prior to 2010) is used instead, the reduction in spending was just under £61 billion (around 4% of GDP). Finally, compared to a situation where public spending remained constant as a share of Gross Domestic Product, the reduction in spending was over £76 billion (around 5% of GDP).

This chapter measures the size of the spending cuts over the 2010–15 Parliament using the RPI inflation measure, on the grounds that this was the default measure of indexation for taxes and most benefits prior to 2010 (when indexation switched to the CPI measure). Thus, it makes sense to measure the size of spending cuts using an equivalent benchmark to the one we use to measure tax and benefit changes.

How the cuts are modelled

The Landman Economics public spending model[10] combines data from two sources:

1. data from HM Treasury on the total extent of cuts to different public services such as health, education, social care, public housing and public transport;
2. data from UK household-level datasets on individual and family use of these public services.

These two sources of data are combined to give an estimate of the amount being spent on services delivered to households with specific attributes (e.g. number of adults in the household, age of adults in the household, number and age of children, housing tenure type, employment status, disability, net income level, etc.) This enables the impact of cuts to spending on different services on each type of household to be modelled.

For some, but not all, types of public service expenditure it would be possible to produce an individual-level breakdown of the impact of service cuts along similar lines to that of tax and social security impacts shown in Figures 7.5 and 7.6 above. In particular, data on health, social care and education service use is available at the individual level. However, for other areas such as public housing and public transport, information is available only at the household level and so cannot be assigned to individuals directly. (This is shown in the right-hand column of Table 7.A2 in the appendix.)

Services included in the model

The model only includes services that can be reasonably allocated to households in the FRS or other datasets based on variables pertaining to service use. The spending analysis here models the extent of spending cuts using data on changes in spending between 2010–11 and 2015–16 from HM Treasury's 'Public Expenditure Statistical Analyses (PESA)' report (2015b), which breaks down expenditure according to the internationally agreed COFOG (Classification Of Functions Of Government) specification.[11] Using this method, the model includes approximately 73% of total public expenditure on services.[12]

The model uses data from five different household datasets on service use – the FRS, Living Costs and Food Survey (LCF), General Lifestyle Survey (GLF), the British Household Panel Survey (BHPS) and the British Crime Survey (BCS). The FRS is the 'base' dataset and data from the other datasets on service use is matched into the FRS using a regression methodology. Table 7.A2 in the appendix explains how the service use variables in the five datasets used are matched to COFOG spending categories in the PESA data.

Table 7.1 shows the implied percentage reductions in spending for all of the modelled categories of spending except for cuts to benefits and tax credits (which

TABLE 7.1 Implied reductions in each category of spending accounting for population change

| | Reduction in spending (%) | |
Spending category	Raw total	Accounting for population change
Police	19.3%	22.3%
Transport: roads	20.9%	24.2%
Transport: buses	14.9%	16.2%
Transport: rail	17.6%	32.4%
Healthcare	3.4%	7.1%
Cultural spending	14.8%	18.1%
Early years	3.6%	12.1%
Education: primary	6.2%	13.1%
Education: secondary	12.4%	9.7%
Education: further and higher	13.6%	13.5%
Social care: old people	15.5%	19.0%
Social care: disabled people	1.0%	4.7%
Social care: families	5.4%	9.8%
Housing	28.2%	33.9%
TOTAL (allocatable)	9.8%	13.1%

are modelled separately using the Landman Economics tax-benefit model). In addition, the modelling takes into account changes in the size of population using each public service to produce a more accurate estimate of changes in spending *per service user* rather than just changes to aggregate spending totals. In most cases, the spending reduction is larger when the change in the population of service users is taken into account, because the size of the population increased between 2010 and 2015.[13] Table 7.1 shows that the largest percentage cuts are for social housing spending, transport (particularly rail subsidies) and police services, while the smallest cuts are for healthcare and secondary education. Overall, excluding social security cuts (which total £21 billion of discretionary reductions in spending), the model allocates around £34 billion of 'raw' spending cuts at 2015 prices. Adjustment for increases in the size of the population receiving these services implies total cuts of just over £45 billion.

The distributional impact of service cuts by income

Figure 7.7 shows the distributional impact of spending cuts (excluding social security measures) expressed in annual cash-equivalent terms, across the distribution of net income (by household income decile). The black line on the figure shows that the total impact of spending cuts is largest in cash terms for the fourth and fifth deciles – just below the middle of the income distribution. Cuts to healthcare and school-level education follow this pattern, being largest in the middle of the distribution. This is because households are more likely to use substantial amounts

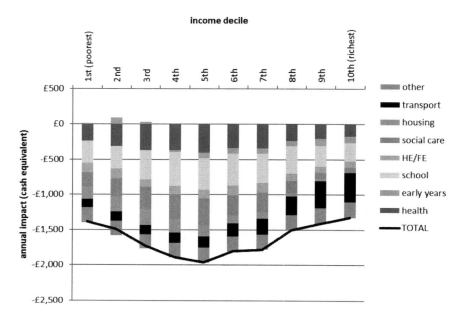

FIGURE 7.7 Distributional impacts of cuts to spending on public services (excluding social security) over the 2010–15 Parliament: annual cash equivalent by income decile

of healthcare if they contain pensioners, while only households with children, who are most likely to be located in the lower-to-middle reaches of the net income distribution, use school-level education. For transport, by contrast, the cuts are largest at the top end of the distribution (mainly because rail and road users tend to be particularly well off). Social care and social housing cuts have the largest cash impact in the lower-to-middle reaches of the income distribution; this is because both of these services are heavily means-tested. Local authorities only fully fund social care for individuals with assets of less than £14,250 per year, and the allocation of social housing is heavily skewed towards households with low incomes. Higher and further education cuts are fairly even across the distribution but slightly smaller at the top end. Changes in early years spending actually result in *increased* expenditure in the second and third deciles (due to the impact of the Early Intervention Grant (EIG) in particular), but cuts further up the distribution. Spending cuts in the 'other' category (including police and cultural spending) are fairly even in cash terms across the distribution. The overall cash-equivalent impact of cuts ranges from around £1,300 to £2,000 per household per year across the distribution, with an overall average of £1,630 across all households.

Figure 7.8 shows the same information on cuts by service category, but as a proportion of total household living standards (defined as household disposable income after taxes and social security payments, *plus* the value of in-kind public services).[14] As a proportion of total living standards, the spending cuts are regressive;

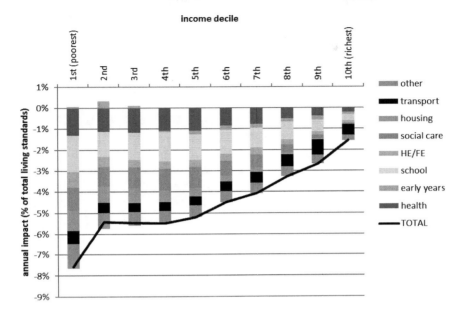

FIGURE 7.8 Distributional impacts of cuts to spending on public services (excluding social security) over the 2010–15 Parliament: as a percentage of net income plus value of services received, by income decile

the lowest income decile experiences an average reduction in living standards of around 7.5%, while the second, third and fourth deciles experience reductions of around 5.5%. Meanwhile, average losses for the top decile are only around 1.5% of living standards, and for the ninth decile only 2.5% of living standards. Spending cuts have a very regressive impact by income decile for most categories; this is because spending in these areas is much larger in relation to disposable income for poorer households than for richer households. The exceptions are early years spending (where the introduction of the EIG leads to an *increase* in spending on average for low-income households) and public transport (where spending is roughly constant as a share of income across the income distribution).

Impact by gendered household type

Figure 7.9 shows the cash-equivalent impacts by household demographic type, disaggregated by gender. Overall, the largest cash impacts are for lone parents, couples with children, and multiple family units (not shown). This result is mainly driven by school-level education, which obviously only affects households containing school-age children. The impacts of cuts to the health budget are largest for pensioners because they are on average more likely to make use of NHS services (such as hospital inpatient and outpatient services, GP visits, etc.) than any other group. Cuts to local authority-funded social care have the largest impact for

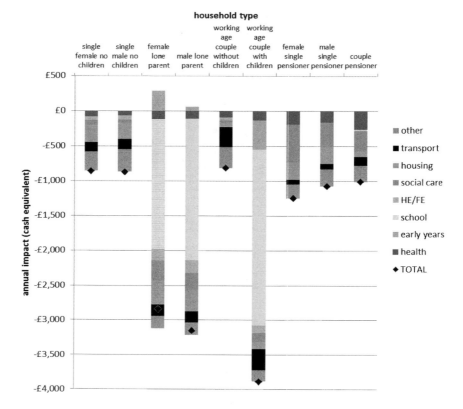

FIGURE 7.9 Distributional impacts of cuts to spending on public services (excluding social security) over the 2010–15 Parliament: annual cash equivalent, by gendered household type

pensioners (especially female single pensioners) as they are the most likely to need formal care services. Single pensioners are more likely to qualify for local authority-funded care services than couple pensioners, mainly because they are less likely to have informal carers (who may provide an alternative to formal care arrangements in some circumstances) because they live alone.

Housing cuts have the largest impact for lone parents as this group is the most likely demographic to be allocated social housing (because of relatively low incomes and acute need for housing). Transport cuts have a particularly large impact on couples (with and without children) as this group is more likely to contain rail commuters (who spend a large amount on fares on average compared with other modes of transport). Cuts to higher and further education (FE and HE) have a relatively large impact on lone parents (who are more likely to be in receipt of grant funding as mature students than other groups) and working age couples with children (who are relatively likely to have HE and FE students still living at home). The effect of early years spending changes is *positive* for lone parents – due to the

The UK under the coalition government   127

relatively low incomes on average of female lone parents in particular. This means that the EIG (which reallocated a proportion of early years funding to particularly disadvantaged children) has a positive impact, which outweighs the cuts to other parts of the early years budget. For couples with children the opposite is true: the impact of overall cuts to the early years budget outweighs any benefit from the EIG.

Figure 7.10 shows the impact of cuts by household type as a percentage of total living standards. The pattern here is different to the cash-equivalent impacts shown above; in percentage terms the cuts are most severe for lone parents, mainly because lone parents have lower average incomes than working age couples with children, which means that the denominator of total living standards is smaller for lone parents and the cuts correspondingly larger as a share of total living standards (around 8% for both male and female lone parents compared to around 7% for working age couples with children). The next worst affected groups are single pensioners, with female single pensioners losing an average of just under 6% due to

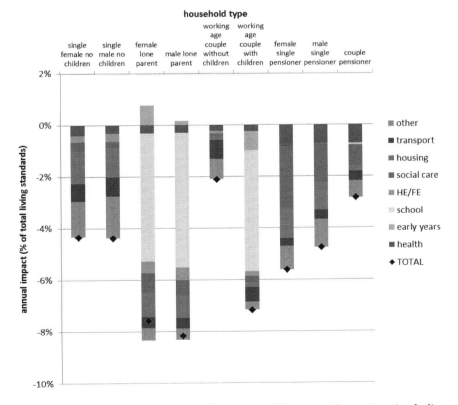

FIGURE 7.10   Distributional impacts of cuts to spending on public services (excluding social security) over the 2010–15 Parliament: as a percentage of net income plus value of services received, by gendered household type

the cuts while male single pensioners lost around 5% on average. This is an interesting finding which goes against the prevailing narrative that pensioners have been relatively insulated from the effects of austerity. Social care cuts and cuts to the health budget both have a large impact on pensioner living standards, with social housing cuts also having a substantial impact. Couple pensioners fare somewhat better with average losses of around 3%, mainly because their losses from social care and housing cuts are much smaller than for single pensioners. Single men and women without children lose out by around 4% of total living standards on average, with housing and 'other services' (police and cultural spending) the biggest contributors to the losses. Couples with no children are the least affected group, with average losses of only just over 2%, mainly as a result of cuts to transport spending and the 'other' category.

Combined impact of tax/benefit measures and cuts to other public services

It is instructive to combine the results on the impact of service cuts described earlier with the distributional analysis of the impact of tax, benefit and tax credit reforms outlined above. Figure 7.11 shows the overall distributional impact of the cuts to spending on public services analysed earlier in this chapter (the 'services' column) combined with the changes to taxes and transfer payments (the 'tax & transfers'

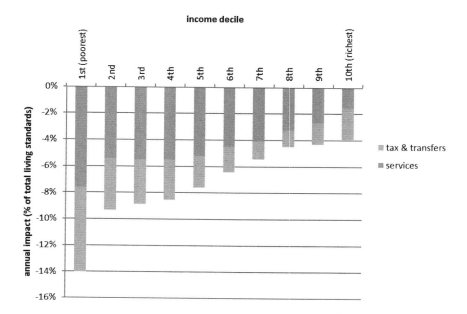

FIGURE 7.11 Combined impact of tax/benefit measures and cuts to other public services, by income decile

column), by household income decile, as a percentage of overall household living standards. The overall impact of all modelled fiscal measures is regressive. The average reduction in living standards as a result of all the modelled tax, transfer and public spending measures is 14% for the bottom decile and between 8% and 10% for the second, third and fourth decile. Meanwhile, for the top three deciles average losses in living standards are around 4%.

Figure 7.12 shows the overall impacts of public spending cuts and tax and transfer payment measures by gendered household type. The largest average negative impacts are for lone parents who lose between 11% and 12% of total living standards. The next biggest losers are working age couples with children, who lose just over 10% of total living standards on average. Cuts to public services make up over two-thirds of the total losses for these groups.

Single pensioners also lose out substantially in total, with average losses of over 8% (for women) and over 7% (for men). Given that around 90% of lone parents and almost three-quarters of single pensioners are women, these results show

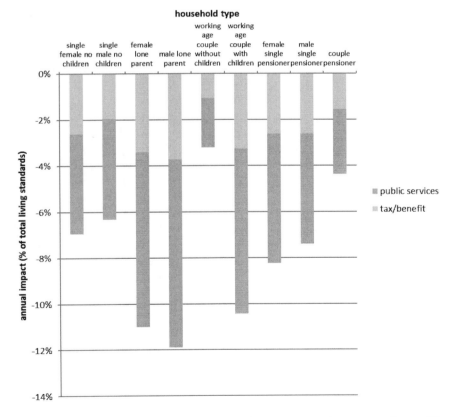

FIGURE 7.12 Combined impact of tax/benefit measures and cuts to other public services, by gendered household type

130 Howard Reed

substantial gender inequalities in the overall impact of austerity, with women losing out more than men. The smallest impacts are for couples without children (a reduction of around 3% in total living standards) and couple pensioners (a reduction of just over 4%).

Conclusions and lessons for policymakers

This chapter has shown that the austerity measures implemented by the UK Coalition Government have been regressive across most of the distribution, with lower-income households losing substantially more as a proportion of total living standards than middle- and higher-income households. Furthermore, the measures have had an unequal gender impact. The analysis of the individual-level impact of tax and welfare reforms by gender in Figure 7.6 shows that women's losses as a share of their income are around twice as large as men's. Furthermore, the cuts to spending on public services (whether considered alone or in conjunction with the tax and social security measures) bear particularly heavily on lone parents, single pensioners and couples with children.

There are several reasons why the austerity measures have had a particularly large impact on women compared to men. One is that lone parents rely particularly heavily on social security payments as a group, and so lose out substantially from cuts to benefits and tax credits – particularly Child Benefit, the Child Tax Credit and the Working Tax Credit, all of which were cut substantially. Secondly, just under three-quarters of single pensioners are women – and single pensioners lose out particularly badly from the cuts to public services, especially health, social care and public housing. Thirdly, and more generally, the Coalition Government's decision to rely mainly on spending cuts rather than tax rises to close the deficit introduced an intrinsic gender bias into its austerity programme. Working age men have a higher employment rate and a higher proportion of full-time employees in the labour force than working age women (because women are more likely than men not to be in paid employment, or to be working part-time rather than full-time, because of childcare responsibilities). This means that men are more likely to be affected by increases in income tax as a group than women. Conversely, women are more likely than men to suffer from reductions in benefits which are aimed at supporting children and low-income families (whether in or out of work).

Finally, the Coalition Government made substantial discretionary *cuts* to income tax – in particular the real-terms increase in the tax-free personal allowance, which cost about £20 billion per year by the end of the 2010–15 Parliament – at the same time as pursuing its stated policy of deficit reduction. This has meant that the government relied even more on spending cuts to reduce the deficit than it would have done had it not made these large-scale discretionary tax cuts.

Sadly, all of these patterns look set to continue under the Conservative Government, elected with a small majority in May 2015, with further substantial reductions to public spending. The experience of the UK, while depressing, is nonetheless helpful in a wider European context as it shows how researchers can

The UK under the coalition government **131**

use data at the individual and household level from survey datasets to model the distributional impact of tax, social security and spending changes by gender. The main priority for future research in the UK is to improve the modelling of the impact of changes to public service spending so that an almost complete picture of the impact of austerity at the individual level can be estimated.[15]

Notes

1 The final Budget of the Coalition Government in March 2015 forecast a budget deficit of around £60 billion for 2014–15, and that the deficit would not be eliminated until 2017–18 – three years later than originally planned. See HM Treasury Budget (2015a) for more details.

2 See Table 7.A1 in the Appendix for details of these plans.

3 Recent guides to the UK tax and benefit system, which explain the terminology used in this section, are provided by the Institute for Fiscal Studies: see Pope, Roantree and Grace (2015) for tax and Hood and Oakley (2014) for benefits.

4 Results for the distributional impact of Universal Credit if it had been fully implemented in 2015 are shown in Reed and Portes (2014: Figures 3.9 and 3.10 and Appendix E).

5 'Working age' here means below the State Pension Age (SPA). The SPA for men is currently 65 in the UK, while the SPA for women is gradually being raised from 60 to 65 between 2010 and 2018. An SPA of 62 for women was used for the modelling in this chapter.

6 It is important to note that male lone parents are a relatively small group. In the 2010–11 Family Resources Survey (which is used for the analysis on the distributional effects of tax-benefit reforms in this chapter), there are only 138 male lone parent households, compared to 1,662 female lone parent households. This means that the confidence intervals around distributional results for male lone parent households are markedly wider than for female lone parent households, and hence the results for male lone parents should be treated with caution.

7 A 'couple pensioner' is any couple where at least one of the adults is at SPA or above.

8 Although the Coalition Government introduced a transferable allowance for income tax for some married couples, which mostly goes to men in single-earner couples, the value of this transferable allowance is relatively small compared to the substantial real-terms increases in the value of the income tax personal allowance made during 2010–15, which means that it does not substantially affect the pattern of results shown here.

9 Couple pensioners see more benefit because this group includes couples where one adult is above the state pension age but the other adult is below it, and the younger adults in these couples *did* gain from the increase in the tax-free personal allowance (if they were in work and earning above the original value of the personal allowance in 2010).

10 For more detail on the methodology used in the Landman Economics public spending model, see Reed and Portes (2014, Chapter 7).

11 It is only since the publication of the most recent PESA statistics in July 2014 that a full breakdown of spending plans at the central government level has been available up to 2015–16. For *local* government, the spending breakdown is only available up to 2013–14 and so expenditure up to 2015–16 has had to be extrapolated using data on the overall local authority spending settlements for 2014–15 and 2015–16.

12 The main exclusions from the model are as follows: foreign affairs (e.g. diplomatic service, etc.); international aid spending; payments to the European Union and other international bodies; debt interest; defence spending; fire protection services; the judicial system and prisons; government support for research and development spending; environmental protection; street lighting and other community amenities; broadcasting and publishing services.

13 An exception is state secondary schools, where statistics from the Department for Education show that overall pupil numbers fell between 2010 and 2014 (the most recent available data). See Department for Education (2015) for more detail.

14 Total household living standards is used as the denominator here rather than just household disposable income (as in Figure 7.2) because it makes it easier to interpret the cuts as leading to a percentage reduction in total living standards. In the lowest income decile in particular, the value of household services received is around two-and-a-half times greater than net income. If net income is used alone as the denominator, this can in extreme cases lead to losses of close to, or more than, 100% of net income, which makes the figures hard to interpret.

15 It is nearly impossible to do a fully complete analysis of the distributional impact of austerity at the individual level in the UK because some of the public service usage data is only available at the household level. However, improvements can be made in some cases by using additional datasets. For example, it should be possible to introduce an individual-level analysis of transport spending using data from the National Travel Survey rather than the Living Costs and Food Survey.

References

Department for Education. 2015. "Schools, Pupils and Their Characteristics: January 2015." Government of the United Kingdom.

HM Treasury. 2015a. "Summer Budget 2015." Government of the United Kingdom.

HM Treasury. 2015b. "Public Expenditure Statistical Analyses." Government of the United Kingdom.

Hood, T. and L. Oakley. 2014. "A Survey of the GB Benefit System." IFS Briefing Note BN13. London: Institute for Fiscal Studies.

Horton, T. and Reed, H. 2010. "The Distributional Impact of the 2010 Spending Review." *Radical Statistics*, 103: 13–24.

Pope, T., B. Roantree and C. Grace. 2015. "A Survey of the UK Tax System." IFS Briefing Note BN09. London: Institute for Fiscal Studies.

Reed, H. and J. Portes. 2014. "Cumulative Impact Assessment: A Research Report by Landman Economics and the National Institute of Economic and Social Research for the Equality and Human Rights Commission." EHRC Research Report 94. Manchester: Equality and Human Rights Commission.

Appendix

TABLE 7.A1 Tax and social security reforms included in the analysis

Tax	Reforms
Income tax	• above-inflation increases in income tax personal allowance; • transferable income tax allowance for married couples; • changes to the income tax higher-rate threshold; and • reduction in 50% additional rate of income tax to 45%.
National Insurance Contributions	• changes to Primary Threshold and Secondary Threshold for Class 1 National Insurance Contributions, and the Lower Profits Limit for Class 4 National Insurance Contributions; and • increases in the rates of employee, employer and self-employed National Insurance Contributions.
Local taxes	• Freeze in nominal rates of Council Tax.
Indirect taxes	• increase in standard rate of VAT from 17.5% to 20%; • changes to excise duties (motor fuels, alcoholic drinks and tobacco products); and • changes to Insurance Premium Tax.
Benefits and tax credits indexation	• Switch from RPI to CPI indexation for most benefits and tax credits.
Tax credits	• increased taper rates; • removal of baby and 50-plus elements; • abolish high income threshold; • 1% nominal uprating for 2013, 2014 and 2015; • increase in working hours' requirement for couples with children to 24 hours; and • reduced percentage of childcare costs met by Working Tax Credit from 80% to 70%.
Pensions	• Triple-lock indexation (by highest of CPI, average earnings or 2.5%).
Other benefits	• Child Benefit frozen in nominal terms for three years from 2011–12; • 1% nominal uprating of most working-age benefits for 2013, 2014 and 2015; • benefit cap (maximum limit on payment of benefits to out-of-work working age households); • 10% reduction in expenditure on Council Tax benefit; and • Child Benefit removed from high-income households.

TABLE A7.2 Spending categories in the Landman Economics public spending model

COFOG category	Service use provision variables used	Individual or household data
3.1: Police	Police services (BCS)	household
4.5: Transport	Spending on petrol/diesel (LCF) Spending on bus fares (LCF) Spending on train fares (LCF)	household
6.1: Social housing development	Social housing tenancy (FRS)	household
7: Health	Hospital inpatient stays (GLF) Hospital outpatient stays (GLF) GP visits (GLF)	individual
8.2: Cultural spending	Museum and gallery attendance (GLF)	individual
9.1: Early years education	Number of children in state-funded nursery education and/or childcare (FRS)	individual
9.1–9.2: School-level education	Number and age of children in state primary and secondary schools (FRS)	individual
9.3–9.4: Further and higher education	Children/adults in further education (FRS) Children/adults in higher education (FRS)	individual
10: Social protection (benefits and tax credits)	Modelled by Landman Economics tax/benefit model (FRS)	individual
10: Social protection (social care spending)	Care received by old people from sources other than household members, means-tested as appropriate (FRS) Care received by disabled people from sources other than household members, means-tested as appropriate (FRS) Family social services (social workers, etc) (BHPS)	individual

PART III

Alternative policies, the role of social infrastructure and the care economy

8

MAKING THE CASE FOR A GENDER-AWARE, INVESTMENT-LED RECOVERY FOR EUROPE

Hannah Bargawi and Giovanni Cozzi

Introduction

Job creation for both women and men should be a high priority for European policy-makers given the unsustainable levels of unemployment and labour force inactivity since the outbreak of the global financial crisis in 2008. However, after earlier piecemeal attempts at a fiscal stimulus – which could have increased aggregate demand, growth and created jobs if continued and boosted – policy responses across Europe have almost exclusively focused on fiscal restraint (austerity) in an attempt to reduce fiscal deficits and government debt. This focus has led European governments to implement harsh austerity policies with negative repercussions on employment (both in the public and private sector), welfare, public and private investment and ultimately growth (IMF 2014). Further, it is becoming increasingly evident that such policies are shifting the burden of debt and budget deficit adjustment onto women (see e.g. Ch.4 by Vertova, Ch.5 by Barry and Ch.6 by Gago in this volume). For example, cutbacks to state-provided care services have led women to return to their traditional gender roles, stepping out of formal employment to take over caring responsibilities no longer funded by the state; precariousness of lone mothers is increasing due to cuts in state-funded services; and cuts in government expenditure have led to a further reduction in female-dominated public sector jobs and pay, particularly in the South Eurozone (i.e. Italy, Spain, Portugal and Greece).

This chapter argues that low investment in both social and physical infrastructure alongside the implementation of austerity policies are at the root of European stagnation, the high levels of unemployment and the worsening of conditions for women in the labour market. As such, an equitable and sustainable recovery for both women and men must be investment-led. Investment, both in social and physical infrastructure, is necessary to cure low aggregate demand and unemployment in the short term. Further, in the long term this type of investment can increase potential output, bring about innovation, improve gender relations, reduce gender inequality in the labour market and increase well-being for both women and men.

Social infrastructure is separated here from physical infrastructure because of the potentially divergent gendered employment outcomes. Social infrastructure includes investment – mainly public – in nurseries, hospitals, prisons, housing and more generally on services providing care, health, education and training. In contrast, physical infrastructure includes transport, environment, energy, telecommunication and defence. There are obvious overlaps between social and physical infrastructure and this chapter addresses the importance of both types of investment in order to achieve truly equitable outcomes.

European institutions are gradually recognising the need to implement EU-wide measures to boost investment and thus return to an era of robust growth and to generate employment. However, the measures implemented to date – and in particular the Growth Compact and EU Commission President Juncker's Investment Plan for Europe – are far from sufficient to spearhead an employment-led economic recovery. Further, their almost exclusive focus on physical infrastructure at the expense of social infrastructure implies that the majority of jobs created by new projects will predominantly go to men rather than to both women and men.

In light of the above, this chapter proposes a two-pronged approach for a gender-aware and sustainable economic recovery. First, it argues for a significant rollback of austerity policies and increases in government expenditure so that public investment, particularly directed towards social infrastructure, can be significantly raised, crowding-in further private investment. Secondly, it argues for both government expenditure and private investment to be targeted towards the expansion of employment for men and women, but with greater weight placed on the latter. In particular, government expenditure should be "gendered"; specifically, increases in government expenditure should be redirected to those areas of investment that can generate jobs for women and improve their well-being. In doing so, the accounting distinction between *current* government consumption spending and longer-term *capital* spending as currently drawn becomes a hindrance. As Himmelweit (2016) has explained, such accounting distinctions need to be redefined in order to appreciate the long-term value of social investments in, for example, care services that at present are counted as expenditure rather than investment.

The chapter starts by sketching out the legacy of the global financial crisis and briefly outlining the current economic situation in Europe. It then traces the evolution of European policies in response to the crisis and recession in order to establish the role of these policies in creating the current economic status quo. The next section then summarises the gendered outcomes of the current policy trajectory. This is followed by an alternative proposal for a gendered, investment-led recovery for Europe, which combines higher levels of government spending that is marshalled towards the generation of more jobs for women, with increases in government revenue and private investment. It is assumed that private investment increases as a result of a stronger role of the European Investment Bank (EIB), the EU Budget and national governments in using public resources to crowd-in private investment. The Cambridge Alphametrics Macroeconomic (CAM) model is then utilised to assess the effectiveness of this alternative, gender-aware, investment scenario vis-à-vis a "business-as-usual" scenario that combines austerity policies with the Investment Plan for Europe (or the Juncker Plan). The final section concludes and provides policy recommendations.

The legacy of crisis and recession in Europe: underinvestment, stagnant growth and unemployment

Europe is suffering from negative or low growth and high unemployment. This is most evident in South Eurozone countries, but is also true for other European nations such as Germany and the United Kingdom. Italy and Spain, for example, saw GDP fall by more than 5% between 2008 and 2014, Portugal by 6% and Greece by over 25%; in Germany and the United Kingdom, output growth averaged little more than 1% per year during the same period (Griffith-Jones and Cozzi 2016).

With the exception of Germany, low growth across Europe over the period since the global economic crisis has been accompanied by increasing levels of unemployment for both women and men. In the South Eurozone, total unemployment as a percentage of the labour force shot up from 7.5% in 2007 to 19.8% in 2014, female adult unemployment increased from 8.1% to 19.1% and male unemployment from 4.9% to 16.1%. However, it was youth unemployment that really spiralled out of control. Female youth unemployment doubled from 22% in 2007 to 44% in 2014 and male youth unemployment nearly tripled from 16% to 40%.[1]

Similar trends, although in more moderate terms, have also been experienced in other areas of the Eurozone. For example, between 2007 and 2014, in France the male adult unemployment rate increased from 6% to 8% and female adult unemployment rose from 7% to almost 9%; female youth unemployment rose from 20% to 22% and male youth unemployment from 18% to 20%. Over the same period, in the United Kingdom total unemployment increased from 5% to 6.3%, male adult unemployment increased from 3.6% to 4.7% and female adult unemployment from 3.5% to 4.4%; female youth unemployment increased from 11% to 15% and male youth unemployment from 12% to 18%.

The gendered outcomes in relation to employment and unemployment for European countries are difficult to fully appreciate when focusing only on the headline data provided above. Countries have followed different trends and gendered outcomes have changed since the outbreak of the crisis. The data can mask shifts in work intensity and underemployment (e.g. increases in part-time over full-time employment or changes to working hours), shifts in those classified as "inactive" and changes to the status or employment category (e.g. increases in recorded self-employment). Clearly, the recession has also had major impacts on men and women outside the labour market, as detailed in a number of other studies (see Karamessini and Rubery 2013). The gendered nature of austerity policies in particular is discussed in more detail below.

This chapter argues that low investment is at the root of the low growth and high levels of unemployment across Europe, and that sustainable economic recovery can only be achieved by significantly increasing investment in both social and physical infrastructure. Investment is necessary to stimulate aggregate demand and reduce unemployment in the short term, but also to reduce gender inequalities in the labour market and increase potential output in the long run.

Gross fixed capital formation, which represents physical investment, for the total economy (including government, business and household), has significantly declined across Europe since the early 2000s. In South Eurozone countries such as Italy such physical investment declined from 20% of GDP in 2000 to 16% in 2014. Over the same period, it fell from 26% of GDP to 19% in Spain, from 23% to 20% in Germany and from 19% to 16% in the United Kingdom. Ultimately, this decline in physical investment has dragged down growth and employment and slowed down economic recovery in Europe (Griffith-Jones and Cozzi 2016).

Tracing European policy responses to the crisis and its aftermath

This section reviews the response of EU and national policy-makers to the global financial crisis and recession, highlighting the rapid and near-universal adoption of austerity policies in Europe. In some cases (e.g. in the UK) such a policy programme was adopted by choice, whereas in others (e.g. in Greece, Italy and Spain) the austerity programme was introduced via the rescue packages negotiated with the EU. Since 2008, the policy trajectory has remained largely unchanged. The rhetoric adopted by EU policy-makers was adjusted in 2012 to suggest a renewed focus on investment. As shown below, whether this adjustment has been large enough to tackle the economic and social challenges confronting Europe remains questionable.

To counter the disappointing trends in investment, growth and unemployment discussed above, powerful action is needed. However, policy responses across Europe, following early, temporary and piecemeal attempts at fiscal stimulus, have mainly focused on fiscal containment and debt reduction rather than promoting investment, growth and job creation (Bettio et al. 2013: 120). If European institutions partly succeeded in curbing financial turmoil, they did not take sufficient action to stimulate the real economy and bring Europe on to a more sustainable and equitable developmental trajectory.

In the immediate aftermath of the global financial crisis of 2008, European governments were confronted with lower government revenues and higher spending as a result of large banking bailouts. The result of these developments was an expected rise in debt-to-GDP ratios and increased fiscal deficits in many

European countries, and in particular across the South Eurozone. The response of EU governments was to implement austerity rather than expansionary fiscal policies combined with strong investment initiatives.

The rationale for this European policy choice was largely based on political motivations and unsound economic arguments (Blyth 2013; Wren-Lewis 2015). One of the economic justifications for austerity policies was the orthodox view put forward by Giavazzi and Pagano (1990) and Alesina and Ardanga (1998), who argued that in times of economic crisis reductions in government spending accompanied by modest tax cuts have a positive impact on investors' confidence and that reduced public investment enables private investment. This strategy would allow crisis-hit countries to reduce deficits and government debt, while higher levels of private investment would increase growth and employment.

However, today, with modest private investment and interest rates at a record low, this argument is particularly weak. With significant underutilised resources in the European economy there is no constraint on the availability of physical or human capital, which would squeeze private investment; further, interest rates are likely to remain at historically low levels (Griffith-Jones and Cozzi 2016). In contrast, public investment in both physical and social infrastructure is much more likely to enable and stimulate private investment. With regards to public investment in physical infrastructure, Stiglitz (2015) has argued that investment in sectors such as energy, transport and telecommunication creates demand in the short term for a range of new goods and services, and in the medium term stimulates growth through an expanded stock of physical capital and higher efficiency. From a gender perspective, the need for public investment to crowd-in private investment is further strengthened. As argued by the ILO (2014), there is an urgent need to integrate social protection, employment and taxation policies in order to foster inclusive growth in the short term and to build human capital and human capacity in the long term. Further, a simultaneous investment in social infrastructure would also generate significant returns in the future as it allows individuals to acquire better economic and social skills as well as higher levels of economic and social well-being (Women's Budget Group 2015).

European institutions have also begun to recognise that European countries need higher levels of investment in order to stimulate growth and create jobs. To this end, European policy-makers argued that fiscal consolidation (austerity) should go hand-in-hand with growth-enhancing policies (Rasmussen and Schulz 2010; Buti and Padoan 2012). At economic policy level this translated into two main initiatives: the Compact for Growth and Jobs (June 2012); and European Commission President Jean-Claude Juncker's Investment Plan for Europe (November 2014).

In June 2012 the European Council approved the "Growth Compact", a document intended to move the focus beyond austerity policies and towards investment. The Growth Compact emphasised the need for further reforms in various fields to deepen the Single Market. Further, in the hope of increasing investment by around €120 billion via leverage, it required member states to provide a total of €10 billion of additional capital to the European Investment Bank. In addition to this, the Compact proposed a reallocation of the EU budget, shifting funds towards programmes aimed at fighting stagnation and unemployment (Griffith-Jones and Cozzi 2016). However, the Growth Compact did not lead to significant increases in economic growth and employment across Europe. One of the reasons for the modest impact of this programme was that investment was not scaled up sufficiently, and it was accompanied by further fiscal consolidation measures at the national level, which more than offset the positive effects the Growth Compact could have had on growth.

By the end of 2014 it was clear that the Growth Compact had not delivered the desired boost to the European economy. European Commission President Juncker therefore proposed the mobilisation of up to €315 billion in additional public and private investment over the following three years. President Juncker argued that additional investment was needed in infrastructure, notably in broadband, renewable energy, energy efficiency, transport, education, and research and development. This proposed "Investment Plan for Europe" further called for a significant amount of investment to be channelled towards projects that could counter youth unemployment.

However, the Plan presented some serious limitations. First, almost nothing was mentioned about boosting investment in social infrastructure, which is essential to improve female labour force participation rates and the well-being of both women and men in the long term. The emphasis of the Juncker Plan has been on investment in physical infrastructure and therefore investment in economic sectors that mainly employ men.[2]

Besides some references to increasing investment in education and training, social infrastructure investment was not included in the Plan. This is because this type of investment is often not seen as strategic capital investment but rather as current spending which governments should not borrow additional money to finance. However, it is argued here that social infrastructure should be included in long-term strategic public investment, as it is an indispensable component of well-being, sustainable economic growth and job creation for women and men (see Ch.2 by Ilkkaracan in this volume).

Public investment in social and physical infrastructure stimulates and complements, rather than competes with, private investment. A well-designed European public-investment strategy would therefore have the potential to crowd-in private investment and increase aggregate demand, with long-term positive effects on growth and employment for women and men. Public investment in social infrastructure is particularly important due to the impact that austerity policies are having on women both within and outside the European labour market.

Secondly, it is questionable that the size of the Juncker Plan is sufficient for stimulating the European economy – €315 billion over three years represents an annual investment boost of approximately 0.75% of EU GDP, which is far too little for what is needed to reignite sustainable growth and create jobs. By comparison, the US Government's 2009–10 stimulus package amounted to around 2.8% of GDP per annum over two years; Griffith-Jones and Cozzi (2016) argue that a stimulus of an order of magnitude closer to this is needed today in Europe. As such, the Juncker Plan is not of sufficient size to provide a significant and sustainable stimulus to the European economy.

The overall picture that emerges is of national governments and European policy-makers having unequivocally adopted austerity policies in response to the global financial crisis and not sufficiently focusing on the need to boost public investment in both social and physical infrastructure across Europe. The next section shows how such a policy stance is hindering progress towards gender equality in the labour market. In particular, it discusses how attempts at promoting investment since 2012 have been directed almost exclusively towards physical infrastructure at the expenses of social infrastructure, thereby exacerbating gender divisions, while being woefully inadequate in the amount of investment actually raised.

A gender-aware investment proposal for Europe

A significant discussion of alternative policy proposals for economic recovery has recently emerged from a number of different arenas. These proposals are based on the recognition that austerity policies are detrimental for Europe and that jobs and growth are created only with the adoption of an expansionary macroeconomic framework and a significant boost to both public and private investment (see e.g. Bagaria et al. 2012; Dauderstaedt and Hillebrandt 2013; Griffith-Jones et al. 2012; Griffith-Jones and Kollatz-Ahnen 2013; McKinley et al. 2013; Szczurek 2014; Griffith-Jones and Cozzi 2016). A particularly illuminating aspect of this research is the demonstration that sustainable long-term economic recovery in Europe can only be achieved by simultaneously increasing private investment and reducing, or even rolling back, austerity policies.

However, currently missing from the above studies is a discussion of the potential gender impacts of different policy scenarios. These studies have focused predominantly on the need to increase investment in physical infrastructure and innovation as a means to create jobs and achieve technological transformation. As such they have not sufficiently explored the need to also invest in social infrastructure (i.e. care services, health and education sectors) in order to further enhance growth and employment and reduce gender inequality within the labour market, as well as to increase the well-being of women and men.

A "gender-aware" alternative to austerity is particularly important due to the impact existing policies are having on women across Europe. It has become increasingly evident that austerity policies are significantly shifting the burden of debt and budget deficit adjustment on to women (Seguino 2010; Gurmai 2013; Karamessini and Rubery 2013; UNISON 2014; see also Ch.4 by Vertova, Ch.6 by Gago and Ch.7 by Reed in this volume).

Initially, the global financial crisis led to a decline in domestic and global demand in male-dominated manufacturing, construction, and financial sectors. However, as crisis turned to recession across Europe, secondary impacts via private sector demand have been less gender-specific, affecting a range of industries and leading to job cuts, wage freezes and increased job insecurity for both men and women (Seguino 2010; Karamessini and Rubery 2013). In a study focusing on the UK, Rubery and Rafferty (2013) concluded that gendered labour market segregation can go a long way to explaining why men and women have been affected differently in this recession. A distinction that can be drawn between this and previous recessions is that women are resisting taking on the role of a flexible and contingent labour force during this recession. Rather than leaving the labour market entirely they are reporting themselves to be unemployed or are involuntarily moving to part-time employment.

Cuts in government expenditure have led to a further reduction in female-dominated public sector jobs and pay. Even early indications from a study conducted in 2010–11 in four countries in Europe indicated that public sector job cuts have been a widespread feature of austerity policies, with women disproportionately affected (European Federation of Public Service Unions 2011). Recruitment freezes or job cuts have also resulted in increased working intensity (i.e. longer hours, fewer holidays and less family-friendly shift patterns) for those remaining in employment. Women have been disproportionately affected by such changes (see Ch.4 by Vertova, Ch.5 by Barry and Ch.6 by Gago in this volume).

Beyond these *direct* labour market impacts, there are a number of ways in which women have been *indirectly* impacted by austerity policies. Increases in the retirement age, the removal or tightening of criteria relating to certain benefits (e.g. housing benefit) and the rise in out-of-pocket health spending are all additional examples of ways in which expenditure cuts are hitting households, and women in particular, outside of the labour market. For example, current pension reforms in Greece illustrate how women can be penalised as a result of having had shorter and irregular work histories (Karamessini 2013). Several chapters in this volume have also outlined the various dimensions in which austerity policies have had pernicious and differential impacts on men and women (see Ch.4 by Vertova, Ch.5 by Barry, Ch.6 by Gago and Ch.7 by Reed in this volume).

This chapter presents a specific proposal to boost investment across Europe while concurrently addressing gender inequalities in the labour market. Using the CAM model (see Appendix I), it demonstrates that such an approach, when compared with continued fiscal consolidation combined with a mild investment boost, can not only lead to higher levels of growth and employment, but also has positive impacts on gender equality in the labour market while not compromising fiscal sustainability.

In order to achieve a gender-equitable and sustainable economic recovery, this chapter proposes a major boost in investment in both physical and social infrastructure in the European economy and a significant reduction in the pace of fiscal consolidation. With regards to the increase in investment, the Juncker Plan should at least double in size to reach a total investment of €630 billion by 2017 across Europe. This would represent a boost in the EU in the order of 1.5% of

GDP per annum. A second round of investment by the end of 2020 of a similar magnitude is also proposed. With reference to the financing of such an investment plan, several proposals have been put forward. This chapter is based on the work of Griffith-Jones and Cozzi (2016), who have argued for various measures to boost private investment, including a boost to the European Investment Bank, the European Fund for Investment and the creation of a Risk Mitigation Fund.

In addition to this significant boost to private investment, expansionary fiscal policies across Europe are also needed in order to halt the fall in public investment. As discussed above, public investment is crucial to crowd-in private investment and to support and develop social and physical infrastructure. As such, fiscal policies should be seen as a tool for increasing aggregate demand, and thus to stimulate growth and increase employment. European governments should thus increase government expenditure in areas such as research and development, innovation, skills upgrading, healthcare, education, childcare services, long-term care services, social security and housing. These are essential long-term investments that have the potential to create more jobs, increase gender equity in the labour market and lead to more sustainable growth and greater well-being.

In addition, increases in government expenditures should be marshalled to target a disproportionate increase in female employment vis-à-vis male employment so that the ratio of female employment to male employment significantly increases. In other words, government expenditure should be "gendered". This is particularly important given the low levels of female employment in Europe, and especially in the South Eurozone, where female employment as percentage of female working-age population stood at 48% in 2014 as compared to 66% for men (UN data via CAM model databank). To this end, redirecting government expenditure towards greater social investment and particularly to the female-dominated public services providing health, education and training would increase female employment.

However, in order to increase female participation in other sectors of the economy and redress gendered occupational segregation it is also important that European governments provide incentives and support for private companies to provide training and skills upgrading for women and offer family-friendly working practices and support for childcare.[3]

The European Union also has a fundamental role to play in supporting investment in social infrastructure. The European Social Fund (ESF) is one of the main tools at European level to support skills development, improve education, encourage the creation of new job opportunities, and invest in better public services. However, the total annual contribution to the ESF only amounted to €10 billion in 2014, which corresponded to 0.07% of EU GDP. The European Union should significantly scale up its contribution to this fund in order to make it an effective pan-European instrument that could complement national government actions to increase female labour market participation rates and create high-quality jobs.

To further mitigate the pressure on fiscal balances there needs to be an increase in the level of government revenues across Europe. This requires more progressive tax systems to be introduced in European countries involving higher rates of direct taxation for top earners and the introduction of taxes on assets and wealth. Such progressive tax policies have the added benefit of addressing gender inequities (Women's Budget Group 2012).

The next section assesses the impact of this proposal on growth, employment and investment, as well as on debt-to-GDP ratios and fiscal deficits (as a percentage of GDP). The results are presented at the aggregate level for the North Eurozone (which comprises Germany, the Netherlands, Finland, Austria and Belgium) and for the South Eurozone (which comprises Spain, Portugal, Italy and Greece), and the United Kingdom.

Projecting the impact of a gender-aware investment proposal for Europe

Using the Cambridge Alphametrics Macroeconomic (CAM) model, two alternative scenarios for Europe for the period to 2020 were examined. The first scenario – "business-as-usual" – models the impact of the €315 billion Juncker Investment Plan for Europe. In addition, it assumes that austerity policies in Europe would be maintained in an attempt to reduce national debt-to-GDP ratios to around 60% and budget deficits below 3% of GDP, as prescribed by the Growth and Stability Pact. In other words, governments would continue to cut their expenditures to reduce government debt and deficits. This translates into a negative effect on public investment, which would continue to fall.

In addition, in the business-as-usual scenario, in order to reduce government deficits we assume that government revenue either increases marginally or remains at 2014 levels throughout the period under investigation. For the United Kingdom, in line with the Spending Review and Autumn Statement 2015, we assume that government revenue as a percentage of GDP increases from 17.3% in 2014 to 18% in 2020. For the North Eurozone government revenue remains at 21% of GDP throughout the period and for the South Eurozone it remains at 16% of GDP over the period 2014 to 2020.

The business-as-usual scenario was then contrasted with a gender-aware investment-led scenario for Europe. In this alternative gender-aware scenario investment is a key strategy to increase employment and economic growth. Based on the proposals set out above, it assumes additional resources for investment compared to the business-as-usual scenario of approximately €315 billion above the Juncker Plan in nominal terms by 2017. It also assumes an additional increase in investment of €630 billion for the three years 2018–20. This enables private investment in the European Union to increase significantly, reaching 22% of GDP across Europe by 2020. Table 8.1 shows the assumed increases in private investment under the two scenarios.

The gender-aware investment scenario also assumes increases in government expenditure across Europe and that government expenditure would be marshalled to target increases in employment. The target is based on the ratio of the number

TABLE 8.1 Projected private investment as % of GDP

	Scenario	Actual		Projections	
		2007	2014	2017	2020
North Eurozone	Business as usual	20.1	15.5	18.7	19.0
	Gender-aware investment			20.2	22.0
South Eurozone	Business as usual	21.5	18.3	18.7	19.7
	Gender-aware investment			19.8	22.0
United Kingdom	Business as usual	16.1	16.5	18.8	19.0
	Gender-aware investment			21.2	22.0

Source: Author's calculations via CAM model.

of people employed to the number of people of working age. The size of the stimulus was calibrated in order to achieve a desirable, but feasible, level of this ratio for each European bloc. In the case of the North Eurozone and the United Kingdom the overall employment target is 72% by 2020 and in the South Eurozone the target is 60%. These targets represent a considerable increase over 2014 levels, particularly for the South Eurozone. In 2014 employment as percentage of working population stood at 70% in the United Kingdom, at 68% in the North Eurozone and at 55% in the South Eurozone.

In addition, it was assumed that government expenditure would be gendered – or, in other words, that government expenditure would be redirected towards those investment areas that can create jobs for women and thus improve the ratio of female employment to male employment. However, the increase in female employment envisaged is still relatively modest in scope, and would not substantially change the basic structure of employment in Europe. Table 8.2 show the impact of these assumptions on the ratio of female employment to male employment.

In order to contain future government deficits, a boost in government revenue in conjunction with projected increases in expenditure was also assumed. So, for the South Eurozone and the UK, it was assumed that government revenue as a

TABLE 8.2 Female employment as % of male employment

	Scenario	Historical		Projections
		2007	2014	2020
North Eurozone	Business as usual	84.3	86.7	87.2
	Gender-aware investment			88.1
South Eurozone	Business as usual	70.6	72.2	69.8
	Gender-aware investment			74.1
United Kingdom	Business as usual	84.9	85.6	86.0
	Gender-aware investment			86.7

Source: Author's calculations via CAM model.

ratio to GDP would rise to 20.5% by 2020. In the UK government revenue as a percentage of GDP in 2014 stood at 18.3% and in the South Eurozone at 16.2%. The target for the North Eurozone in this scenario was 22% (increased from 21% in 2014). These increases, particularly for the South Eurozone and the United Kingdom, represent substantial increases over 2014 levels, but are all below historical peaks.

Table 8.3 shows the projected average GDP growth rate for the two scenarios under investigation. For the period 2015–20, under the business-as-usual scenario, the increase in investment resulting from the Juncker Plan leads to a small increase in the average GDP growth rate. However, with the exception of the North Eurozone, projected growth rates under the business-as-usual scenario remain much lower than for the period 2000–08. In the South Eurozone, average GDP growth falls to 0.7% for the period 2018–20.

This is in sharp contrast with the gendered scenario where GDP growth averages 2.9% for the period 2018–20. A similar analysis can be done for the United Kingdom, where GDP growth stagnates in 2018–20 under the business-as-usual scenario, whereas under the gender-aware investment scenario GDP growth is well above 2%. Also, the North Eurozone achieves higher levels of GDP growth under the gender-aware investment scenario.

So the combination of a €315 billion Investment Plan with a reduction in both government expenditure and revenue – i.e. the business-as-usual case – will not allow Europe to return to pre-crisis levels of economic growth. On the other hand, under the gender-aware investment scenario, a larger investment boost combined with an increase in government spending that is targeted to boost female employment, funded by higher government revenue, would lead to much higher growth rates across Europe.

These projections also reveal important gains in terms of the number of people in employment across Europe. Table 8.4 shows the projections for female and male employment (in millions) by 2020. In the North Eurozone, under the business-as-usual scenario, the number of people employed marginally increases by 2020, and in the United Kingdom remains virtually unchanged. In the South Eurozone,

TABLE 8.3 Projected average GDP growth (%)

	Scenario	Actual		Projections	
		2000–08	2009–14	2015–17	2018–20
North Eurozone	Business as usual	1.9	0.4	1.5	1.8
	Gender-aware investment			2.8	3.2
South Eurozone	Business as usual	2.3	−1.3	1.2	0.7
	Gender-aware investment			3.7	2.9
United Kingdom	Business as usual	2.7	0.7	1.8	0.3
	Gender-aware investment			2.9	2.2

Source: Author's calculations via CAM model.

TABLE 8.4 Projected total employment (millions)

	Scenario	2007			2014			2020 Projections		
		F	M	T	F	M	T	F	M	T
North Eurozone	Business as usual	39.8	48.7	88.5	41.8	48.1	89.9	42.6	48.8	91.4
	Gender-aware investment							44.2	50.2	94.4
	Difference							1.6	1.4	3
South Eurozone	Business as usual	23.1	33.5	56.6	21.6	29.9	51.4	21.6	31	52.6
	Gender-aware investment							23.6	32	55.6
	Difference							2	1	3
United Kingdom	Business as usual	13.6	16.3	29.9	14.0	16.3	30.3	14.0	16.3	30.3
	Gender-aware investment							14.6	16.8	31.4
	Difference							0.6	0.6	1.1

Source: Author's calculations via CAM model.

Notes: F—Female employment; M—Male employment; T—Total employment.

total employment marginally increases from 51.4 million in 2014 to 52.6 million in 2020. Furthermore, with the exception of the North Eurozone, female employment remains at 2014 levels. This indicates that the combination of a "minor" investment plan for Europe with austerity policies will lead to poor gains in terms of job creation and especially for female employment.

Significant employment gains, particularly for women, are instead projected under the gender-aware investment scenario. Compared with the business-as-usual scenario, this alternative scenario has the potential to generate 7.1 million additional jobs across Europe, of which 4.2 million are allocated to women and 2.9 million to men – reflecting the importance of marshalling government expenditure towards activities that can stimulate employment creation for women. This constitutes significant progress towards closing the gender employment gap – and it also generates employment for men.

The model was also used to assess the effect of these two scenarios on government balances. Table 8.5 shows the historical trends and projections of government spending as a percentage of GDP for the two scenarios under investigation. Under the business-as-usual scenario reductions in government spending were exogenously determined by the requirement to bring government deficits below the 3% of GDP threshold imposed by the European Growth and Stability Pact for Eurozone countries and towards a surplus in the United Kingdom, as recommended by the 2015 Spending Review and Autumn Statement (HM Treasury 2015).

150 Hannah Bargawi and Giovanni Cozzi

TABLE 8.5 Government spending as % of GDP

	Scenario	Historical		Projections
		2007	2014	2020
North Eurozone	Business as usual	22.4	23.8	21.3
	Gender-aware investment			22.7
South Eurozone	Business as usual	22.4	21.2	18.1
	Gender-aware investment			23.3
United Kingdom	Business as usual	22	23.4	18.9
	Gender-aware investment			21.3

Source: Author's calculations via CAM model.

In contrast, under the gender-aware scenario, government spending is endogenously determined on the basis of set employment targets. In addition, in the gender-aware scenario government spending is gendered and marshalled more towards employment creation for women. The data clearly shows that in order to boost employment for men and women across Europe higher levels of government spending are required, and that in order to help close the gender employment gap government expenditure should also be redirected towards investment in social infrastructure. However, although government spending is higher in this alternative gender-aware scenario this is still well below historical peaks (25.9% of GDP in the South Eurozone, 25% in the United Kingdom and 24% in the North Eurozone in 2009).

Table 8.6 shows the impact of these assumptions for government spending, revenue and private investment on government sector net lending and government debt as a percentage of GDP. The gender-aware investment scenario also leads to favourable results in terms of debt-to-GDP ratios and fiscal deficits. With regards to government debt, the decrease in government debt is more pronounced under the gender-aware investment scenario. The underlying reason for this is the higher

TABLE 8.6 Projections for government debt and fiscal sustainability

	Scenario	Government debt (% GDP)			Government sector net borrowing (% GDP)		
		2007	2014	2020	2007	2014	2020
North Eurozone	Business as usual	61.5	78.0	66.7	−0.73	−2.01	−0.2
	Gender aware investment			59.8			−0.4
South Eurozone	Business as usual	74.2	118.9	119.0	−0.72	−5.16	−2.1
	Gender aware investment			103.0			−2.5
United Kingdom	Business as usual	43.4	84.1	85.6	−2.83	−4.61	−1.1
	Gender aware investment			68.5			−0.6

Source: Author's calculations via CAM model.

level of GDP growth achieved under this scenario compared with the business-as-usual case, and the increase in taxation revenues that result from higher levels of employment and higher GDP growth. With reference to fiscal deficits, government sector net borrowing in Table 8.6 improves under the gender-aware scenario. This means that by 2020 deficits as a percentage of GDP are above the −3% required by the Fiscal Compact across the Eurozone, and almost approach a balanced budget in the United Kingdom. As a result, the gender-aware scenario cannot be dismissed for creating more debt or for increasing fiscal deficits.

Conclusion

The collection of chapters in this volume have demonstrated the myriad ways in which continued austerity policies are doing more harm than good for the economies and societies of Europe, and have shown the value of a gendered analysis for understanding the impacts of austerity policies and for building an alternative sustainable vision for Europe. Taking this one step further, this chapter has made the case for a gender-aware macroeconomic framework for Europe by comparing its projections with those of the business-as-usual scenario over the next five years.

Crucially, the analysis presented has shown that the aims of economic growth and increased employment targeted at women can be achieved via the adoption of gender-aware expansionary macroeconomic policies. Such a macroeconomic strategy is economically feasible, leading to substantial gains in terms of job creation for women and men, as well as accelerated growth *and* reductions in government debts and fiscal deficits. Thus, the recommendations that stem from this analysis are to increase public *and* private investment in both social and physical infrastructure significantly; and to roll back austerity policies. Further, it is recommended that governments should embark on a new gender-aware expansionary economic trajectory and to do this should marshal public investment into those areas that will lead to higher female employment (e.g. healthcare, long-term care, education, and so forth). Europe urgently needs a gender-aware investment strategy. The time to act is now!

Notes

1 Unemployment data source: ILO Global Employment Trends (GET), aggregated at country group level by the authors.
2 See Barry, Ch.5 in this volume, for further analysis on the marginalisation of gender equality priorities within EU policy frameworks since 2010.
3 See Ch.9 by Andersen and Dahl and Ch.10 by De Henau for a detailed analysis of the importance of investing in childcare across Europe and in the UK.

References

Alesina. A. and A. Ardanga. 1998. "Tale of Fiscal Adjustment." *Economic Policy* 13: 459–585.

Bagaria, N., D. Holland and J. Van Reenen. 2012. "Fiscal Consolidation in a Depression." *National Institute Economic Review* 221.

Bettio, F., M. Corsi, C. D'Ippoliti, A. Lyberaki, M. Samek Lodovici and A. Verashchagina. 2013. *The Impact of the Economic Crisis on the Situation of Women and Men and on Gender Equality Policies.* Luxembourg: European Union.

Blyth, M. 2013. *Austerity: The History of a Dangerous Idea.* Oxford: Oxford University Press.

Buti, M. and P.C. Padoan. 2012. "From a Vicious to a Virtuous Circle in the Eurozone – the Time is Ripe." Vox CEPR's Policy Portal. www.voxeu.org/article/vicious-virtuous-circle-eurozone (accessed 29 February 2016).

Cripps, F. 2014. "Macro-model Scenarios and Implications for European Policy." In J. Eatwell, T. McKinley and P. Petit (eds). *Challenges for Europe in the World, 2030.* Farnham, Surrey: Ashgate Publishing.

Dauderstaedt, M. and E. Hillebrandt (eds). 2013. *Alternatives to Austerity: Progressive Growth Strategies for Europe.* Berlin: Fridrich-Ebert Stiftung.

European Federation of Public Service Unions. 2011. *Widening the Gender Gap: The Impact of Public Sector Pay and Job Cuts on the Employment and Working Conditions of Women in Four Countries.* Brussels: EPSU.

Gago, E.G. and M.S. Kirzner. 2013. "Women, Gender Equality and the Economic Crisis in Spain." In M. Karamessini and J. Rubery (eds). *Women and Austerity: The Economic Crisis and the Future for Gender Equality.* Oxford: Routledge.

Giavazzi, Francesco and Marco Pagano. 1990. "Can Severe Fiscal Contractions Be Expansionary? Tales of Two Small European Countries". *NBER Macroeconomics Annual* 5: 75–122.

Griffith-Jones, S. and G. Cozzi. 2016. "Investment-led Growth: A Solution to the European Crisis." In M. Jacobs and M. Mazzucato (eds). *Rethinking Capitalism: Economic Policy for Sustainable and Inclusive Growth.* London: Whiley-Blackwell.

Griffith-Jones, S. and M. Kollatz-Ahnen. 2013. "Europe's Economic Crisis: Some Ideas for Recovery and Growth." *The Guardian* (16 August). *www.the guardian.com/* (accessed 25 January 2014).

Griffith-Jones, S., M. Kollatz-Ahnen, L. Andersen and S. Hansen. 2012. "Shifting Europe from Austerity to Growth: A Proposed Investment Programme for 2012–2015." FEPS-IPD-ECLM Policy Brief.

Gurmai, Z. 2013. "More Gender Equality is Needed as a Response to the Current Economic and Financial Crisis." Party of European Socialists. www.pes.eu/ (accessed 3 February 2014).

International Labour Office. 2014. *Social Protection Global Policy Trends 2010–2015: From Fiscal Consolidation to Expanding Social Protection: Key to Crisis Recovery, Inclusive Development and Social Justice.* Geneva: ILO.

IMF. 2014. *World Economic Outlook 2014: Legacies, Clouds, Uncertainties.* Washington: IMF.

Himmelweit, S. 2016. "Childcare as an Investment in Infrastructure." In J. Campbell and M. Gillespie (eds). *Feminist Economics and Public Policy.* Oxford: Routledge.

HM Treasury. 2015. "Spending Review and Autumn Statement 2015." Policy Paper. HM Treasury. www.gov.uk/government/publications/spending-review-and-autumn-statement-2015-documents/spending-review-and-autumn-statement-2015 (accessed 29 February 2016).

Karamessini, M. 2013. "Structural Crisis and Adjustment in Greece." In M. Karamessini and J. Rubery (eds). *Women and Austerity: The Economic Crisis and the Future for Gender Equality.* Oxford: Routledge.

Karamessini, M. and J. Rubery. 2013. "Economic Crisis and Austerity: Challenges to Gender Equality." In Karamessini, M. and J. Rubery (eds). *Women and Austerity: The Economic Crisis and the Future for Gender Equality.* Oxford: Routledge.

McKinley, T., G. Cozzi, J. Michell and H. Bargawi. 2013. *Could Employment-Focused Policies Spearhead Economic Recovery in Europe?* Policy Brief No.4. FEPS-CDPR.

Rasmussen, P. and M. Schulz. 2010. "It's Time for a New Deal on European Economic Policy." PES. http://pes.eu/en/news/its-time-new-deal-european-economic-policy (accessed 1 March 2016).

Rubery, J. and A. Rafferty. 2013. "Women and Recession Revisited." *Work, Employment & Society,* 27: 414–432.

Seguino, S. 2010. "The Global Economic Crisis, its Gender Implications, and Policy Responses." *Gender and Development* 18(2): 179–199.

Stiglitz, J. 2015. "Stimulating the Economy in an Era of Debt and Deficit." *The Economists' Voice* (March).

Szczurek, M. 2014. "Investing for Europe's Future." Speech delivered at Bruegel Institute, September 2014. http://voxeu.org/article/investing-europe-s-future (accessed 15 February 2016).

UNISON. 2014. "Counting the Cost: How Cuts are Shrinking Women's Lives." London: UNISON.

Women's Budget Group. 2012. "Women's Budget Group Pre-Budget Briefing March 2012." WBG. http://wbg.org.uk/pdfs/0-WBG-pre-budget-FINAL.pdf (accessed 29 February 2016).

Women's Budget Group. 2015. "The Impact on Women of the Autumn Statement and Comprehensive Spending Review 2015: Still Failing to Invest in Women's Security." http://wbg.org.uk/wp-content/uploads/2015/12/WBG_CSR_FullResponse_final_8Dec15.pdf (accessed 15 February 2016).

Wren-Lewis, S. 2015. "The Austerity Con." *London Review of Books* 37(4): 9–11.

Appendix I: The Cambridge Alphametrics Macroeconomic (CAM) model

The Cambridge Alphametrics Macroeconomic (CAM) model of the world economy is a structuralist growth model that is primarily used to make medium- to long-term projections of historical trends of the global economy, blocs of countries, and major individual countries. This macroeconometric model does not have any single, well-defined equilibrium path to which the economy tends to return. Being an open disequilibrium system, a wide variety of outcomes may be simulated with different growth rates and end points (see "Technical Appendix" in Cripps 2014). CAM model projections draw on continuous historical data from 1970 to the latest year available (2014 for this exercise).

In the CAM model, the world economy is regarded as an integrated system in which the behaviour of different countries and blocs differs and changes progressively through time because of their specific situation in terms of geography, level of development, financial position, etc. The macro-model has a common set of identities and behavioural equations for all blocs to reflect that they are part of the same world economy. This allows for panel estimation methods.

In the model, aggregate demand and technical progress are the principal drivers of growth. Thus the long-term growth rate is best understood as reflecting the growth of aggregate investment and government spending in the world as a whole. These variables in turn reflect confidence, expectations and policy (Cripps 2014). Further, as in many structuralist growth models, full employment is not assumed.

9

A EUROPEAN GENDERED INVESTMENT PLAN WITH FORMAL CHILDCARE AS A CORNERSTONE

Lars Andersen and Signe Dahl

The repercussions of the crisis and austerity on employment in Europe

The expected demographic changes in the EU in the years to come will result in fewer children being born, more people retiring, and ultimately fewer people in the labour force. In order for Europe to maintain its growth potential in the long run and regain momentum in growth, it is necessary to bring more people into work. One option to both increase the employment rate and to promote gender equality is to enhance the public childcare system.

On top of these demographic challenges, Europe is still struggling to recover from the global financial crisis of 2007/08. It is now more than eight years since the outbreak of the worst economic crisis since World War II, however the EU employment rate has still not returned to its pre-crisis level. In 2014, the EU unemployment rate was 3.2 percentage points higher than in 2008; in the Euro area this number was 4.1 percentage points. Further, even though it may seem as though the gender imbalance has decreased, there was still over ten percentage points difference in the male and female employment rates in both the EU and the Euro area in 2014.[1] Therefore, action is required.

This chapter presents an alternative approach to create jobs and stimulate growth in Europe – an alternative not only to austerity, but also one that takes the future demographic challenges into account.[2] It comes in the form of a gendered European investment plan that will result in a recovery based on increased investment in childcare, as well as economic growth in Europe. The outcome of the alternative is based on calculations from the international macroeconomic model HEIMDAL, which is explained in more detail below.

The chapter begins by presenting some of the core reasons for the difference in female and male activity rates in Europe. Before the investment plan is presented,

156 Lars Andersen and Signe Dahl

the positive effects of formal childcare on women's activity rates and growth are discussed. The impact on the total labour force is also considered, as well as the effects of formal childcare on children.

A glance at female employment

The activity rates in Europe vary significantly between countries and so does the share of women who are active in the labour market. The activity rate of men exceeds that of women in all Member States of the EU, according to data from Eurostat. In 2014, the EU male activity rate was 11.8 percentage points higher than the female rate – this gender gap indicates the employment potential of increasing the female activity rate. In general, the gender gaps in activity rates are smallest in the Nordic countries with gaps of around 4–7 percentage points in 2014. The gender gaps are largest in some Southern European countries and some Central and Eastern European countries – e.g. in 2014, Spain and Hungary had gender gaps of 10.6 and 13.6 percentage points respectively, while Malta had a gap of as much as 26.1 percentage points.

There are many reasons for the difference between male and female activity rates, such as historic gender patterns, caring obligations for children and the elderly, and the cost of formal care. For the younger generations of women, caring obligations for children and the cost of formal care tend to be of most significant concern. There are large variations in the opportunities to acquire formal childcare among European countries. In 2013, the Nordic countries had enrolment rates of up to 80%, representing some of the highest rates of zero- to three-year-olds in formal care. These countries have substantial support from the state, e.g. the Danish state pays around 75% of the total price of formal childcare. This commitment to available and subsidised childcare impacts directly on female employment rates and is often compared to Southern Europe, where the picture is quite different.

Across countries, the more children and the younger they are, the lower the activity rate for women. In the EU, only one quarter of women with three children (where at least one of them is less than six years old) work full-time. In general, one third of the women that are working only work part-time. Therefore, there is huge potential in both getting more women into the labour market, as well as increasing the hours worked by women who are already employed. Further, the countries with high female employment rates tend to also have a large group of part-time workers, such as the Netherlands, Austria, Germany and Belgium. Figure 9.1 shows the main reasons for part-time employment in 2014 – it is clear that men and women work part-time for different reasons.

Around 30% of females indicated "looking after children or incapacitated adults" as the main reason for working part-time. Combined with the 15% who indicated "other family or personal responsibilities" as the main reason, family responsibility can be identified as the main explanation of why females work part-time. Twenty-six per cent of females said they worked part-time because they could not find a full-time job. On the other hand, 40% of males said that they

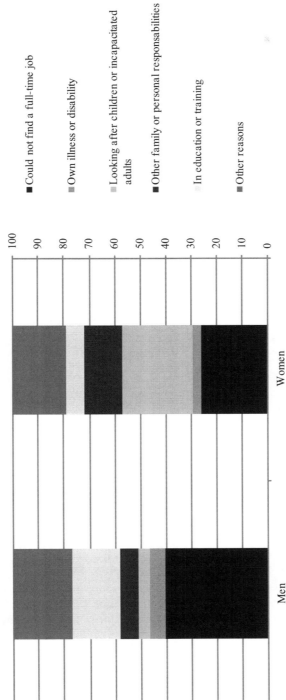

FIGURE 9.1 Main reasons for part-time employment in the EU, 2014

Source: Eurostat

Note: this figure considers the main reasons for part-time employment for the age group 15–64 years old

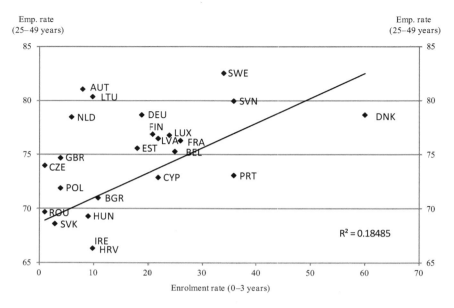

FIGURE 9.2 Share of 0–3 year old children in childcare and female activity rate (25–49 years)

Source: Eurostat

could not find a full-time job, while only 11% of males indicated family responsibilities and looking after children or incapacitated adults as the main reason for working part-time. Overall, Figure 9.1 indicates that good and inexpensive formal childcare has the potential to move a significant portion of part-time employed women into full-time employment.

As discussed above, there are large differences in childcare enrolment rates across the EU (also, see Figure 9.2). Within countries, the enrolment rates also vary depending on the age of the child. Denmark stands out as having by far the largest enrolment rate of pre-school children (60%), the majority of whom attend for more than 30 hours per week. In Belgium, pre-school education is free from the age of three and enrolment rates are as high as 25% for children under the age of three and close to 100% for children aged three to five years. On the other hand, Eastern European countries such as Poland, Slovakia and the Czech Republic have enrolment rates of less than 5% for children under the age of three. For children over three years, Poland has enrolment rates of over 40%, while Slovakia and the Czech Republic have rates of over 70%. In general, enrolment rates rise with the age of the child.

Publicly subsidised childcare increases the labour supply of women (mothers) significantly, as it frees up both parents to be active in the labour market. The parents who work instead of taking care of their children can make use of their education and will thereby be more productive, which will benefit society.

Therefore, publicly subsidised childcare will not only increase activity rates, but also result in greater specialisation and in this way productivity gains. Further, many children will also benefit from the provision of good-quality formal care; it has been proven to be very beneficial for child development, especially for children who grow up in less fortunate surroundings (Havnes and Modstad 2009), as discussed below.

As depicted in Figure 9.2, data shows that there may be a correlation between the enrolment rate in childcare and female activity rate for women aged 25–49 years (whom we presume could have small children because of their age). The figure compares the female employment rate with the proportion of children in childcare in a number of European countries. The overall picture suggests a correlation between the percentage of children in childcare and the female employment rate. For example, the Nordic countries have both high enrolment rates and high activity rates – Sweden has an enrolment rate of almost 35% and a female employment rate of 82.5%, whilst Denmark has an enrolment rate of 60% and a female employment rate of 78%. On the other hand, some Southern and Eastern European countries have both low enrolment rates and low activity rates – Croatia has an enrolment rate of 10% and a female employment rate of 66%.

Childcare is a good investment

There are numerous studies that show why publicly subsidised childcare is a good investment (see e.g. Glavind 2000; Buxbaum and Pirklbauer 2013; De Henau, Ch.10 in this book); the results from some of these are presented in this section. Overall, when parents can send their children to childcare during the day, both sole parents and couple parents have the opportunity to take a job outside the home. The release of labour occurs because childcare staff and educators – as a result of their training and institutional frameworks – can take care of more children at one time than parents.

As a concrete example of the positive employment effects that can be obtained from formal childcare, Glavind (2000) calculated an example of the effects on labour supply of increased spending on childcare. The example was based on Danish conditions and considered the effect of a situation where either 100 nursery places (for children aged zero to two) or 100 kindergarten places (for children aged three to five) were created. When establishing respectively 100 nursery places or 100 kindergarten places, it was estimated that the total required resources for educators, caretakers and construction workers corresponded to respectively 37 or 22 full-time employees. In the case of 100 nursery places, the 37 full-time employees were compared to the expectation of an increase in employment of 47 full-time employees since the parents of children now in childcare would also increase their labour supply. This meant that the creation of formal childcare would lead to a net gain of ten employees. When it came to the creation of 100 kindergarten places, the 22 full-time employees required were again compared to 47 freed full-time employees who would have their children in formal childcare. In this case, it resulted in a net gain of nearly 25 full-time employees. The difference between the two examples arises in the fact that children in nurseries require more caretakers, and so the nursery example resulted in a smaller net gain in full-time employees compared to the kindergarten example. Nevertheless, in both cases there was a notable net gain, indicating that formal pre-school childcare has positive effects on employment even when taking into account the resources needed to run the institutions.

Other angles on the issue also provide results that encourage focus on investments in formal childcare. Buxbaum and Pirklbauer (2013) concluded that expansion and improvement of childcare in Austria would be self-financing within a 10-year period. The calculations were based on a situation where 35,000 new childcare places were created and opening hours were increased, corresponding to 70,000 childcare places. Further, the quality of the childcare offer was increased through better child/educator ratios, corresponding to an increase of 35,000 childcare places. Overall, such an investment in the expansion and improvement of the Austrian childcare system was estimated to cost €566 million. It was shown that the size of the economic gains depends on the proportion of the released labour that enters employment. Therefore, three scenarios were considered: in the most pessimistic scenario, it was assumed that only 25% of mothers with children now in formal childcare would be employed; in the average scenario, up to 37%; and in the most optimistic scenario, up to 50%. Buxbaum and Pirklbauer showed that even in the pessimistic scenario, the investment could be self-financing after 10 years with a positive budgetary effect of €8 million. This means that after 10 years, the savings and increased tax revenues would surpass the cost of establishment by €8 million. While the average scenario would lead to positive budgetary effects of €104 million over the 10-year period, the optimistic scenario would result in budgetary effects of €200 million. In this case, where half of the released labour comes into work, the investment would be self-financing after only four years. Overall, according to the study, investment in formal childcare in Austria would have positive outcomes.

In another study based on UK data, Ben-Galim (2011) found that each woman who rejoins the British labour market after maternity leave would provide a public return of £20,050 over a four-year period (based on full-time employment, median income and 25 hours of childcare per week). In a more pessimistic scenario, where the women were not assumed to be employed full-time at the median wage, the public return was still positive. Even after accounting for different work patterns, as well as hourly income rates, there would still be a public return of £4,860. Further, De Henau (see Ch.10 in this book) also points out that universal childcare provision for pre-school children along with a reduction in working time to accommodate childcare needs could lead to the creation of 2.3 million more jobs in the UK in the coming years. Further, De Henau argues that investment in universal childcare would also improve women's employment opportunities as well as promote more equal employment and working hours between women and men in the UK.

The issue of formal childcare is not only present in Europe. A paper by Fairholm (2011) looked at the economic effects of the introduction of a universal childcare system in Canada. It found that over an eight-year period the introduction of a universal childcare system increased the employment rate of women in Quebec by 3.8% and Quebec GDP increased by 1.7%.

Compared to the above studies that generally consider the economic effects of formal childcare, Simonsen (2005) used Danish panel data to analyse Danish women's participation as a result of access to day care. The analysis only included women where the cost of childcare is not income dependent (i.e. relatively well-off women). Simonsen found that women living in municipalities with a childcare guarantee were 6% more likely to be in employment 8–13 months after they gave birth, compared to municipalities without a childcare guarantee. This study showed that for women to return to employment, the availability of formal childcare is important.

In the studies mentioned above, the focus was mainly on the positive budgetary effect from extended and improved childcare. This effect arises because of the release of labour supply – more parents have the chance to work and thereby raise employment and increase overall productivity by working in their speciality. This is true for different countries, as the studies show. In addition to the direct effects on labour supply are the effects of increased consumption, which in turn will generate both increased tax revenues and employment, as well as the long-term positive effects on children's human capital.

The effects of formal childcare on children

The focus of the chapter so far has been on the positive economic effects of formal childcare as well as the positive effects on female employment rates. Whilst such gains are an essential component of the investment plan, it is also important to examine how children are affected by formal childcare. First, it is noteworthy that the study by Paull and Taylor (2002) found that formal care tends to be associated with more positive outcomes than informal care. Several studies have shown that children can benefit from formal childcare of good quality in different ways. The experiences one gains as a child have long-term effects on cognitive abilities, which can in turn influence income, education and other socioeconomic factors. Because teachers and social workers employed in formal care are trained professionals, studies have shown there are social and educational advantages for the child, and high-quality care has been associated with improved cognitive learning and better language skills.

Heckman et al.'s (2005) renowned empirical research on the efficacy of early childhood education programmes showed that the evolution of skills is a process that starts early on in life and continues every day. The skills gained in one stage of life affect the ability to gain further skills later in life – i.e. the earlier the investment in the child, the bigger the effect. Based on this, formal childcare should be offered to children from an early age. Also, it is to be expected that children from less advantaged backgrounds should gain from formal childcare of high quality.

162 Lars Andersen and Signe Dahl

Several studies have focused on specific positive effects of formal childcare. One study from the Norwegian Institute of Health found fewer late talkers among children who attend formal childcare (Lekhal et al. 2011). Another Norwegian study by Havnes and Modstad (2009) investigated the long-term consequences of formal childcare. Using a sample of 17,500 persons, they found that the risk of a young person dropping out of school was reduced by almost 6% if the young person had received formal childcare as a child. Also, the chance of being accepted in an institution of higher education was found to increase by almost 7% for people who had received formal childcare, and the risk of long-term dependency on transfer payments fell by 5%. The effects were most significant for children of unskilled parents and decreased as the parents' level of education increased.

The discovery that there are the biggest gains for children who grow up in less fortunate surroundings is not new. Early in life, it has been shown that there are considerable differences in the skills of children who grow up with parents of different backgrounds. It was found by Hart and Risley (1995) that a three-year-old child who grows up with parents who have a university degree tends to be familiar with more words and has a vocabulary double that of a child whose parents receive transfer payments; this gap increases as elementary school approaches for the child. This means that for children with weak backgrounds the offer of formal childcare may have positive long-term consequences and help break the negative social legacy.

Obviously, there are differences in the quality of formal childcare, which Nielsen and Christoffersen (2009) considered in their study. They did not specify the quality of formal childcare in different institutions or countries; instead, they found that factors such as the child/caretaker ratio, the education of the caretakers, the activities in the care centre, and the physical surroundings are main determinants of the quality of childcare.

Overall, there are strong indications that childcare has positive effects for the child – especially for children from weak backgrounds and when the childcare is of high quality. There are therefore two particular reasons why childcare is a good investment: it has positive effects on female employment; and the children benefit from formal care.

A gendered investment plan for Europe: accounting for formal childcare

This section looks at the effects of a gendered investment plan that has formal childcare as its cornerstone. As discussed above, expansion of the public childcare system is one way to increase female labour supply. There is great potential in terms of women's activity rates being lower than men's and many women working part-time due to care obligations (as seen in Figure 9.1). Further, formal childcare is also a good investment for the child.

The gendered investment plan involves investment in the childcare system that aims to both improve the existing system, as well as to develop and extend it. In addition, it should stimulate the European economy via government investments financed by taxes. The taxes are imposed in order to ensure a balanced investment plan – the increases in income tax correspond to the expenses of the investments. The results of the plan, as presented below, show how the negative effects from taxes (in the form of decreased consumption, for example) are offset by the positive effects on employment and growth.

The gendered investment plan is calculated using the international macroeconomic model, HEIMDAL. HEIMDAL focuses on the world economy from a European perspective and describes the European economies both on a country and on an aggregated EU level. Besides the US and Japan, there are 13 European countries in the model. Each country is described using its own country model with several sectors and the relations are estimated based on annual data (the data used originates primarily from the OECD Outlook database, which is published every six months). The economies in the model are interlinked via a broad range of transmission mechanisms. The individual country models are based on a Keynesian theoretical background in the sense that production and employment are determined by aggregate demand in the short run; in the long run, prices and wages would react to changes in unemployment and capacity utilisation.[3]

The gendered plan is based on two pillars: first, investments in childcare in order to increase women's labour supply; and secondly, a more traditional investment plan with a special focus on female employment in order to increase the demand for female labour. The countries that have been used as case studies in the strategy are the southern Eurozone countries of Italy, Spain, Greece, Portugal and Ireland, the western Eurozone countries of Germany, France, Holland, Belgium and Austria, and the UK.

In the model's calculations, it is assumed that the framework conditions for women to participate in the labour market are improved. That means investing heavily in expanding and improving childcare facilities in Europe, with a special focus on Southern European countries (as the potential for increasing the female participation rate is largest in this area). It is assumed that the improvement in childcare would gradually increase public employment by 0.5% towards 2020 (0.75% for the southern Eurozone countries), and the improved framework would gradually increase the labour force during the next five years, resulting in a 1% increase by 2020.

The countries would simultaneously increase public investments, starting with 1% of GDP in 2016 and gradually increasing this to 1.5% in 2020; southern Eurozone countries would invest 1.5% of GDP in 2016 and gradually increase this to 2.5% in 2020.

As mentioned above, taxes would also be increased in a balanced way so that the total effect on the public budget would equal zero. Whereas the investments would be spread so that the investment level would be increased more in the southern Eurozone than in the rest of the countries, the increase in taxes would be spread evenly among the case study countries.

Through this model and the aforementioned calculations, the gendered investment plan is shown to have positive effects on the European economy and result in a recovery based on investing in childcare as well as in the creation of growth in Europe that focuses on female employment. The effects on the GDP of the EU are also estimated from the period 2016–20 using HEIMDAL. In 2016, the effects of the gendered investment plan would raise GDP by just over 1%. The plan would cause a further rise in GDP each year until 2020 where the effect would be a rise of 2.4%. These effects are compared with the situation where the gendered investment plan does not take place – therefore the improvements in childcare and increased investments are shown to be the source of the rise in GDP during the period.

A similar effect is seen if the focus is narrowed to only the Eurozone – in 2020, GDP would be elevated by 2.6%. The larger effect on the Eurozone is due to the fact that it is mainly Eurozone countries that are included in the simulation of the gendered investment plan.

The gendered investment plan is also shown to have positive effects on European employment, as can be seen in Figure 9.3. The massive investment in childcare as well as other investments would boost employment in Europe. In its first year, the gendered investment plan would create close to 1.4 million new jobs in Europe, of which there would be an increase in female employment of 725,000 jobs and an increase in male employment of 645,000 jobs – female employment would therefore increase by 12% more than male employment in the first year. As the childcare system is improved and expanded all over Europe, more women would supply their labour and more jobs for women would be created. The ratio of new female jobs to new male jobs would therefore increase. Cumulatively, from 2016–20, the gendered investment plan would create 4.8 million jobs in the EU, of which more than 2.7 million jobs would be female jobs and 2.1 million jobs would be male jobs. Further, from 2016–20, the gendered investment plan would create

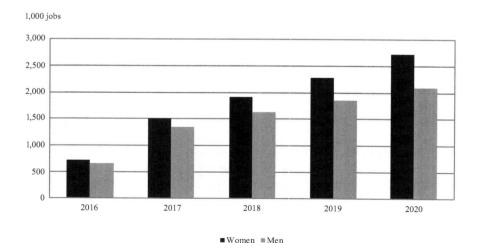

FIGURE 9.3 Effect on EU employment (male/female)

Formal childcare as a cornerstone **165**

30% more female jobs than male jobs, showing how targeting investments at childcare can add a significantly larger share of female jobs compared to an investment plan without a gendered approach. Figure 9.3 shows how the gap between the two pillars would widen over time.

Table 9.1 shows the effect of the gendered investment plan on GDP and employment in a number of countries and regions. In the period from 2016–20, GDP in the EU would grow by 2.4% more than in the scenario with no investment plan. In employment terms, the total effect on the EU would be more than 4.8 million extra people employed in 2020. Again this is compared to a situation where nothing is done. The spread between male and female job creation would widen over time, so that relatively more and more female jobs would be created in the period. In the Eurozone, the gendered investment plan would create 3.5 million jobs by 2020, where the majority of the jobs (in absolute numbers) would be located in the western Eurozone. However, in relative terms the job creation in the western Eurozone and in the southern Eurozone would be about the same.

In the gendered investment plan, the investments in the southern Eurozone are intensified so that government investments start at 1.5% of GDP in 2016. This would be gradually increased to 2.5% of GDP in 2020. In comparison, the other countries in the scenario would have government investments starting at 1% of GDP in 2016 and increasing to 1.5% of GDP in 2020. The reason why the job creation (in relative terms) would be the same in the western Eurozone and in the southern Eurozone despite this difference is due to the underlying multipliers and the openness in the economies. The total employment effect is the sum of the domestic employment effect (from the investments within the country) plus the spill-over effect (the effect from an increase in demand from other European

TABLE 9.1 Growth and employment effects on selected regions and countries, cumulative effect 2016–2020

	Employment (1,000 jobs)			GDP growth (%)
	Women	Men	Total	
Southern Eurozone	690	540	1,230	2.6
Italy	260	200	470	2.3
Spain	290	220	510	3.0
Western Eurozone	1,300	1,010	2,310	2.6
Germany	650	500	1,150	3.0
France	270	210	480	1.6
Belgium	50	40	90	2.4
UK	240	190	430	2.0
EUROZONE	1,990	1,540	3,540	2.5
EU	2,710	2,100	4,810	2.4

Source: ECLM based on calculations on HEIMDAL.

Note: The southern Eurozone includes Italy, Spain, Greece, Portugal and Ireland. The western Eurozone includes Germany, France, Holland, Belgium and Austria.

166 Lars Andersen and Signe Dahl

TABLE 9.2 Examples of spill-over effects to EU countries that are not part of the strategy, cumulative effect 2016–2020

	Employment (1,000 jobs)	GDP growth (%)
Poland	270	2.1
Sweden	60	1.8
Denmark	30	1.6
Finland	20	1.4

Source: ECLM based on calculations on HEIMDAL.

countries). Because of the larger spill-over effects in the western Eurozone compared to the southern Eurozone, the western Eurozone would experience the same relative increase in employment even though the investment level is higher in the southern Eurozone.

It can also be seen in Table 9.1 how the GDP multiplier varies between countries depending on their openness and spill-over between countries. The GDP and employment effects would be higher in countries that greatly depend on exports – e.g. in the German export-oriented economy, GDP would increase by 3% over the five-year period.

As explained above, some of the positive effects in this scenario are due to the fact that a number of the European countries would be acting simultaneously. There would therefore be positive spill-over effects on each individual country that would enlarge the effects on employment and wealth. Table 9.2 gives examples of these spill-over effects on countries that are not part of the gendered investment plan. Sweden, for example, would experience a GDP increase of 1.8% and 60,000 jobs would be created in the period from 2016–20 due to the gendered investment plan. In this scenario it is only the countries that are part of the gendered investment plan that provide the financing; however, with the spill-over effects in mind, one could argue that it would only be fair if all European countries, in some way, provide the financing as all countries to some extent would benefit from the plan.

Conclusions

This chapter has introduced a gendered investment plan that increases employment (especially female) and increases GDP. The plan includes as its cornerstone investments in formal childcare – this is based on the potential for a big release of labour supply from parents and especially mothers when they are offered formal childcare of high quality. Further, as the parents work within their speciality there should be productivity gains, which is also an explaining factor behind the forecast rise in GDP.

Several studies have shown that early, formal childcare of high quality has positive effects on the child. High-quality care is associated with improved cognitive learning and better language skills. This is especially true for children

Formal childcare as a cornerstone **167**

from weak backgrounds. The effect of formal childcare on children is therefore an important consideration of the plan.

The gendered investment plan would draw Europe in the right direction, create 4.8 million jobs, increase the female participation rate and promote gender equality by reducing the gender gap in the labour market. Also, it would ensure a quicker return to Europe's historical growth path, and would face the challenge of the demographic changes in the EU. Significant improvements can be made to the labour market when implementing the gendered investment plan, and so whilst increasing the female participation rate may result in a higher unemployment rate in the short term, if active labour market policies are implemented in order to help women to get jobs and to be quickly integrated on the labour market then female employment may increase even more than expected.

Notes

1 The main data source in this paper is Eurostat (2013).
2 See Barry (Ch.5) and Bargawi and Cozzi (Ch.8) in this book for a thorough discussion of policies implemented at EU level since the crisis.
3 For more information about the HEIMDAL model, see Bjørsted and Dahl (2012).

References

Ben-Galim, D. 2011. "Making the Case for Universal Childcare." London: IPPR.
Bjørsted, E. and S. Dahl. 2012. "HEIMDAL – Model Description and Properties." Copenhagen: ECLM Arbejderbevægelsens Erhvervsråd.
Buxbaum, A and S. Pirklbauer. 2013. "Social Investment Growth, Employment and Financial Sustainability Economic and Fiscal Effects of Improving Childcare in Austria." AK Position Paper. Brussels: AK Europa.
Eurostat. 2013. "European System of Accounts ESA 2010." Publications Office of the European Union. Luxembourg.
Fairholm, R. 2011. "Economic Impacts of Early Learning and Care." Canada: The Centre for Spatial Economics.
Glavind, N. 2000. "Børn i kroner og ører." Copenhagen: Bureau 2000.
Hart, B. and T.R. Risley. 1995. *Meaningful Differences in the Everyday Experience of Young American Children*. Baltimore: Brookes Publishing.
Havnes, T. and M. Modstad. 2009. "No Child Left Behind. Universal Child Care and Children's Long-run Outcome." Bonn: IZA.
Heckman, J.J., F. Cunha, L. Lochner and D.V. Masterov. 2005. "Interpreting the Evidence on Life Cycle Skill Formation." University College London.
Lekhal, R., H.D. Zachrisson, M.V. Wang, S. Schjølberg and T. von Soest. 2011. "Does Universally Accessible Child Care Protect Children from Late Talking? Results from a Norwegian Population-based Prospective Study." *Early Child Development and Care* 181(8): 1007–19.
Nielsen, A.A. and M.N. Christoffersen. 2009. "Børnehavens betydning for børns udvikling." Copenhagen: SFI.
Paull, G. and J. Taylor. 2002. "Mothers' Employment and Childcare Use in Britain." London: The Institute for Fiscal Studies.
Simonsen, M. 2005. "Availability and Price of High Quality Day Care and Female Employment." Copenhagen: Department of Economics, University of Copenhagen.

10

COSTING A FEMINIST PLAN FOR A CARING ECONOMY

The case of free universal childcare in the UK

Jerome De Henau

Introduction

Since 2010, a Conservative–Liberal Democrat Coalition Government followed in 2015 by a Conservative-majority Government have implemented a vast austerity plan in the United Kingdom to deal with the budget deficit and rising public debt in the aftermath of the financial crisis of 2007–08. The claim was that there was no alternative to this "Plan A", which involved drastic spending cuts in social security and public services, to rebalance public finances and the economy. Low-income households and particularly lone parents and single pensioners – the vast majority of whom are women – have been found to have borne the brunt of the cumulative spending cuts in services and tax-benefit changes (see Reed in this volume (Ch.7); Reed and Portes 2014). Not only have the changes damaged women's economic security and employment opportunities but they have also disrupted the social infrastructure of the UK, with potential long-term negative consequences for the economy, while doing nothing to provide upwards convergence in both men's and women's economic positions.

This chapter examines an alternative settlement for the UK, one that aims at achieving a caring economy that works for people and for gender equality. The Women's Budget Group (an independent think-tank analysing gender implications of fiscal and social policies) have devised a Plan F – a feminist plan for a caring economy (WBG 2015a). They argue that investing in care services, guaranteeing decent working conditions in paid care and supporting more equitable sharing of unpaid care between men and women are at the core of such an economy. Part of this alternative requires the government to secure funding for the social infrastructure – care, health, education and training services, social security and housing – alongside funding already earmarked for investment in the physical infrastructure of transport and technology, albeit with modest ambition

The case of free universal childcare in the UK **169**

compared to what the country needs. Fostering social reproduction and investing in social infrastructure (not just building schools and hospitals but paying teachers, nurses and carers) are essential to both improving well-being and increasing productivity in the short and longer term (Braunstein et al. 2011). In some ways this approach is in line with a "social investment strategy" aimed at increasing equal opportunities of future generations through integrating their parents (and themselves later on) into the labour market (Morel et al. 2012). However, the idea of the care economy goes beyond the often too narrow and instrumental perspective of the social investment approach, which has been the accepted social policy paradigm in Europe since the turn of the century. From a care economy perspective, providing high-quality care is seen not just as a means to achieve greater (female) employment by reducing constraints on labour supply, but also as a necessary feature of a civilised society that offers social equality and improves the security and quality of life of its population.

In light of these aims, this chapter investigates the fiscal space available for such an alternative vision and focuses on universal childcare provision for pre-school children as one of the bedrocks of the social infrastructure that is currently deficient in the UK. Along with the reduction in working time to accommodate childcare needs and a better sharing of caring tasks between parents, costings are estimated using various assumptions about childcare coverage and staff pay. Funding options are explored, including by reversing tax giveaways identified as having benefited men disproportionately, such as rises in personal tax allowances and cuts in fuel and alcohol duties. Other options are examined and alternative employment multipliers discussed. The model proposed is one in which dual-earner, dual-carer parents operate in partnership with universal and high-quality public care services, which could be termed a "triple-carer model" (dual-carer in the case of lone parents).

Making the case for free universal pre-school childcare

The main problems with childcare provision in the UK and elsewhere in Europe have long been identified, and childcare accessibility and affordability have been scrutinised by a number of researchers (De Henau et al. 2007a). The cost to parents is very high in the UK compared to its European neighbours, and cost rises have been outstripping general inflation over the last 10–15 years (Rutter and Stocker 2014; Rutter 2015). Rutter and Stocker (2014) also point to the lack of places for young children, even among private providers, due to a lack of public funding. Indeed, current state support is too low or inadequate: in 2015, public subsidies to providers to offer free childcare for three- to four-year-olds (and disadvantaged two-year-olds) only covered for 15 hours per week and for 38 weeks of the year (Rutter and Stocker 2014; WBG 2014).[1] Moreover, the payment to providers per hour of childcare is below their supply cost, leading providers to recoup the shortfall by raising fees for hours purchased by parents – thereby increasing the already high costs of UK childcare. In addition, a complex system of means-tested cash transfers (tax credits) to families with children, including subsidies to pay for childcare expenses, leads to heavy costs being borne by second earners if they work more than short part-time weeks. Besides inadequate provision, the UK is also characterised by high levels of inequality in childcare use, partly driven by its high costs, even when subsidised. Van Lancker (2013), using 2009 EU-SILC data on full-time equivalent (FTE) childcare use by household income quintiles, calculated that children under three in the top 20% of families were six times more likely than those in the bottom 20% to be in childcare, compared to 1.5 times more likely in Germany, Belgium and Italy and 1.2 times in Denmark and Sweden.

Research has consistently shown that lack of affordable and accessible childcare provision is associated with lasting negative effects on gender inequalities over the life course, as families adopt a one-and-a-half breadwinner model that reinforces intra-household inequalities (De Henau et al. 2007a, 2007b; Lewis 2006; De Henau and Himmelweit 2013). Moreover, access to high-quality formal childcare for a significant number of hours during the week is crucial to improving children's outcomes and life chances, even for very young toddlers and infants, especially those from more disadvantaged backgrounds (Havnes and Mogstad 2011, 2014; Karoly et al. 2005; Babchishin et al. 2013; Li et al. 2013; see also Van Lancker 2013 for a fuller discussion).

One solution is thus to invest on a broad scale in free full-time formal childcare for all children, with highly trained and well-paid staff (De Henau et al. 2007a; Mohun Himmelweit et al. 2014; Ben Ghalim 2011). Therefore this chapter looks at the costing and funding possibilities of such investment for children aged between six months and five years (when they enter primary school) in the UK. It also explores the synergies between free formal childcare and a reformed parental leave system for children in their first year. A large part of the cost calculations build on a previous study on costing free universal childcare for children under three in England, carried out by the New Economics Foundation (NEF) in 2014 (Mohun Himmelweit et al. 2014). The scope of the NEF study is extended here to all pre-school children in the UK and the chapter further analyses different coverage scenarios. It also goes beyond calculating direct employment effects by investigating indirect and induced employment job creation, interactions with the tax credit system, funding sources from taxation and a reformed parental leave system.

The premise of this chapter is that there is enough fiscal space, even within existing current resources, to fund such radical policy. It explores how this could be done, comparing the childcare funding needs to some of the tax giveaways afforded during successive budgets since 2010, despite a commitment to austerity in public finances. The justification for some of these tax cuts was that they would contribute to boosting employment; comparatively little "new" money was invested into childcare support (WBG 2014).

Costing the free delivery of full-time universal childcare

The cost of providing free childcare for all pre-school children depends on five main criteria:

1. the number of children in each age group;
2. the ratio of staff to children for each age group;
3. the ratio of supervisory care staff (highly qualified) to less-qualified staff for each age group;
4. the remuneration of both levels of staff; and
5. the opening hours per week (and per year) and percentage of children covered.

The maximum scenario assumes 100% of children are covered for a FTE week of work, accounting for commuting time of one hour per day. A full-time working week is assumed to be 35 hours in this model, as it represents the average working time of women who were employed full-time in 2014 (ONS 2014b). Hence childcare is available for 40 hours per week.[2] Childcare provision is also assumed to be available for 48 weeks per annum, allowing for a conservative four-week holiday period.

Numbers for the first three criteria are taken from population statistics and existing quality regulations, as shown in Table 10.1. It is also assumed that childcare centres have one manager and each centre has 41 children of mixed ages (Mohun Himmelweit et al. 2014). Supervisory staff are assumed to have higher educational qualifications than other caring staff, and so proportionally more of them are allocated to older children (see Table 10.1).

The fourth criterion for high-quality childcare provision relates to staff pay, and thus higher levels of pay for childcare workers are included. Two possible salary profiles are provided, following some of the suggestions of Mohun Himmelweit et al. (2014). The first, "high-quality", option is based on a teacher's salary (in primary school, distinguishing between supervising and non-supervising levels using official pay scales); the second, "decent-quality", option is based on the average living wage. The living wage is paid to the lowest qualified category of staff (other staff) with the wages of supervisory childcare workers and centre managers calculated to maintain the same pay ratio between staff categories observed in the high-quality

TABLE 10.1 Number of children and staff ratios

	No. children in UK (mid-2014)	Staff:child ratio	% Supervisory staff	No. places in centre
Children aged 6–24m	1,188,872	0.333	33%	9
Children aged 24–36m	828,035	0.250	50%	16
Children aged 36–60m	1,620,554	0.125	50%	16

Source: population from ONS (2015a); other data from Mohun Himmelweit et al. (2014).

172 Jerome De Henau

option. Table 10.2 shows the hours and pay for each category of staff. Comparatively, mean weekly earnings of childcare workers were £224.80 in 2014, approximately £11,690 annually (ONS 2014c).

This information is used to calculate a cost per child per hour for each type of staff and for each age group. It is assumed, following Mohun Himmelweit et al. (2014), that:

- non-wage costs are 23% of unit cost (per child per hour); and
- gross earnings attract pension contributions of 14.1%.

Because managers' costs are per centre and not per age group, Table 10.3 shows the cost per child per hour with the manager's cost being apportioned per capita to each child.

If childcare workers were paid a teacher's wage, £49 billion would be required per annum to provide universal free childcare, reduced to £28 billion if workers were paid at living wage levels.

This is a huge amount, equivalent to 3% of GDP in the high-quality scenario and compares to a mere £5 billion of current annual expenditure that goes towards the three main forms of childcare support (tax-free vouchers from some employers, childcare support in the Working Tax Credit, and free childcare for 15 hours for three- to four-year-olds and 40% of two-year-olds), some of which goes to older children.[3]

The net cost to the Exchequer would be reduced through additional revenue raised from newly generated employment in childcare. Spending on means-tested tax credits and cash transfers would also be reduced for those taking up paid

TABLE 10.2 Childcare workers' annual and hourly pay and weekly hours (2014)

	Supervisory staff (Level 6 qual.)[a]	Other staff (Level 3 qual.)[a]	Centre manager
No. hours per week[b]	29.7	29.7	35
"High-quality" option			
Teacher salary (£, hourly)[c,d]	17.85	13.73	26.46
Teacher salary (£, yearly)	27,534	21,185	48,156
"Decent-quality" option			
Living wage (£, hourly)[c]	10.41	8.01	15.38
Living wage (£, yearly)	16,052	12,351	28,074

Source: Department for Education (2014) and Living Wage Foundation (2015).

Notes: (a) Level 6 qualification is a first degree and level 3 corresponds to A-level (upper secondary school). (b) Carers' hours are based on teachers' hours in both salary options and calculated as follows: 1,265 hours of teaching for 260 paid days = 82% of working time per day, so total per week = 1,265/260/0.82*5 = 29.7. This assumes that carers spend 18% of their day on other activities than direct contact with children (administration, meetings, etc). (c) Teachers' salaries are mid-point of the scale. (d) Figures for both types of salaries account for London's higher rates.

The case of free universal childcare in the UK **173**

TABLE 10.3 Total cost of free universal full-time childcare

	No. children covered	Teacher wage		Living wage	
		Cost per hour per child (£)	Total cost per annum (£m)	Cost per hour per child (£)	Total cost per annum (£m)
6–24m	1,188,872	10.05	22,950	5.70	13,018
24–36m	828,035	8.13	12,918	4.62	7,339
36–60m	1,620,554	4.27	13,280	2.43	7,550
All	3,637,461	7.04	49,149	4.00	27,907

Source: author's calculations.

Note: the cost per hour per child is that of hours of direct care of the child, not hours of carer's work.

employment. Moreover, there would be indirect and induced multiplier employment effects in the rest of the economy, generating further net revenue to the Exchequer (provided there is spare capacity in the economy – i.e. enough people looking for work or wanting to increase their working hours, including parents newly available because of the increased childcare provision, to take up these jobs). These employment effects are considered below.

Employment effects

Labour demand effects

The main immediate employment effect is to create jobs in the care sector. The number of FTE caring jobs created as a result of the maximum scenario is shown in Table 10.4. The calculation reflects the number of working hours of staff of each category needed per hour of care per child multiplied by the number of children and the number of hours covered. Total working hours account for regulatory staff:child ratios and non-care time as explained above. The number of jobs created considers childcare workers on a 30-hour full-time shift (in line with teachers). Therefore the number of FTE jobs created is calculated on a 35-hour week basis.

TABLE 10.4 Number of jobs created in childcare services (universal full-time coverage)

	Supervisory care staff	Other care staff	Centre manager	Total
Children aged 6–24m	217,203	434,405		651,608
Children aged 24–36m	170,189	170,189		340,378
Children aged 36–60m	166,539	166,539		333,078
Total	553,931	771,134	101,393	1,426,457
Total (35h FTE basis)	469,527	653,634	101,393	1,224,554

Source: author's calculations.

174 Jerome De Henau

When based on a 35-hour full-time working week, the 1.2 million new jobs created correspond to 34 full-time jobs for every 100 children offered a full-time slot in a childcare centre.[4]

Of course not all of these jobs would be new since childcare providers already exist. In April–June 2014 in the UK, there were 337,000 people employed in the main three occupations of childcare workers (namely, nursery nurses, childminders and playworkers),[5] 98% of whom were women and 55% full-time employed (ONS 2014b). This is approximately 260,000 FTE jobs (or 19% of the total FTE jobs that would be created by the universal childcare reform).[6] Accounting for existing jobs, net job creation would be equal to a 3% increase in the FTE employed population of 28 million in 2014 (OECD 2014b).

A second type of employment effect is the indirect multiplier (also known as Type I multiplier) stemming from employment created through increased demand for inputs from other sectors into the additional childcare services (e.g. food, construction, transport, etc). One method of estimating such effects is by using input-output tables (Antonopoulos et al. 2010; De Henau et al. 2015). The Office for National Statistics (ONS), using 2010 data, provides estimates on such indirect effects for different sectors of the UK economy. The social sector classification, which includes childcare services, had a multiplier of 2.76 (for non-market activities, i.e. those that are provided publicly). However, given the structure of childcare services (mainly procured from private providers), it is not clear what this multiplier would be if the childcare provision was fully publicly funded and publicly delivered. In comparison, private sector care services activities (childcare and social care combined) had a multiplier of 1.34. Perhaps the multiplier for the education sector is closer to what this exercise is assuming, i.e. the childcare workforce resembles the primary school teachers' workforce (in terms of pay and qualifications). In this sector, the multiplier was much lower at 1.17. This would still add an extra 208,000 FTE jobs, to make the total 1.43 million.

A third type of employment multiplier (also known as Type II) is the induced impact on economic growth due to an income effect on consumption and thus internal demand by the newly employed population. Estimates of this multiplier are not available for the UK but Scotland has carried out an exercise in calculating both Type I and Type II multipliers using Scottish input-output matrices. Given the sector analysed – education – which is expected to attract mainly local employment, the Scottish estimate could be used as proxy for the UK induced employment multiplier. In 2010, the indirect multiplier was 1.10, while the induced multiplier was 1.27 (Scottish Government 2015). Since the induced effect applies to both directly and indirectly generated employment, if the same ratio is applied to the UK indirect multiplier of 1.17 then the induced multiplier for the UK would be 1.35. This means an additional 221,000 FTE jobs.[7]

However, estimating such effects with more accuracy would require a full-blown macroeconomic simulation tool outside of the scope of this chapter (see Ch.8 by Bargawi and Cozzi, and Ch.9 by Andersen and Dahl in this volume). The same goes for estimating a fourth employment effect over the longer run related to

The case of free universal childcare in the UK **175**

TABLE 10.5 Job creation in childcare and other sectors

	Direct	Direct + indirect	Direct + indirect + induced	Women (total)	Men (total)
No. FTE jobs created					
Direct (care)	1,224,554	1,224,554	1,224,554	1,200,063	24,491
Indirect	0	208,174	208,174	104,087	104,087
Induced	0	0	221,422	110,711	110,711
Total	1,224,554	1,432,729	1,654,150	1,414,861	239,289
% rise in employment rate (16–64y)	3.0	3.5	4.1	6.9	1.2

Source: author's calculations using multipliers from ONS and Scottish Government (2015).

improved child outcomes, such as through increased productivity due to a higher quality and more inclusive early education system. Table 10.5 summarises the estimates of these different employment effects.

The overall female employment rate (aged 16–64) in 2014 was 68% in headcount and 53% in FTE (based on female full-time hours). Depending on the multiplier and if all the new jobs are taken up by women (given the potential supply effect among mothers of young children discussed below), the increase in female employment rate would be between 6% (if only direct effects considered) and 8% (if induced effects are included).

The 8% increase in the female employment rate in the full multiplier scenario of 1.35 would mean nearly closing the 10% headcount employment gap between all men and women aged 16–64, which has remained unchanged since 2009.

Freeing up labour supply

Figures calculated in Table 10.5 provide only a demand-side picture of the jobs created. In general, it is possible to assume that any job that cannot be filled by the resident population (i.e. if there isn't enough spare capacity) would be by calling upon the immigrant workforce (as in the case of the healthcare system). Nevertheless, it is useful to consider the supply-side effects of such policy, especially given the constraints that childcare costs and availability impose on (mainly) mothers' employment prospects.

Indeed boosting availability of high-quality childcare is expected to free up time of the current unpaid carers of pre-school children so that they can take up employment or increase their working hours. The magnitude of this supply-side effect will depend on the number of unpaid carers whose time would be freed up relative to the number of jobs created in the childcare sector, and on the unpaid carers' willingness and capacity to supply more labour.

Using data on FTE employment rates for parents whose youngest child is under the age of five, we can estimate the employment gap between fathers and mothers

176 Jerome De Henau

and use it as an indicator of the potential increase in labour supply for mothers if it is assumed that fathers do not face caring time constraints. This is one way of estimating an upper bound of labour supply in a model that assumes fathers' and mothers' characteristics (such as education, skills, motivations and experience) do not differ, and so employment rates would be the same if this caring time constraint was alleviated. This makes sense insofar as such gender differences in personal characteristics have significantly reduced over the past few decades (Goldin 2006).

Based on a 35-hour week model, the FTE employment rate of mothers of children aged zero to four years was 41% in 2014 and that of corresponding fathers was 84%.[8] The model assumes that if 84% of such fathers are able to work the equivalent of 35 hours per week then so could mothers if their childcaring constraints were fully alleviated, thereby increasing their FTE employment rate by 43%.

In 2014, there were approximately 2.9 million mothers of children aged six months to five years (ONS 2014b). The supply-side effect would thus be 43% of that figure – i.e. approximately 1,269,000 new FTEs. This is just above the direct demand for childcare employment (and 30% more if existing childcare jobs are taken into account). Overall the remaining demand of just under 400,000 FTE jobs (considering induced effects) would potentially reduce unemployment by a fifth, according to 2014 figures, and by even more (30%) if it is assumed that the 134,000 unemployed women with a child aged zero to four years would also acquire employment (ONS 2014b).

Interaction with means-tested benefits

Providing free childcare to all is expected to increase the labour supply of mothers of young children in both high- and low-income families. However, for the latter, the interaction with means-tested benefits needs to be considered to assess the strength of these supply-side effects, given that childcare support is intertwined with in-work benefit payments.

The main existing in-work benefit payment, Universal Credit (UC), is a system of cash benefits (tax credits) intended to "make work pay" for low-income households. Because of its household means-tested structure, it provides little incentive to second earners in low-income families to take up employment or work longer hours, up to a certain level of wage rates. The analysis that follows looks at the UC system since it is meant to overhaul the existing Working and Child Tax Credits system gradually. Universal Credit will reduce the level of benefit paid by 65p for every additional net pound earned by the household, above a certain level of income (known as a "work allowance"), a threshold that is more likely to be attained if one member of the couple is already in (full-time) employment.

There is no single way to analyse work incentives for second earners. One approach examined here is to calculate the gain in net household income after childcare costs for a non-employed partner in a couple to take up paid employment

The case of free universal childcare in the UK **177**

at 35 hours per week, when the other partner is already in full-time employment, under a regime of UC and compare this gain with that if in-work benefits were not in place. If the income generated after childcare costs is lower in the former regime, then the system is said to create disincentives for the second earner. These effects can then be compared with a system in which provision of childcare is free.

Using an example of couples where both partners' wage rate is the median wage of £11.61 per hour and with two children aged four years and one year, we can calculate the net household income gain for taking up 35 hours' employment for the second earner (the first earner being on 40 hours per week) in four situations to be compared with one another:

a. with existing childcare costs and UC (and thus available childcare support within the UC system);
b. with existing childcare costs but without UC or any other system of in-work benefits (and therefore no childcare support);
c. without childcare costs (free universal provision) but with whatever UC support is available (if any); and
d. with no childcare costs and no UC.

At median-wage rates, the increase in gross annual household income owing to the partner taking up full-time employment (35 hours) is £21,130 (see Table 10.6). In net terms and after childcare costs, the gain in household income is £2,890 (14% of gross gain) under the planned UC system (situation (a)) and £3,199 (15% of gross gain) if there was no tax credit support available (situation (b)).[9] At this level of wages, the UC system doesn't do anything to relieve the high costs of childcare on the employment incentives of second earners (though it does make the family better off). Note that in either situation the net gain is rather small (only 15% of additional income retained) and could be entirely swallowed by other work-related costs, such as commuting. Hence, in situations (a) and (b), high childcare costs don't quite make full-time employment for second earners pay much at median-wage levels.

In comparison, looking at situations (c) and (d), for the same gross gain, the net gain for the household in a system where free universal childcare is provided (full-time) is £13,765 (65% of gross gain) under the UC system (situation (c)) and £17,323 (82% of gross gain) if there was no tax credit system (situation (d)). Interestingly, when childcare is free, the disincentive provided by means-testing in the UC system becomes clear. That said, the net gain with free childcare remains higher than in either (a) or (b), which is expected.

Also, within a free-childcare system, the lower the wage rate, the larger the disincentive effect of the means-tested benefits. For example, at living wages, the respective net income gains from employment would be 40% of gross gains with UC (situation (c)) compared to 89% without UC (situation (d)).

A more complete analysis of the interaction between the different elements of the tax-benefit system that relate to employment disincentives in the presence of

178 Jerome De Henau

TABLE 10.6 Net household income gains from employment with and without Universal Credit and childcare costs (couples on median wages and with two pre-school children)

	(a) Childcare costs with UC	(b) Childcare costs w/o UC	(c) Free childcare with UC	(d) Free childcare w/o UC
Gross income 0h (£, yearly)	24,149	24,149	24,149	24,149
Gross income 35h (£, yearly)	45,279	45,279	45,279	45,279
Gross income gain (£, yearly)	21,130	21,130	21,130	21,130
Net income 0h (£, yearly)	24,705	21,147	24,705	21,147
Childcare costs (if 35h work) (£, yearly)	14,124	14,124	0	0
Net income 35h (£, yearly)	27,595	24,346	38,470	38,470
Net income gain (£, yearly)	2890	3199	13,765	17,323
Net income gain (% gross gain)	14%	15%	65%	82%

Source: author's calculations based on tax year 2014–15. Couple with two children aged four and one, one partner in full-time employment at 40 hours. Both partners on median wage rates. Gain is calculated for second partner to move from zero to 35 hours of employment.

young children would require a full-blown tax-benefit simulation tool such as that used in Reed's chapter in this volume (see Ch.7), accompanied by an econometric behavioural model of employment. This would also allow a more accurate estimation of the reduction in total spending on tax credits and other means-tested benefits from providing universal childcare and thus increasing employment.

Net funding needs

Given these employment considerations, it is possible to assess the revenue streams that would go to the Treasury, thereby reducing the net bill necessary to fund the investment in free universal childcare.

First, the amount currently spent on childcare subsidies (£5 billion in 2014–15) would obviously be absorbed by the new investment (apart for a minor amount going to some older children using out-of-school childcare). Secondly, direct revenue would arise from income tax and national insurance levied on the newly created jobs; tax revenue would also come in the form of indirect taxation as a result of increased consumption. Thirdly, spending on tax credits (i.e. UC) could be reduced as employment and earnings increase.

A rough estimate of the last of these can be calculated as follows (assuming mothers of young children took up employment at earnings levels described above). The total tax credit bill paid to families with children aged between six months and five years and excluding childcare subsidies was just under £10 billion in 2014.[10] As Table 10.6 shows, couple families at median wage levels would no longer be entitled to any UC if childcare was free and both parents were employed full-time (in fact, at least 30 hours per week). Lone parents would still get substantial amounts of tax credit, even if working full-time. Using data from the Family Resources Survey, lone parents accounted for 39% of families with children under five years of age receiving tax credits in 2013–14, approximately 600,000 families.[11] Simulating their entitlement on a 35-hour working week basis and averaging between one- and two-child families, the remaining total bill in non-childcare UC would be an average £1.7 billion at median wages and £3.6 billion at living wages.[12] Therefore the tax credit bill excluding childcare subsidies would be reduced by £8 billion and £6.1 billion respectively.

Revenue from the new jobs in the form of income tax and national insurance contributions of employees and of employers can also be estimated. Jobs resulting from indirect and induced effects are assumed to be paid at the full-time median salary per annum of £23,889. Table 10.7 summarises the tax revenue from all new jobs created. It also shows the remaining net funding needs for the government, taking into account the current £5 billion annual childcare budget and the reduced tax credits bill estimated above. Revenue from indirect taxation has also been

TABLE 10.7 Tax revenue from job creation and net funding needs

Employment effect	Teacher wage			Living wage		
	Direct	Direct + indirect	Direct + indirect + induced	Direct	Direct + indirect	Direct + indirect + induced
Gross funding need (£m)	49,149	49,149	49,149	27,907	27,907	27,907
Tax revenue from jobs (£m)						
Care	10,987	10,987	10,987	3,957	3,957	3,957
Other	0	1,434	2,959	0	1,434	2,959
Total	10,987	12,421	13,946	3,957	5,391	6,916
Indirect tax revenue (£m)	6,200	7,046	7,945	3,615	4,460	5,359
Reduced UC bill (£m)	8,000	8,000	8,000	6,200	6,200	6,200
Current funding cc (£m)	5,000	5,000	5,000	5,000	5,000	5,000
Net funding need (£m)	18,962	16,683	14,258	9,135	6,856	4,432
% of gross funding	39%	34%	29%	33%	25%	16%

Source: author's calculations.

Note: "UC" stands for Universal Credit and "cc" for childcare.

considered, using a rough estimate based on the average tax incidence on gross household income (17%) for non-retired households in the middle quintiles (second, third and fourth) in 2013–14 (ONS 2015b).[13]

As the net funding needs remain significant in either pay scenario (£14 billion and £4 billion respectively, assuming induced effects), funding from other sources would need to be brought in. One possibility would be to reverse some of the tax giveaways afforded since 2010. Successive above-inflation rises in personal income tax allowance (and the introduction of a transferable tax allowance for married couples) amounted to foregone revenue of £13 billion per year in 2015–16 and freezes or cuts in alcohol and fuel duties added up to £7 billion per year (OBR 2015). These giveaways were criticised for being ill targeted, expensive and less advantageous for women (IFS 2015; WBG 2014, 2015b). Reversing the personal income tax giveaway would almost entirely cover the shortfall in the teacher scenario (induced effects), while reversing the excise duties giveaway would more than fill the gap in the living wage scenario (even if only indirect effects are considered).

In addition, companies could fund the shortfall: the successive cuts in the corporation tax rate were forecast to add up to approximately £7.6 billion per year in foregone revenue in 2015–16 (HMRC and HM Treasury 2013). The government justified the successive cuts in the corporation tax rate as a means to boost investment and thus employment levels since 2010 (HMRC and HM Treasury 2013). Together with the other tax reductions, they are claimed to have contributed to the 1.8 million rise in employment numbers observed between 2010 and 2015, which is 1.65 million in FTEs. Interestingly, this is equivalent to the 1.6 million FTE jobs the free childcare plan would create, accounting for its indirect effects.

Hence if the government claim is correct, the same case could be made to reverse these giveaways to fund employment in childcare, and although the total employment effect might be neutral (same total employment "created") the gender implications would likely be very different with a large reduction in the gender employment gap in the case of childcare. Incidentally, if only half of the total amount of these three giveaways was reversed (i.e. £13.8 billion), this would be just as much as the £13.8 billion shortfall in the teacher scenario.

In any case, the net funding needs – even in the higher-quality scenario – are well below the annual foregone revenue due to tax avoidance and evasion, even using the government's cautious estimate of £34 billion (which may in fact be up to £120 billion according to Sikka 2015).

Alternative scenarios for childcare provision

If the sources of additional revenue and funding explored above are too speculative or politically infeasible, other avenues for spending on childcare could be explored. This could be achieved by reducing the number of children or hours provided for by the free high-quality childcare places (either by targeting specific children or on

The case of free universal childcare in the UK   **181**

the assumption that not all parents will want to take up a full-time childcare place for every child from six months old until school age). Another option could be to charge a fee to parents, which for the purpose of looking at total costs would be equivalent to reducing the proportion of children that are covered free of charge and/or full-time. If we were to look at distributional and incentive aspects then this option should be considered separately from other alternatives because of potential differences in the take-up effects of fees according to parental income levels.[14]

Notwithstanding costing issues, alternative policies could also be designed to require fewer hours in centre-based care and more equally shared parental caring time (for couples).[15] For example, in the case of couples, with a reduced working week spanning four days (seven hours per day to tie in with the 35-hour week discussed above), and assuming alternate days of care by each parent, centre-based coverage would only be provided for three days per week, thereby reducing total funding needs. Option 2 below is based on this premise. It would be adapted to lone parents' four-day working week so as to provide 32 hours of childcare. Other options are also discussed below and reflect what some political parties have pledged to achieve (albeit at a different – lower – level of wages).

The following options are examined:

- Option 1 is the scenario above with 40 hours' coverage, including one hour per day for commuting.
- Option 2 covers all children for three days per week at eight hours per day, and four days per week for lone parents (averaging 26 hours in total,[16] in line with Labour and SNP 2015 general election proposals of 25 hours).
- Option 3 is the existing (pre-2015 election) provision of 15 hours free but extended to all pre-school children (and at higher wage levels).
- Option 4 is the planned (2015 Conservative Government) provision of 30 hours free for working parents (assumed to cover 75% of children in each age group).

Note that Option 4, the current government's proposal, offers longer hours than Option 2 but is restricted to working parents. This would be an issue for parents looking for work or in full-time education and is also problematic for those parents at home with disabilities or long-term conditions who may need help looking after their child. It also implies that childcare is a benefit only for the parents, not the child.

All of the options offer a more generous scenario than any party's proposal in their 2015 election manifesto. The Conservative Government elected in May 2015 is committed to offer 30 hours' free childcare for three- to four-year-olds (which is also SNP policy in Scotland). Labour's proposal was for 25 hours (supported by the SNP for England). The Liberal Democrats' long-term plan was to aim for 20 hours for all children aged from nine months to five years, starting with 15 hours to all two-year-olds. However, all parties explicitly focused on access to children whose parents are both in paid employment. Only the Greens pledged a free

182 Jerome De Henau

childcare scenario for all children regardless of the working status of their parents but they did not give a figure of hours per week. None of these parties made clear whether they would extend the free hours offer from 38 weeks to 48 weeks a year (as in the options above). Given the costing included in some of the manifestos, it is unlikely that the proposals envisaged subsidising the care staff at rates corresponding to a living wage, let alone a teacher's wage.

Table 10.8 summarises the main results for each option and for both types of pay for carers, using the full (induced) employment multiplier.

The net cost (net funding need) of £6 billion in Option 2 (teacher's salary) is below the £7 billion annual tax giveaways in excise duties cumulated between 2010 and 2015. In the living wage scenario it is entirely self-funded from increased direct and indirect tax revenue and a reduced UC bill, as are Options 3 and 4.

The "cheapest" option is obviously Option 3 and the teacher wage scenario would require a net amount (£450 million) – this is less than the extra £1 billion commitment by the government in 2015 to fund the extra hours of free childcare. However, providing 15 hours of childcare, albeit with well-paid staff, failing to even cover two days of work including commuting time, would not be considered sufficient to promote a triple-carer dual-earner model, as it is unlikely that both parents would reduce their hours in equal measure to fill the gap.

On the other hand, a commitment could still be made to find additional funding (from reversing tax giveaways or curbing tax avoidance schemes) so that Option 1 is pursued. Then if Option 2 was eventually chosen as a better way to foster gender

TABLE 10.8 Cost of free childcare for alternative hours and coverage

| | Option 1 | Option 2 | Option 3 | Option 4 |
| | *100% cov. /* | *100% cov. /* | *100% cov. /* | *75% cov.* |
	40h pw	*26h pw*	*15h pw*	*/ 30h pw*
Total cost (£m)				
Teacher wage	49,149	31,947	18,431	27,646
Living wage	27,907	18,140	10,465	15,698
No. FTE care jobs	1,224,554	795,960	459,208	688,812
No. FTE non-care jobs	429,596	279,237	161,098	241,648
Tax revenue from jobs (£m)				
Teacher wage	21,891	14,229	8,209	12,314
Living wage	12,276	7,979	4,603	6,905
Reduced UC bill (£m)				
Teacher wage	8,000	6,800	4,600	5,100
Living wage	6,200	5,400	2,000	4,050
Net funding need (£m)				
Teacher wage	14,258	5,918	622	5,233
Living wage	4,432	−240	−1,138	−257

Source: author's calculations.

Note: "UC" stands for Universal Credit

The case of free universal childcare in the UK **183**

equality and parental involvement in sharing some caring time, the difference in funding requirements between the two options (£8 billion of net funding needs) could be directed to investing in other aspects of the caring economy and its social infrastructure. An obvious area that crucially needs additional funding is adult social care services. The final report of the independent Commission on the Future of Health and Social Care in England estimated that making sufficient care to provide for all critical and substantial needs free at the point of use for older people would require approximately £3 billion in the short term rising to £14 billion by 2025 (Barker 2014).

Besides providing high-quality childcare to all children, promoting a more gender-equal care and employment system would also require reforming the maternity and paternity leave system so as to enhance the chances of equal parenting in the first months of a child's life. This might have knock-on effects on the time organisation of both parents when the child enters formal childcare, improving the chances of adopting a reduced four-day working week as in the model of Option 2 above (or even Option 1 with a 35-hour week for both parents). Research has shown that relatively short periods of individual well-paid leave were attractive to fathers and beneficial to mothers' long-term prospects (see De Henau et al. 2007b).

One possibility could therefore be to offer six months of individual leave to each parent paid as a relatively high proportion of earnings, to accompany universal childcare provision. A fiscally neutral solution could be to use the amount spent per child during the first year (from existing parental leave spending and the first six months of the gross funding of free childcare provision). This would be equivalent to £347 per week on average per child over the first year (and thus for each parent), using Option 1 costing. This is 70% of median full-time earnings (ONS 2014c), and is more than double the current amount of statutory maternity and paternity leave available per child over the first year. The amount could be allocated on a flat-rate basis (thus more generous for lower earnings) or as a proportion of earnings (as in Germany and Sweden), between certain limits. This would affect take up incentives for parents on different income levels and thus the way children of different socioeconomic backgrounds are looked after. However, if the leave period is capped at six months per parent and generous high-quality childcare is offered afterwards, limited differential impact on children's outcomes and career prospects of parents between those choosing the leave and those opting for formal childcare would be expected (Ray et al. 2010).

Conclusion

This chapter has demonstrated that investing in free childcare is a costly but feasible endeavour using existing resources more effectively. The UK Chancellor claimed in his 2015 summer budget that the 2.3 million jobs created since he took office in 2010 (2 million FTE) were made possible by the tax and spending cuts his government introduced. Whether they have caused the increase in employment remains to be shown. In any case, the childcare policy presented above shows that

184 Jerome De Henau

almost the equivalent in terms of FTE employment could be created, with much clearer causal effects (given the direct investment in public employment), and with more decent working conditions and earnings than many of the private sector jobs (25% of which were self-employment, many with low earnings) created since 2010 (WBG 2015b). Moreover, such investment would improve women's employment opportunities and earnings, promote more equal employment and working hours between men and women, and reduce spending on means-tested social security benefits.

Be that as it may, building the social infrastructure and providing the care that people need is not just about creating employment, boosting economic growth and therefore investing in productive assets – children – for the return they can bring. The case made here is about what we should expect from a civilised society. Providing free and universal childcare will enhance children's social interaction and education, which may have positive knock-on effects on their future outcomes. Significant amounts of resources are required – full-time universal childcare coverage at teachers' wages amounts to 3% of GDP. However, between 70% and 100% of the gross amount could be self-funded through tax revenue stemming from direct and indirect job creation and subsequent consumption and reduced social security benefit payments, while reversing some of the main three tax giveaways of the Coalition 2010–15 Government could fund the remaining shortfall. Even if not strictly self-funding (as in Option 1 or Option 2 at teachers' wages), investing in free universal childcare of high quality would still be worthwhile on the grounds of improving well-being, quality of life and social cohesion.

The chapter also explored issues around fostering more equal parenting time. Transforming labour markets, childcare provision and parental leave systems could contribute to developing a high-quality triple-carer/dual-earner model that fosters gender equality in both spheres of paid and unpaid work. At the core of this plan would be the move towards reducing the full-time working week to a four-day week, so that parents of young children can alternate one day of full-time care at home. This is an essential step towards building a caring economy that doesn't only rely on formal services but also on providing quality time and protection to unpaid carers, both men and women.

Notes

1 This is effectively equivalent to 10 hours of parental opportunity to take employment if 48 working weeks per annum and commuting time are to be accounted for.
2 Note that by taking the women's average as reference instead of the overall average, the author does not imply that such a system is designed around childcare remaining solely a women's issue. Benchmarking on 35h implies that both men and women would work shorter hours in order to have more time to get involved in caring activities, which is the way forward within a triple-carer model.
3 The 2015 Spending Review announced increased investment in childcare provision set to reach £6 billion by 2020 (with increased free childcare hours for children of working parents). Despite the announcement this would actually be a fall as a proportion of GDP (WBG 2015c).

The case of free universal childcare in the UK **185**

4 This is higher than the headline staff:child ratio of 23 carers for every 100 children (see Table 1). The difference is due to the fact that carers' full-time equivalent week is only 35 hours while children are to be looked after for 40 hours in the full-time scenario. Also, not all the carers' time is spent with children (18% was factored in for administration and meetings, as in Table 2).

5 Respectively, categories 6121, 6122 and 6123 of the SOC 2010 occupations in the Labour Force Survey (ONS 2014b).

6 Although it would be slightly more when accounting for the current teaching professionals in nursery education and managerial staff, the numbers of whom are difficult to estimate given the existing statistical classification that treats, for example, primary school and nursery school professionals (the latter being for some of the three- and four-year olds) as part of the same occupation.

7 Existing jobs were not subtracted from the direct and indirect effects when computing the induced effects since they would experience increased earnings that also have induced effects.

8 Headcount rates are derived from the ONS series on working families and FTE calculations are based on proportions of employed men and women with young children working part-time (15% and 55% respectively), using average working hours of part-time men and women overall (around 16 hours). We assume a full-time working week based on the female full-time average of 35 hours. All data are from ONS 2014b.

9 The planned system of UC covers 85% of childcare costs up to a limit. In situations (a) and (c) childcare costs are assumed to be at an average of £4.4 an hour per child (based on Rutter and Stocker 2014) for 48 weeks. However, 15 hours of free childcare per week for 38 weeks are taken up by the oldest child aged four (the youngest is one year old and not entitled to the current provision of free hours).

10 Thirty-nine per cent of the non-childcare tax credit bill went to families with children aged zero to four years in 2012–13 (HMRC 2014), and the total tax credit bill was £30 billion in 2014, with £2 billion in childcare subsidies (DWP 2014).

11 Data kindly provided by Howard Reed's Landman Economics simulation model.

12 These wage rates represent the respective minimum wages assumed in each childcare model (teacher option and living wage option). In the former option, teachers' wages are higher but median wages are assumed for indirect and induced employment effects.

13 Keeping a constant rate is a plausible method: the incidence is 18% for households in the second quintile and 15% for those in the fourth quintile (so the range around the average is small). Moreover the difference in average gross income between the two groups is just above the median gross earnings, which is in the range of the increase in household income if one member was taking up one of these extra jobs/hours.

14 Of course, fees could be adapted to parents' income, as in many countries with subsidised childcare places (Van Lancker 2013).

15 See also discussion in Mohun Himmelweit et al. (2014).

16 Eighty per cent of parents on 24 hours (couples) and 20% on 32 hours (lone parents), as per ONS figures (ONS 2014a).

References

Antonopoulos, R., K. Kim, T. Masterson and A. Zacharias. 2010. "Investing in Care: A Strategy for Effective and Equitable Job Creation." Working Paper No. 610. Levy Economics Institute.

Babchishin, L., K. Weegar and E. Romano. 2013. "Early Child Care Effects on Later Behavioral Outcomes Using a Canadian Nation-Wide Sample." *Journal of Educational and Developmental Psychology* 3(2): 15–29. www.ruor.uottawa.ca/bitstream/10393/31986/1/Romano.pdf (accessed 23 April 2015).

186 Jerome De Henau

Barker, K. (ed.). 2014. "A New Settlement for Health and Social Care." Final Report of the Independent Commission on the Future of Health and Social Care in England. London: King's Fund.

Ben Ghalim, D. 2011. "Making the Case for Universal Childcare." Briefing. London: Institute for Public Policy Research.

Braunstein, E., I. Van Staveren and D. Tavani. 2011. "Embedding Care and Unpaid Work in Macroeconomic Modelling: A Structuralist Approach." *Feminist Economics* 17(4): 5–31.

De Henau, J. and S. Himmelweit. 2013. "Examining Public Policy from a Gendered Intra-household Perspective: Changes in Family-related Policies in the UK, Australia and Germany since the Mid-nineties." *Oñati Socio-Legal Series* 3(7): 1222–48.

De Henau, J., S. Himmelweit, Z. Lapniewska and D. Perrons. 2015. "Investing in the Care Economy. A Gender Analysis of Employment Stimulus in Seven OECD Countries." Women's Budget Group Report to the International Trade Union Confederation (November), Brussels.

De Henau, J., D. Meulders and S. O'Dorchai. 2007a. "Making Time for Working Parents: Comparing Public Childcare Provision across EU-15." In D. Del Boca and C. Wetzels (eds). *Social Policies, Labour Markets and Motherhood: A Comparative Analysis of European Countries*. Cambridge: Cambridge University Press, pp.28–62.

De Henau, J., D. Meulders and S. O'Dorchai. 2007b. "Parents' Care and Career: Comparing Parental Leave Policies across EU-15". In D. Del Boca and C. Wetzels (eds). *Social Policies, Labour Markets and Motherhood: A Comparative Analysis of European Countries*. Cambridge University Press, pp.63–106.

Department for Education. 2014. "School Teachers Pay and Conditions, September, London." Government of the United Kingdom. www.gov.uk/government/uploads/system/uploads/attachment_data/file/341951/School_teachers__pay_and_conditions_2014.pdf (accessed 21 February 2015).

Department for Work and Pensions (DWP). 2014. "Outturn and Forecast – Autumn Statement 2014, Benefit Expenditure and Caseload Tables." Government of the United Kingdom. www.gov.uk/government/statistics/benefit-expenditure-and-caseload-tables-2014 (accessed 11 November 2015).

Goldin, C. 2006. "The Quiet Revolution that Transformed Women's Employment, Education, and Family." *American Economic Review* 96: 1–21.

HM Revenue & Customs. 2014. "Child Benefit, Child Tax Credit and Working Tax Credit, Take-up Rates 2012-13." Government of the United Kingdom.

HM Revenue & Customs and HM Treasury. 2013. "Analysis of the Dynamic Effects of Corporation Tax Reductions." Government of the United Kingdom. www.gov.uk/government/uploads/system/uploads/attachment_data/file/263560/4069_CT_Dynamic_effects_paper_2013031 (accessed 11 November 2015).

Havnes, T. and M. Mogstad. 2011. "No Child Left Behind: Universal Child Care and Children's Long-Run Outcomes." *American Economic Journal: Economic Policy* 3(2): 97–129.

Havnes, T. and M. Mogstad. 2014. "Is Universal Child Care Leveling the Playing Field? Evidence from Non-Linear Difference-in-Differences." IZA Discussion Paper 4978. www.econstor.eu/bitstream/10419/36832/1/62740314X.pdf (accessed 23 April 2015).

IFS. 2015. *Green Budget 2015* (February). London: Institute for Fiscal Studies.

Karoly, L.A., M.R. Kilburn and J.S. Cannon. 2005. *Early Childhood Interventions: Proven Results, Future Promise*. Santa Monica: RAND Corporation, CA.

Lewis, J. (ed.). 2006. *Children, Changing Families and Welfare States*. Cheltenham: Edward Elgar.

The case of free universal childcare in the UK **187**

Li, W., G. Farkas, G.J. Duncan, M.R. Burchinal and D.L. Vandell. 2013. "Timing of High-quality Child Care and Cognitive, Language, and Preacademic Development." *Developmental Psychology* 49(8): 1440–51. www.ncbi.nlm.nih.gov/pmc/articles/PMC4034459/ (accessed 23 April 2015).

Living Wage Foundation. 2015. "Calculation of the Living Wage." www.livingwage.org.uk/calculation (accessed 21 March 2015).

Mohun Himmelweit, J., A. Coote and J. Hough. 2014. *The Value of Childcare*. London: New Economics Foundation.

Morel, N., B. Palier and J. Palme (eds). 2012. *Towards a Social Investment Welfare State? Ideas, Policies and Challenges*. Bristol: The Policy Press.

OBR. 2015. "Budget/PBR/Autumn Statement Measures Database." Office for Budget Responsibility. http://budgetresponsibility.org.uk/policy-measures-database/ (accessed 14 August 2015).

ONS. 2014a. "Population Estimates for UK, England and Wales, Scotland and Northern Ireland, Mid-2014, Reference Tables." Office for National Statistics. www.ons.gov.uk/ons/publications/re-reference-tables.html?edition=tcm%3A77-368259 (accessed 25 July 2015).

ONS. 2014b. "Labour Force Survey, Reference Tables." Office for National Statistics. www.ons.gov.uk/ons/datasets-and-tables (accessed 23 April 2015).

ONS. 2014c. "Annual Survey of Hours and Earnings, Provisional Tables 2014." Office for National Statistics. www.ons.gov.uk/ons/datasets-and-tables (accessed 12 February 2015).

ONS. 2015a. "Births in England and Wales, 2014." Statistical Bulletin (15 July). Office for National Statistics. www.ons.gov.uk/ons/dcp171778_410897.pdf (accessed 24 July 2015).

ONS. 2015b. "The Effects of Taxes and Benefits on Household Income, 2013–14, Reference Tables." www.ons.gov.uk/ons/rel/household-income/the-effects-of-taxes-and-benefits-on-household-income/2013-2014/index.html (accessed 27 November 2015).

Ray, R., J. Gornick and J. Schmitt. 2010. "Who Cares? Assessing Generosity and Gender Equality in Parental Leave Policy Designs in 21 Countries." *Journal of European Social Policy* 20(3): 196–216.

Reed, H. and J. Portes. 2014. "Cumulative Impact Assessment: A Research Report by Landman Economics and the National Institute of Economic and Social Research (NIESR) for the Equality and Human Rights Commission." EHRC Research Report 94.

Rutter, J. 2015. *Childcare Costs Survey 2015*. London: Family and Childcare Trust.

Rutter, J. and K. Stocker. 2014. *Childcare Costs Survey 2014*. London: Family and Childcare Trust.

Sikka, P. 2015. "This Election, Remember that Cracking Down on Tax Avoidance Could End Austerity." *The Conversation* (9 March). http://theconversation.com/this-election-remember-that-cracking-down-on-tax-avoidance-could-end-austerity-38464 (accessed 19 March 2015).

Scottish Government. 2015. "Input-Output Tables 1998-2012 – Leontief Type 1 Table." www.gov.scot/Topics/Statistics/Browse/Economy/Input-Output/Downloads/IO1998-2012L1 (accessed 23 July 2015).

Van Lancker, W. 2013. "Putting the Child-centred Investment Strategy to the Test: Evidence for the EU-27." *Journal of Social Security* 15(1): 4–27.

Women's Budget Group (WBG). 2014. "The Impact on Women of Budget 2014: No Recovery for Women." Women's Budget Group Budget Analysis. http://wbg.org.uk/wp-content/uploads/2015/04/WBG-Budget-2015.pdf (accessed 20 April 2015).

Women's Budget Group (WBG). 2015a. "PLAN F: A Feminist Economic Strategy for a Caring and Sustainable Economy." Women's Budget Group Briefing Paper. http://wbg.org.uk/wp-content/uploads/2015/02/PLAN-F-2015.pdf (accessed 20 April 2015).

Women's Budget Group (WBG). 2015b. "Response to Budget 2015 – The WBG Calls for Rebuilding the Foundations before Fixing the Roof." Women's Budget Group Budget Analysis. http://wbg.org.uk/wp-content/uploads/2015/04/WBG-Budget-2015.pdf (accessed 20 April 2015).

Women's Budget Group (WBG). 2015c. "The Impact on Women of the Autumn Statement and Comprehensive Spending Review 2015: Still Failing to Invest in Women's Security." Women's Budget Group Analysis. http://wbg.org.uk/wp-content/uploads/2015/04/WBG_AFS_CSR_2015_report_2015_12_07_final3.pdf (accessed 12 January 2016).

CONCLUSION

Explaining austerity and its gender impact

Susan Himmelweit

Introduction

Despite being compiled more than seven years after the financial crisis of 2007–08, this book's chapters show that the effects of the crisis, and those of the austerity policies implemented across Europe in its wake, are far from over.

The recession consequent upon the financial crisis started as a "mancession", hitting men's employment more than women's in all European countries, with the majority of jobs initially lost being in male-dominated, pro-cyclical industries, primarily manufacturing and construction (OECD 2010). Greater numbers of women were working in the public sector and in basic services that were less subject to cyclical downturns, especially immediately after the financial crash when governments tended to increase public spending rather than cut it (Ch.6 by Gago in this volume).

Austerity and its effects

But that changed rapidly as one government after another subscribed to the austerity agenda, or had it imposed upon them, despite the continuing recession in many countries. Austerity was justified by a number of core beliefs: first, that current levels of public debt were unsustainable; second, that the priority had to be fiscal consolidation, to reduce and eventually eliminate any fiscal deficit; third, that the way to do so was to tackle the fiscal deficit directly, even if that resulted in more unemployment or an economic downturn making fiscal consolidation harder to achieve; and finally, that fiscal consolidation had to be carried out primarily by cutting spending rather than raising taxes. All of these were justified by reference to "the markets" that in the absence of such policies might render a country's existing debt impossible to finance.

190 Susan Himmelweit

Özlem Onaran's chapter (Ch.3 in this volume) shows the weakness of this argument, while other chapters in this volume demonstrate its effects (Chapters 4 by Vertova, 5 by Barry, 6 by Gago and 7 by Reed in this volume). The mancession had not in itself been easy for many women who had to cope not only with managing reduced household budgets, but in some cases if they could find a job also working long hours themselves to compensate for a man's lost wages. Then as governments turned from stimulus policies to austerity, expenditure cuts directly hit women's jobs that made up the majority of frontline public sector employment in most countries (Karamessini and Rubery 2014). The recovery has been slow and fragile with little net job creation, and with Greece expected to continue to show negative growth until 2017, and Belgium, Greece, Spain and Italy expecting to see a fall in real wages in 2016 (European Union 2015). And in all the countries considered in this book, austerity has ground on relentlessly.

Women's unemployment levels rose faster than men's, and continued to rise in many countries after men's peaked. Although women's unemployment rates are now falling this may well conceal hidden unemployment: for example, in the UK the rise in the economic activity rate of women - a key indicator of women's attachment to the labour market that had been converging to that of men - has slowed considerably, with the number of economically inactive women who want employment rising between the first quarters of 2012 and 2015 (TUC 2015).

Where there has been growth, it is through previous public sectors jobs being replaced by private sector jobs, but not necessarily in the same numbers and not necessarily given to women in the same proportions as the public sector jobs they replaced. Further those private sector jobs have been of worse quality on a number of dimensions (TUC 2012). In particular, private sector employment has a considerably larger gender pay gap in nearly all countries and rarely matches the family-friendly conditions of employment that have been pioneered in the public sector (OECD 2014).

The earlier trend of the gender pay gap narrowing through upward convergence of women's wages to men's has been replaced by a widening gap, or one that has fallen only through downward convergence as many men's wages and conditions fall to those more typical of women's jobs (Bettio et al. 2013). Similarly, the gender gap in employment rates has narrowed across the EU, but only due to the worsening employment situation of men (Ch.5 by Barry in this volume: Table 5.1). In Italy where, unusually, women's employment levels rose while men's continued to fall after 2010, this exception was achieved only by a huge growth in involuntary part-time working among women, thus suggesting a substitution of women working under inferior conditions for the jobs men had lost (Ch.4 by Vertova in this volume).

Another particularly worrying trend throughout Europe is for gender equality as a goal to be side-lined, with equality in general seen as a low priority compared to fiscal consolidation, despite heavy reliance on a rhetoric of citizens needing to pull together. As Vertova notes, this can better be called "gender blindness" because only a few countries carried out any gender impact assessment of their

Austerity and its gender impact **191**

recovery programs, despite the latter tending to target any initial stimulus packages on heavily male-dominated industries (European Commission 2009: 10; Bettio et al. 2013; Ch.4 by Vertova in this volume). And gender specific employment targets that were included in the European Employment Strategy when it was first developed in the 1990s have all but disappeared from EU policy documents (European Commission 2009, 2012).

Some women have been hit harder than others. Howard Reed's chapter (Ch.7 in this volume) shows that in the UK it is lone parents who have lost most through benefit cuts and tax changes, while they and single pensioners constitute the groups that have been impacted most by cuts in public services, particularly in social care. While we do not have such detailed analysis for other European countries, similar types of cuts have been implemented in many countries and so we can expect those two groups to have been particularly impacted elsewhere too (Ch.5 by Barry in this volume; Keane et al. 2014).

Cuts to social care provision that have been implemented in many countries impact more severely on women than men, as care recipients, as employees in paid care and as the providers of unpaid care; in all of these groups women form the majority (Bettio 2013). There can be considerable regional variation within countries on the gender impact of austerity measures, as Gago's chapter shows (Ch.6 in this volume). She found considerably greater regional variation in the impact of austerity on women's employment rates than on men's, and that gender employment gaps seem to have increased most in those regions that already had larger than average gaps before the crisis. In other words, rather than seeing any convergence, regional disparities in gender inequalities have significantly increased.

The chapters together show that there has been considerable variation across European countries. Nevertheless, the direction of travel has been similar, with women in general, and additionally particular groups of women, lone mothers, the elderly and women needing care for themselves or for a disabled child, bearing a disproportionate share of the effects of austerity.

Alternative policies

The chapters in this book have also documented that austerity has not been particularly effective in achieving recovery (among others Ch.1 by Elson in this volume). Indeed, as the chapter by Onaran (Ch.3 in this volume) shows, there is good reason to expect that for Europe as a whole, and many of the larger countries individually, higher wages rather than higher profits are needed to generate employment and growth. Austerity has had the opposite effect, leading to stagnation and recession in many countries. Although some countries are slowly recovering, the austerity policies conventionally credited with this unspectacular recovery have in practice slowed it down, and have been far less effective than some alternative policies would have been in promoting employment (Rosnick and Weisbrot 2015). As I write in early 2016 it is not clear whether this fragile recovery in some European countries is set to continue or will stall.

192 Susan Himmelweit

Further the particular policies adopted have set back the cause of gender equality, by directly taking more from women than from men through tax-benefit systems and by imposing cuts on the forms of public expenditure which matter most to women (Ch.7 by Reed in this volume). Other chapters have shown that there are alternative polices which would be much more effective in generating employment and growth, while at the same time promoting greater gender equality. In particular boosting public spending in ways that are targeted specifically at reducing the gender employment gap would be more effective than a less targeted approach in generating overall employment and growth (Chapters 8 by Bargawi and Cozzi and 9 by Andersen and Dahl in this volume).

Like other forms of stimulus spending, one would want such targeted spending to be in a form of investment with long-term benefits to the economy and to be sustainable, in terms of both the environment and gender relations. The latter is an important but largely unrecognised aspect of sustainability since depending on unequal gender norms is unlikely to be sustainable in the long run as women's employment rates increase. Ipek Ikkaracan's chapter (Ch.2 in this volume) makes the case for investment that is simultaneously "green", in being environmentally sustainable, and "purple", in promoting gender equality. Jerome De Henau's chapter (Ch.10 in this volume) shows that a form of social investment that would generate significant impacts on gender equality, the provision of universal free childcare by a well-paid childcare workforce, while expensive, costs no more than the annual revenue given away in successive tax cuts in the UK since 2010, despite that being a period of fiscal consolidation.

Explanations needed

Given this, some explanation is needed of why, to a greater or lesser extent, governments throughout Europe have adopted policies that have held back recovery and set back gender equality. The rest of this chapter will suggest one possible answer to this puzzle. It will first consider the interests that have been served by such policies and the shifts within global capitalism that enabled those interests to achieve hegemony. And second it will consider why those policies have had such different effects on men and women. To explore both these questions we need to examine trends that were in place well before the financial crisis.

Why austerity policies have been adopted: shifts within global capitalism

Historically, the development of European welfare states was based on the recognition of shared interests of capital and labour in the social reproduction of a national working class (Wahl 2011). Here "social reproduction" means everything a society does to reproduce its people and the social relations into which they enter. The term covers not just material consumption, but also the services that people require to be functioning members of society and its potential labour force.

These services include, but are not limited to, the different forms of care that people need at various stages of their life course. The services contributing to social reproduction that the state provides have been termed the "social wage" by analogy with the wage that workers receive from their employers. Rather than being paid by individual capitalists, the social wage is paid through the state by "capital in general" that, in a Marxist account at least, represents those interests of the capitalist class that require collective action.

The class compromise that led to state involvement in the process of social reproduction was based on the existence and political influence of a national capitalist class that made its profits through employing workers within that country, and therefore had an interest in their social reproduction. It was that interest that led to the development of state-funded national education, health and care systems, providing the vital services that contribute to social reproduction for which the wage system and the family does not adequately cater and could be better provided collectively. It is important to recognise that such state support augments and underpins but is never designed to replace either the wage system or unpaid family care. These remain the more fundamental contributors to social reproduction in a capitalist economy – even in Sweden, the country with the most developed welfare state, twice the amount of paid care provided to elderly people is given unpaid within families, while for people with dementia the amount of unpaid care is about 8.5 times greater than that provided by formal services (Wimo et al. 2002).

The class compromise that led to the development of the welfare state was not automatic; it depended on a number of factors that were in place to differing extents in most European countries in the post-Second World War period. These factors included the recognition by both labour and capital that as classes they have shared interests in social reproduction that are best met collectively. Labour movements have varied across Europe in the extent to which they have supported the social wage, collective provision for social reproduction, or have focused more narrowly on improving the pay and working conditions of their members. Capital's willingness to support collective provision depends, among other factors, on how dependent it is on any particular national working class, or whether it can pick and choose where to employ workers to make its profits; mobility and the possibility of outsourcing and offshoring in a globalising world undermines capital's dependency and hence its support for collective provision. The relative powers of capital and labour and how they can be exercised is also influenced by global international conditions: whether there is more of a focus on short-term competitive pressures and driving down wage rates and taxes on capital or, alternatively, whether welfare states are being built-up to improve the conditions of social reproduction for their populations and the economy's long-term competitiveness.

Broadly, Western European welfare states were and still are more in favour of collective provision than the United States, but within Western Europe there is considerable variation. On one end of the European continuum is the UK, with its long history of capital mobility, outsourcing and immigration through the British Empire and Commonwealth, a labour movement that was relatively quiescent politically and a liberal "safety-net" welfare state. At the other end there are the far more generous and inclusive social-democratic Scandinavian welfare states, built on strong labour movements and an initial reluctance to let immigration dilute relatively homogenous and cohesive populations.

Finance capital is the ultimate in internationally mobile capital: David Harvey (2005) calls it "butterfly capital" (Durand and Boulet 2013). It makes little of its profits directly from its own workforce and far more from the profits of other capitals and thus indirectly from their workers, who may be anywhere in the world. It is therefore dependent for its profits on workers, but not on any particular set of workers. In particular, finance capital has no stake in the conditions of social reproduction of whatever country it happens to have located its headquarters, or where it chooses to pay any taxes. Indeed the power that it has to make such a choice, including to shelter in tax havens, undermines governments' abilities to raise revenue through corporate taxation.[1] Instead finance capital has an interest in undermining collective provision for social reproduction, because many financial services, such as insurance and particularly types of savings products, are required when individuals and households are left to make their own provision. Finance capital does not want to see its potentially lucrative markets in these areas undermined by often more efficient collective provision. Once it sufficiently dominates an economy, finance capital's mobility gives it the power to set political agendas, through the threat, and in some cases the reality, of capital flight.

During the 1980s the growing power of internationally mobile finance capital resulted in the election of governments fully or partially espousing neoliberal programmes to reduce the power of the state, initially by deregulation of the financial sector and reduction in the progressivity of the tax system (Stiglitz 2012a). This happened first in the US and the UK, with the election of the Reagan and Thatcher governments, but their programmes were internationally influential and many other parties, even those of the left, adopted significant parts of the neoliberal agenda. Harvey (2005) sees neoliberalism both "as a utopian project to realize a theoretical design for the reorganization of international capitalism [that is one with a much smaller welfare state]" and "as a political project to re-establish the conditions for capital accumulation and to restore the power of economic elites", in which the second of these objectives has in practice dominated (Harvey 2005: 19).

The economic elites Harvey refers to are primarily constituted by those who derive their huge incomes from finance capital. Joseph Stiglitz makes the same point in different language. He talks of the financial sector, as "the rent-seeking sector par excellence" where rent-seeking means having the power through the ownership of property to appropriate income produced elsewhere so that rents are "nothing more than re-distributions from one part of society to the rent seekers". This he sees as a political problem because "when one interest group holds too much power, it succeeds in getting policies that help itself in the short term rather than help society as a whole over the long term" (Stiglitz 2012b). Such policies include dismantling the welfare state as well as deregulation and tax cutting.

Neoliberalism's attack on the welfare state is therefore based on a rejection of any notion of shared national interest in social reproduction by an increasingly financialised and thus internationally mobile capital that has no interest in the social reproduction of any particular national working class, but instead an interest in promoting working-class households' engagement in the market for financial services.

This attack limited the expansion of the welfare state even before the financial crisis, and led to "welfare reforms" being introduced in many countries. Typically, such reforms were imposed through the privatisation of public services, imposing private sector working conditions on a public sector workforce, a redesign of the benefits system, as in Germany and the UK, to recommodify labour and incentivise employment for all (with sticks as well as carrots) and creating a market for new financial "products".

Although neoliberal policies had been adopted previously, the financial crisis provided an opportunity to further that agenda, with the cuts to state spending to achieve fiscal consolidation presented as all what "the markets" required. Many countries chose or were forced to adopt neoliberal policies that entailed further cuts in the role of the state in social reproduction, thereby reducing aggregate demand even while unemployment and under-employment rates were high. As the chapters in this book have shown, there was some variation in how such cuts were imposed, with policy makers in a few places trying to resist their inequality creating effects. But in general the needs of social reproduction were subordinated to those of finance capital; it was policies conducive to *its* reproduction that dominated. In practice this meant that policies were followed that favoured the interests of finance capital, including some costly privatisations, despite undermining growth and even deficit reduction (Chapters 1 by Elson and 3 by Onaran in this volume).

Austerity was presented as a way out of the crisis through fiscal consolidation. However, given its lack of success in meeting even its own stated aims, it can be seen as in practice directed more at changing the norms of social reproduction and attitudes to the state. Real household incomes fell for a considerable period in most states that adopted fiscal consolidation policies. Even now as incomes are starting to rise again in many countries, they are highly unlikely ever to match where they would have been without the period of austerity, and what are seen as acceptable minimum standards will have fallen, possibly permanently. However, and perhaps more significantly, such austerity policies have also resulted in falls in the social wage, through public service cuts, with previous levels of service provision argued to be "unaffordable" and heavy emphasis put on the need for individuals and families to provide for their own needs (through the purchase of appropriate financial products). Public service cuts should not be seen as an unfortunate side effect of austerity policies, but a measure of their success in achieving neoliberal objectives.

The continuation of crisis conditions has enabled such policies to be adopted and normalised. There has been little initial resistance to the hegemonic power of the household analogy – that nations, like households, should not live beyond their means – and an acceptance that market "discipline" is needed to reduce "wasteful" spending on public services and "responsiblise" households into making their own provision. The household analogy underpinned the argument that the fiscal deficit had to be reduced, despite finance being available at near-zero interest rates for infrastructure projects whose long-term benefits easily outweighed their initial costs. Indeed, that analogy worked in the opposite direction, combined with the idea of public spending as wasteful, providing fertile ground for the view that families should be doing more to provide for their own needs. The argument that budget deficits were an indication of excessive costs of social reproduction was thus successfully presented as common sense, with the high levels of unemployment consequent on austerity policies leading to working-class quiescence.

Even if the economies of European do pick up again and see a more sustained recovery than has appeared to date, the effects of austerity in lowering expectations of state provision and in promoting the acceptance of more individualised responsibilities may be long-lasting, and possibly irreversible.

And why have they impacted particularly on women?

It was inevitable that such austerity programmes should have impacted particularly on women. Across Europe, women rely more on state support than men. This is for a number of reasons.

First, women are greater users of public services (Ch.7 by Reed in this volume). This is in part due to childbirth and greater longevity, so that women make more use of the medical services that in all European countries are at least partly publicly provided. Women are also more likely to live on their own when old because women tend to outlive their male partners due to their greater longevity being compounded by a traditional age gap between spouses. Women thus eventually require a range of other public services, above all social care, which men can often rely on their wives to provide.

Second, women are also likely to be poorer than their male counterparts, so more dependent on public services, and more likely to be eligible for, and in receipt of, means-tested benefits (Ch.7 by Reed in this volume). Women's lower incomes and their greater risk of poverty follow largely from their greater involvement in care, partly through the greater tendency for women to experience breaks and periods of part-time working in their employment history. That women's lives are more varied in this respect than men's is as much a cause of the gender pay and employment gaps as outright discrimination; though the impact of a reduced employment history varies across Europe (O'Reilly and Bothfeld 2002; Manning and Petrongolo 2004; Russo and Hassink 2008) and can itself be discriminatory, with women's careers suffering more and for longer after a period of part-time working than men's (Francesconi and Gosling 2005; Kröger and Yeandle 2013). Such differences in earnings and other benefits from employment cumulate through the life course and follow women into retirement (OECD 2015a). Considerably smaller retirement pensions, particularly occupational superannuation and other private pensions, leave women in old age more dependent than men on the rules determining their state pension and thus more vulnerable to austerity measures that reduce the value of pensions or tighten eligibility criteria (D'Addio 2014).

Third, women are more likely to be employed by the state than men, and therefore their employment is more likely to be impacted by public sector job cuts. This is partly for historical reasons: women entered employment in large numbers as public services expanded in the second half of the twentieth century; not surprisingly they took many of those newly created jobs. Relatedly, the conditions of public sector employment are often more favourable for women than those of the private sector (Stanley 2010; TUC 2012, 2014). In particular, the public sector has in many countries taken the lead in adopting family-friendly employment policies that have not been matched in the private sector. Such policies were needed to retain women in employment, because women's lives are more structured by care responsibilities than men's.

Finally, women are more affected by austerity because they are the ones who are likely to put in the unpaid time required to make up for absent public services. Women are more likely than men to put family care responsibilities before their careers in all European countries, even the most egalitarian – though in practice what these gendered care norms mean and their consequences for gender equality in the labour market vary a great deal over the different welfare states of Europe. And within families these gendered care norms are compounded by the greater earning power of men, so that when care needs necessitate someone cutting down their employment hours, less household income is lost through a woman doing so. Gender norms thus reinforce and perpetuate these domestic inequalities. In particular, when childcare becomes less available, or too expensive, it is likely to be women more than men who reduce their employment hours and juggle them around their children's needs. Even where employment hours stay the same, women find themselves doing more in the home to make up for reduced incomes and cuts in social services.

In other words, women's lives are more intimately connected with social reproduction and tend to be less fully integrated into the labour market than men's. Consequently, any reduction in the state's contribution to social reproduction inevitably impacts more on women, who are also less well-prepared by the labour market to shift from public support to reliance on the market for their own care needs.

This would be true for a rolling-back of the state's contribution to social reproduction at any time, but has been particularly acute in the recent period of austerity. In the period immediately preceding the recession much of the growth in welfare state provision was specifically targeted at enabling women to take employment: by providing or subsidising childcare services; by legislating for parental leave and other employment practices to encourage women with care responsibilities to stay in the workforce; and by redesigning social security systems around a dual earner model.

198 Susan Himmelweit

Increasing women's labour force participation was a crucial part of European Union economic strategy. Indeed, the European Employment Strategy (EES), the cornerstone of the EU's employment policy introduced by the 1992 Lisbon treaty, saw the revenues raised from increased labour market participation as essential to the continued funding of the European Social Model of support for social reproduction. The two groups the EES had targeted as having lower than average labour force participation rates were women and the over 50s, the groups most likely to reduce, interrupt or terminate their employment because of care responsibilities. The EES specifically saw increased childcare for pre-school children as the way to encourage women's employment and set targets for its coverage of the pre-school population of member states, though it did not consider targets for adult social care (Lisbon European Council 2000).

The adoption of such policies at both European and national levels were important steps in reducing gender inequalities within both employment and the home throughout Europe. Until the recession there were steady, if at times glacially slow, falls in the gender pay and employment gaps in most European countries (OECD 2015b). The male breadwinner/female care giver model of family life gradually gave way to at least a one and a half breadwinner model even in the most conservative of European states, while in the more progressive states men's and women's working hours, although still unequal, began to converge, despite gendered norms about care responsibilities changing much more slowly (Pascall and Lewis 2004).

However, although gender equality was one of the four pillars of the European Employment Strategy, its main concern and that of member states was the more instrumental one of increasing employment rates in order to raise state revenues. As a result, despite the commitment to providing public support for care, there were always concerns about its costs rising.

Costs were always going to rise for a number of reasons. To take long-term care, rather than the more instrumentally motivated childcare, to start with: on average across the OECD, spending on long-term care is predicted to increase between two- and four-fold by 2050 (Appleby 2013: 7). The explanation most often offered for these rising costs is the ageing of societies due to greater life expectancy and falling birth rates. However, needs vary and ageing in itself does not create greater need for care – it is the average number of years for which care is needed that matters (Bardsley et al. 2011). Second, older people look after each other, and frequently care for the young too. Greater life expectancy also means more couples surviving into old age. If medical research prioritised improving the length of disability-free life, it could be that rising life expectancy means less not more need for care. It is also possible that investment in better preventative care can reduce the need for spending on long-term care (European Commission 2013, 2014).

Care costs more generally rise for a different, and more optimistic, reason. Care is a highly labour intensive industry in which, if quality is to be maintained, unit costs must rise at least in line with wages, which cannot be too far below wages elsewhere without creating recruitment and retention problems in the industry. If

Austerity and its gender impact **199**

quality is to be improved, training and wage levels throughout the industry will need to rise (Quilter and Himmelweit 2015). And as care costs rise fewer households will be able to pay the full market cost of care. Hence more state support will be needed if women's employment levels are going to continue to rise, especially if nothing is done to tackle the rising inequality that makes purchasing care unaffordable for low earners. These non-demographic factors will have a bigger impact across the OECD on long-term care spending than demographic factors (Appleby 2013: 7).

It is unfortunate that a rising state contribution to social reproduction has not been accepted as the necessary cost of a more gender-equal society. It can be seen as a mark of civilisation that an increasing proportion of government revenues should go into care and that the care industry in its various forms, both public and private, makes up an increasing portion of the economy. The ambivalent view, prevalent in much of Europe, that women's employment is to be encouraged but that spending on care services should be contained, has in practice meant relying on outdated gender norms with respect to unpaid care that are likely to be unsustainable, including long hours for those combining care with paid work, and poor pay and working conditions in paid care.

Indeed, it is likely that only a portion of the increased revenue from women's employment has been invested in funding replacement care services, with the remainder spent elsewhere or used to reduce taxes – though there has been some recognition with respect to childcare, at least, that the market will not provide care at a cost that makes employment pay for all earners, and that some form of state intervention is necessary (Lisbon European Council 2000; European Commission 2011)

Care provision became one of the first and easiest victims of austerity. Relative to rising need, reductions in state funding for care, typically imposed through marketisation as well as through direct cuts, have restricted who is eligible to receive care, shifted more costs onto families, lowered standards of state-financed care and imposed casualised labour market conditions on care workers. If the aim is to provide the conditions for renewed growth these moves are chronically short-sighted. If labour markets become tight again and women's employment increases, the care industry will need to grow at a faster rate than the rest of the economy, but it will not be able to do so if its pay and conditions remain inferior to those in nearly every other sector, as they are in most European countries today.

As with other public services, whether austerity is successful in changing care norms depends on whether the responsibility for falling standards is successfully individualised onto care recipients and their families, and whether there are political and other limits to this process.

Conclusion: resisting the politics of austerity

The effect of austerity has been to privatise more of the costs of social reproduction; this has reduced women's prospects for equality and made lone mothers and others who need state support to combine earning and caring roles more vulnerable to poverty. In dismantling public support for social reproduction, new outlets for financial capital have also been provided, both in financing increased household debt, and in providing new insurance markets and new forms of financing for privatised care services.

This suggests that generating the conditions for renewed growth should not be seen as the main aim of the neoliberal push for austerity policies. Rather, if the view taken earlier that neoliberalism is a political project to augment or restore the power of finance capital is correct, then there are only certain conditions under which it would find renewed growth desirable. In the previous section I suggested that these conditions included changing the norms of social reproduction so that expectations of the state were reduced and those of individuals or families increased. Until such conditions are met, the continuation of austerity, as a way to undermine resistance, may well be preferable to encouraging growth.

If this chapter is right about the reasons for austerity, it will be necessary to accept that politicians who argue for yet more austerity are not being stupid in implementing policies that fail to achieve their stated objectives. Whether deliberately or through external pressure, they are working to a completely different agenda that is supported by a further continuation of crisis conditions and perpetual austerity. With women at the sharp end of cuts to the welfare state, the successful pursuit of this agenda will continue to set back women's equality. Even where greater equality is achieved on some measures, it will inevitably be a harsher world for women, because there will be less support both for women themselves, and for what women, through the lives that they lead, show themselves to care about most.

Even before the crisis, policies being implemented on care relied on outdated gender norms: long hours for women combining work and care responsibilities, poor conditions for paid care workers and in most, but not all, European countries, inadequate care provision particularly for older single women. This was already becoming unsustainable (Himmelweit and Land 2008). Austerity intensified the already existing care deficit and delayed finding any sustainable or equitable solution; care responsibilities just continued to be individualised and financialised.

This is why the focus on investing in the care economy advocated by many chapters in this book is central to finding concrete alternative policies for equitable and sustainable economic recovery in Europe (Chapters 1 by Elson, 2 by Ilkkaracan, 3 by Onaran and 10 by De Henau in this volume). For any policy for recovery to be sustainable, attention will have to be paid to its impact on gender norms and relations. An example of where that has been done is in the UK and Scottish Women's Budget Groups' "Plan F: a long term feminist economic plan to invest in creating a caring and sustainable economy". With budget savings identified that could fund the plan, its measures include: investing in the infrastructure needed for social reproduction; reversing cuts to public services and social security; improving the pay and conditions of those employed in social reproduction by both public and private sectors; improved support for those who provide unpaid care, including well-funded care leave schemes and a reduction in full-time working hours to support men to contribute more unpaid care; and a social security system that provides adequate independent income for all, over the life course, and is designed to support fairer sharing of caring (UK and Scottish Women's Budget Groups 2015).

Such a programme will be difficult to achieve because those who benefit from austerity are increasingly rich and powerful, and Europe is not invulnerable to globalisation pressures. However, Europe has a big internal market and its component countries are still democracies. There are new parties in many Southern European countries, such as Podemos in Spain and Left Bloc in Portugal, who have shown themselves in 2015 able to win support in elections and not only challenge austerity, but also take gender equality more seriously than older parties. In the UK, the surprising but overwhelming win of the anti-austerity candidate for the leadership of the opposition Labour Party marked a decisive rejection by the party's members and supporters of the neoliberal policies it had itself implemented when in power from 1997–2010.

If this really is a new politics, it means that resistance is still possible, but continual pressure will be needed to keep gender issues on the agenda. Above all we need a sense of urgency; time is running out.

Note

1 All multinationals have such power to a greater or lesser extent. But the financial activities of multinationals are increasingly so dominant that it is hard to distinguish their activities and interests from those of finance capital.

References

Appleby, J. 2013. "Spending on health and social care over the next 50 years: why think long term?" The King's Fund. www.kingsfund.org.uk/sites/files/kf/field/field_publication_file/Spending%20on%20health%20…%2050%20years%20low%20res%20for%20web.pdf (accessed 28/12/2015).

Bardsley, M., J. Billings, J. Dixon, T. Georghiou, G. Hywel Lewis and A. Steventon. 2011. "Predicting who will use intensive social care: case finding tools based on linked health and social care data." *Age and Ageing.* 40 (2): 265–70. doi: 10.1093/ageing/afq181.

Bettio, F., M. Corsi, C. D'Ippoliti, A. Lyberaki, M. Samek Lodovici and A.Verashchagina. 2013. "Impact of the Economic Crisis on the Situation of Women and Men and on Gender Equality Policies." Synthesis Report of EU Network on Gender, Equality and Employment. www.ingenere.it/sites/default/files/ricerche/crisis%20report-def-7web.pdf (accessed 28/12/2015).

D'Addio, A. C. 2014. "Pension entitlements of women with children in OECD countries." Presentation to Second Cinitia Conference, Torino, 24–25 November 2014. http://fileserver.carloalberto.org/cerp/d%20addio%20torino_cintia.pdf (accessed 28/12/2015).

Durand, C. and E. Boulet. 2013. "An interview with David Harvey." *X-pressed.* (15 March). www.x-pressed.org/?xpd_article=an-interview-with-david-harvey-2-2-2 (accessed 28/12/2015).

European Commission. 2009. "Opinion on the Gender Perspective on the Response to the Economic and Financial Crisis." Report of the European Commission. http://ec. europa.eu/social/BlobServlet?docId=2878 (accessed 28/12/2015).

European Commission. 2011. "Early Childhood Education and Care: Providing all our children with the best start for the world of tomorrow." European Commission Communication. Summary at www.early-years.org/policy/briefings/ECEC_COM 2011 66 Summary.pdf (accessed 28/12/2015).

European Commission. 2012. "The Impact of the Economic Crisis on the Situation of Women and Men and on Gender Equality Policies." Report of the European Commission. http://ec.europa.eu/justice/gender-equality/files/documents/130410_crisis_report_en.pdf (accessed 2/3/2016).

European Commission. 2013. "Long-term care in ageing societies – Challenges and policy options." Commission Staff Working Document. http://ec.europa.eu/social/Blob Servlet?docId=12633 (accessed 28/12/2015).

European Commission. 2014. "Adequate social protection for long-term care needs in an ageing society." Report jointly prepared by the Social Protection Committee and the European Commission. http://ec.europa.eu/social/BlobServlet?docId=12808 (accessed 28/12/2015).

European Union. 2015. "European Economic Forecast – Autumn 2015: Statistical Annex." http://ec.europa.eu/economy_finance/eu/forecasts/2015_autumn/statistical_en.pdf (accessed 28/12/2015).

Francesconi, M. and A. Gosling. 2005. "Career paths of part-time workers." EOC Working Paper Series no 19. No longer available but summarised on: www.eurofound.europa. eu/observatories/eurwork/articles/working-conditions/career-paths-of-part-time-workers (accessed 28/12/2015).

Harvey, D. 2005. *A Brief History of Neoliberalism*. Oxford: Oxford University Press.

Himmelweit, S. and H. Land. 2008. "Reducing gender inequalities to create a sustainable care system." Joseph Rowntree Foundation. www.jrf.org.uk/report/reducing-gender-inequalities-create-sustainable-care-system (accessed 28/12/2015).

Karamessini, M. and J. Rubery (eds). 2014. *Women and Austerity*. Abingdon and New York: Routledge.

Keane C., T. Callan and J. R. Walsh. 2014. "The Gender Impact of Tax and Benefit Change; A Microsimulation Approach." Economic and Social Research Institute, Ireland. www. esri.ie/publications/gender-impact-of-tax-and-benefit-changes-a-microsimulation-approach (accessed 28/12/2015).

Kröger, T. and S. Yeandle (eds). 2013. *Combining Paid Work and Family Care: Policies and Experiences in International Perspective*. Bristol: The Policy Press.

Lisbon European Council. 2000. Presidency Conclusion. (23 and 24 March) www. consilium.europa.eu/en/uedocs/cms_data/docs/pressdata/en/ec/00100-r1.en0.htm (accessed 28/12/2015).

Manning, A. and B. Petrongolo. 2004. "The part-time pay penalty." Report for the Women and Equality Unit, London: Department of Trade and Industry.

OECD. 2010. "Mancession." OECD Observer 278 (March). http://oecdobserver.org/ news/archivestory.php/aid/3240/Mancession_.html (accessed 28/12/2015).

OECD. 2014. "Women, Government and Policy Making in OECD Countries: Fostering Diversity for Inclusive Growth." Paris: OECD Publishing.

OECD. 2015a. "New OECD data and analysis revealing the wide gap in pension benefits between men and women." www.oecd.org/gender/data/newoecddata andanalysisrevealingthewidegapinpensionbenefitsbetweenmenandwomen.htm (accessed 28/12/2015).

OECD. 2015b. "Gender wage gap." Gender Data Portal. www.oecd.org/gender/data/genderwagegap.htm (accessed 28/12/2015).

O'Reilly, J. and S. Bothfeld. 2002. "What happens after working part time? Integration, maintenance or exclusionary transitions in Britain and Western Germany." *Cambridge Journal of Economics*, 26(4): 409–39.

Pascall, G. and J. Lewis. 2004. "Emerging gender regimes and policies for gender equality in a wider Europe." *Journal of Social Policy* 33(3): 373–94.

Quilter, I. and S. Himmelweit. 2015. "Social Care for the Elderly in England." A briefing from the UK Women's Budget Group. http://wbg.org.uk/wp-content/uploads/2015/07/social-care-briefing-june-2015.pdf (accessed 28/12/2015).

Rosnick, D. and M. Weisbrot. 2015. "Has Austerity Worked in Spain?" Center for Economic and Policy Research, Washington DC. http://cepr.net/publications/reports/has-austerity-worked-in-spain (accessed 28/12/2015).

Russo, G. and W. Hassink. 2008. "The part-time wage gap: a career perspective." *De Economist,* 156 (2): 145–74.

Stanley, N. 2010. "Public/private sector pay – what about gender?" *Touchstone blog* (21 January). http://touchstoneblog.org.uk/2010/01/publicprivate-sector-pay-what-about-gender (accessed 28/12/2015).

Stiglitz, J. E. 2012a. *The Price of Inequality*. New York and London: W. W. Norton & Company, Penguin.

Stiglitz, J. E. 2012b. "The One Percent: The 1 Percent's Problem." *Vanity Fair* (31 May) www.vanityfair.com/news/2012/05/joseph-stiglitz-the-price-on-inequality (accessed 28/12/2015).

TUC. 2012. "Women's pay and employment update: a public/private sector comparison." www.tuc.org.uk/sites/default/files/Womenspay.pdf (accessed 28/12/2015).

TUC. 2014. "Outsourcing Public Services." www.tuc.org.uk/sites/default/files/TUC%20and%20NEF%20Outsourcing%20Public%20Services.pdf (accessed 28/12/2015).

TUC. 2015. "Women want work: 'want work' levels and women's labour market participation." www.tuc.org.uk/sites/default/files/Women%20want%20work.pdf (accessed 28/12/2015).

UK and Scottish Women's Budget Groups. 2015. "Plan F: a Feminist Economic Strategy for a Caring and Sustainable Economy." http://wbg.org.uk/wp-content/uploads/2015/02/PLAN-F-2015.pdf (accessed 28/12/2015).

Wahl, A. 2011. *The Rise and Fall of the Welfare State*. London: Pluto Press.

Wimo A., E. von Strauss, G. Nordberg, F. Sassi and L. Johansson. 2002. "Time spent on informal and formal care giving for persons with dementia in Sweden." *Health Policy.* 61(3): 255–68.

INDEX

2008 financial crisis 76, 88–9; employment changes 79–80; EU gender equality policies 76–8; gender-equitable macroeconomic framework 15, 23; global perspective 81; *see also* 2008 financial crisis (Ireland); 2008 financial crisis (Spain); investment-led recovery

2008 financial crisis (Ireland) 81–2, 82–4, 85–7; impact of crisis 84–5; low-income households and single parents 87–8; recession 82–4; Universal Social Charge 87

2008 financial crisis (Spain) 91–2, 92–4, 106–9; fiscal consolidation measures 95–8; gender effects 101–6; labour market reform 98–100; pensions reform 100–1; policy response 94–101

added worker effect 62

austerity and gender impact 5–7, 189–91, 196–9, 192, 199–201; global capitalism 192–6; overview and structure of book 1–2, 7–9; policies 4–5, 191–2

austerity, definitions of 2–4

austerity measures (Ireland) 82–4, 85–7

austerity under Coalition Government 113–4, 130–1; data sources 115; service cuts 114, 121–30; tax and benefit reforms 114, 115–21, 128–30, 133–4

Austria 33

benefit reforms (Coalition Government) 114, 128–30, 133–4; analysis by demographic 116–9; analysis by household income 115–6; individual-level analysis of gender impacts 119–21

Braunstein, E. 47, 49–50

Braunstein et al.'s model 44–5

buffer effect 63

Cambridge Alphametrics Macroeconomic model 139, 146, 153–4

caring economy *see* free universal childcare

childcare *see* free universal childcare; gendered investment plan with childcare

class-without-gender 60

Coalition Government *see* austerity under Coalition Government

Conservatives *see* austerity under Coalition Government

demand-led growth models 41, 43, 49–50; feminist macroeconomic models 43–5; gendered macro model 46–9; Post-Keynesian and neo-Kaleckian models 41–3

discouraged worker effect 62

discrimination 79–80

distributional impact of service cuts 121, 128–30; extent of cuts 121; impact by demographic 125–8; impact by income

123–5; Landman Economics public spending model 122–3

distributional impact of tax and benefit reforms: analysis by demographic 116–9, 128–30; analysis by household income 115–6; individual-level analysis of gender impacts 119–21

economic crisis *see* 2008 financial crisis; 2008 financial crisis (Ireland); 2008 financial crisis (Spain)

economic models *see* equality-led growth strategies

economic performance 19–20

employment *see* labour markets

equality-led growth strategies 40–1, 53; demand-led growth models 41–3, 43–9, 49–50; feminist macroeconomic models 43–5; gender-aware policies 51–3; gendered macro model 46–9; Post-Keynesian and neo-Kaleckian models 41–3

equality policies in EU 76–8

equality reforms (Spain) 95

European policies 4–5, 76–8

extended gendered macro model 46–9

familiar social reproduction system 71

female employment 156–9

feminisation of labour markets 67–9

feminist alternative to austerity *see* purple economy

feminist economics: Braunstein, E. 47, 44–5, 49–50; effects of gender integration 49–50; feminist macroeconomic models 43–5; gendered macro model 46–9

feminist macroeconomic models 43–5

finance capital 194

financial crisis *see* 2008 financial crisis; 2008 financial crisis (Ireland); 2008 financial crisis (Spain)

financial governance 23–4

fiscal consolidation measures (Spain) 95–8; gender equality reforms 95; paternity leave 96–7; public enterprises 97; social care 95–6

fiscal policies 4–5

free universal childcare 168–9, 183–4; alternative scenarios 180–3; benefits

169–70; costs 171–3; employment effects 173–8; net funding needs 178–80

gender *see* austerity and gender impact

gender-aware policies 51–3

gender budget 64

gender equality policies 76–8

gender equality reforms (Spain) 95

gender-equitable macroeconomic framework 15–16, 24–5; financial governance 23–4; gross domestic product 19–20; measurements and indicators 19–20; social and physical infrastructure 20–1; taxation 22–3; unpaid work 16–18

gender impact analysis 5–7

gender impact of austerity on women 189–91, 196–9

gender integration effects 49–50

gender norms (Italy) 71

gender pay gap 190; Spain (financial crisis) 97; Italy (mortgage crisis) 67–9

gender-without-class 59–60

gendered alternative to austerity 7

gendered investment plan 143–6; impact 146–51; labour market 143–5

gendered investment plan with childcare 155–6, 166–7; benefits of childcare investment 159–61; benefits to children 161–2; female employment 156–9; impact 162–4; *see also* free universal childcare

gendered macro model 46–9

global capitalism 192–6

green economy 27, 29

gross domestic product 19–20

Growth Compact 141–2

HEIMDAL 163–4

household expenditure 80

indicators of economic performance 19–20

infrastructure 20–1; 142; *see also* physical infrastructure; social care and infrastructure

investment-led recovery 137–9, 151; Cambridge Alphametrics Macroeconomic model 153–4; gendered investment plan 143–51; low growth

206 Index

and unemployment 139–40; policy responses to crisis 140–3
Investment Plan for Europe 142–3
Ireland (financial crisis) 81–2, 82–4, 85–7; impact of crisis 84–5; low-income households and single parents 87–8; recession 82–4; Universal Social Charge 87
Italy (mortgage crisis) 65; feminisation of labour markets 67–9; production system 67–71; social reproduction system 65–7, 71

Juncker Plan 142–3

labour markets: 2008 financial crisis 79, 98–100, 101–6; free universal childcare 173–6; gendered investment plan 143–5; mortgage crisis 62–3; women 67–9, 156–9
Landman Economics public spending model 122–3
Landman Economics tax-benefit model 115
Lethbridge, J. 81
Liberal Democrats *see* austerity under Coalition Government
literature: feminist macroeconomic models 43–45; gender perspective 60–2
lone parents (Ireland) 87–8
low growth 139–40
low-income households (Ireland) 87–8

macroeconomic models *see* equality-led growth strategies; gender-equitable macroeconomic framework
means-tested benefits 176–8
measurement of economic performance 19–20
mortgage crisis *see* subprime mortgage crisis

negative growth 139–40
neo-Kaleckian model 41–3
neoliberalism 194–5

overview of book 1–2, 7–9

paternity leave (Spain) 96–7
patriarchal dimensions 64–5
pay: Italy (mortgage crisis) 67–9; Spain (financial crisis) 97, 104

pensions reform (Spain) 100–1
physical infrastructure 20–1, 142
policies 4–5, 191–2; 2008 financial crisis 94–101, 140–3; gender-aware policies 51–3; gender equality policies 76–8, Post-Keynesian model 41–3
production system (Italy) 62–3, 67–71
public enterprises (Spain) 97
public social reproduction system (Italy) 65–7
purple economy 27–9, 36–7; green economy 27, 29; pillars 29–31; social care 31–6

recession 82–4; *see also* 2008 financial crisis; 2008 financial crisis (Ireland); 2008 financial crisis (Spain)
recovery *see* investment-led recovery
reduction and redistribution of unpaid work 17–18

salaries: Italy (mortgage crisis) 67–9; Spain (financial crisis) 97, 104
segmentation hypothesis 63
service cuts (Coalition Government) 121, 128–30; impact by demographic 125–8; impact by income 123–5; Landman Economics public spending model 122–3
single parents (Ireland) 87–8
social care and infrastructure: Austria 33; gender-equitable macroeconomic framework 20–1; policy responses to crisis 142; purple economy 31–6; Spain 95–6; South Africa 34; South Korea 32; Turkey 34–5; United States 33; *see also* free universal childcare
social reproduction 192–3
social reproduction system 63–4; familiar SRS 71; public SRS 65–7
social security reforms *see* austerity under Coalition Government
South African social care 34
South Korean social care 32
Spain (financial crisis) 91–2, 92–4, 106–9; fiscal consolidation measures 95–8; gender effects 101–6; labour market reform 98–100; pensions reform 100–1; policy response 94–101

Index **207**

spending cuts *see* service cuts (Coalition Government)
statutory paid leave 18
structure of book 1–2, 7–9
subprime mortgage crisis 59–60, 72; gender perspective literature 60–2; Italy 65–71; theoretical framework for analysis 62–5

tax reforms (Coalition Government) 114, 128–30, 133–4; analysis by demographic 116–9; analysis by household income 115–6; individual-level analysis of gender impacts 119–21
taxation 22–3
theoretical framework for mortgage crisis analysis 62; gender budget 64; labour market 62–3; patriarchal dimensions 64–5; production system 62–3; social reproduction system 63–4
Time Use Survey 50, 64, 71
Turkey 34–5

unemployment 139–40; *see also* labour markets
United Kingdom *see* austerity under Coalition Government
United States: social care 33; *see also* subprime mortgage crisis
universal childcare *see* free universal childcare
Universal Social Charge (Ireland) 87
unpaid work 16–17; reduction and redistribution 17–18; statutory paid leave 18

wages: Italy (mortgage crisis) 67–9; Spain (financial crisis) 97, 104
welfare cuts *see* austerity under Coalition Government
welfare states 192–5
women: impact of austerity 189–91, 196–9; labour markets 67–9, 156–9

Taylor & Francis eBooks

Helping you to choose the right eBooks for your Library

Add Routledge titles to your library's digital collection today. Taylor and Francis ebooks contains over 50,000 titles in the Humanities, Social Sciences, Behavioural Sciences, Built Environment and Law.

Choose from a range of subject packages or create your own!

Benefits for you
- Free MARC records
- COUNTER-compliant usage statistics
- Flexible purchase and pricing options
- All titles DRM-free.

Benefits for your user
- Off-site, anytime access via Athens or referring URL
- Print or copy pages or chapters
- Full content search
- Bookmark, highlight and annotate text
- Access to thousands of pages of quality research at the click of a button.

REQUEST YOUR **FREE** INSTITUTIONAL TRIAL TODAY

Free Trials Available
We offer free trials to qualifying academic, corporate and government customers.

eCollections – Choose from over 30 subject eCollections, including:

Archaeology	Language Learning
Architecture	Law
Asian Studies	Literature
Business & Management	Media & Communication
Classical Studies	Middle East Studies
Construction	Music
Creative & Media Arts	Philosophy
Criminology & Criminal Justice	Planning
Economics	Politics
Education	Psychology & Mental Health
Energy	Religion
Engineering	Security
English Language & Linguistics	Social Work
Environment & Sustainability	Sociology
Geography	Sport
Health Studies	Theatre & Performance
History	Tourism, Hospitality & Events

For more information, pricing enquiries or to order a free trial, please contact your local sales team:
www.tandfebooks.com/page/sales

 | The home of Routledge books | **www.tandfebooks.com**